THE UNIVERSITY OF MICHIGAN
CENTER FOR CHINESE STUDIES

MICHIGAN ABSTRACTS OF CHINESE AND
JAPANESE WORKS ON CHINESE HISTORY

Mark Elvin, Editor

D0071624

Ann Arbor, Michigan

COMMERCE AND SOCIETY IN SUNG CHINA

by

SHIBA Yoshinobu

Translated by Mark Elvin

Michigan Abstracts of Chinese and
Japanese Works on Chinese History

No. 2

1970

Originally published in Japanese as

Shiba Yoshinobu
斯波義信
Sōdai shōgyō- shi kenkyū
宋代商業史研究
(Tokyo: Kazama shobo, 1968)
風間書房

ISBN 0-89264-902-X

Translation © 1970

by

Center for Chinese Studies
The University of Michigan

Contents

The illustration on the cover, showing operations at a government saltern, is taken from the Cheng-ho Reign-period Herbal in Readiness for Emergencies, Drawn from the Classics and Histories and Verified According to Category edited by T'ang Shen-wei and printed in 1116.

The five maps in this volume were drawn by Miss Karen Ewing, whose help is gratefully acknowledged.

Map data after E. Balazs, Annales Economies - Societés - Civilisations, XII, iv., 1957.

Editor's Foreword

It has long been apparent to teachers of Chinese history at universities that a major obstacle in the way of creating a balanced syllabus is the uneven coverage of the subject-matter provided by secondary works in the English language. At the same time there has existed for many decades a rich and important secondary literature in Chinese and Japanese, and one that is constantly growing. The language barrier is such as to make this literature almost inaccessible to undergraduates and still difficult for students at the post-graduate level, while the cost of making full and accurate translations, in terms of the few scholars qualified to do so, is prohibitive. The present series is designed to find a way around this impasse, in the belief that if the major results of this Chinese and Japanese secondary literature can be made widely available to those studying Chinese history at universities, this will raise the level of knowledge and understanding with a speed possible in no other way.

The approach adopted here is that of the long summary, more substantial than the customary abstract, but still confining itself only to essentials and stripped of critical apparatus and notes. It approximates to the working notes that one makes when reading an important Chinese or Japanese secondary work for the first time, and the immediate historical precursor of the series is of course the exchange of such notes which has long been customary among colleagues working in this particularly exacting field. A primary advantage of a condensation of this kind is that it is much less demanding of a contributor's time than a full-dress translation would be, while omitting little if anything of significance to the general student or reader.

The course which I teach on the economic and social history of China at the University of Glasgow has shown the great value of abstracted translations such as the present one for undergraduates. Hopefully, they may also prove of help to research students who need to read around the edges of their main area of concentration, to maturer scholars working in areas of Chinese studies relatively remote from the subject of a given abstract but anxious to fill in the background for the purposes of teaching or general interest, and to those pursuing comparative cross-cultural studies in the social sciences at large.

ii

This series owes its existence to the generosity and vision of Professor Rhoads Murphey and Professor Albert Feuerwerker of the Center of Chinese Studies at the University of Michigan. I should like to conclude by acknowledging with gratitude their continuing enthusiasm and support.

Mark Elvin
Series Editor

Translator's Introduction

The full dimensions of the medieval Chinese economic revolution are still almost unknown to economic historians in the Western world, and the manifold problems that it raises for accepted theories of economic development have hardly yet begun to be systematically considered. Japanese scholars have been the pioneers in opening up this field, and Professor Shiba's Commerce and Society in Sung China is among the most recent and the most impressive fruits of their labors. For the first time it is possible to be relatively confident, as the result of the author's systematic exploitation of an enormous range of source materials, about the parts played by transport, trade, business organization and urbanization in this revolution. It is hardly necessary to labor the significance of this advance. China's was beyond any reasonable doubt the most developed economy in the medieval world, and the investigation both of the causes that made this possible and of those that subsequently prevented a take-off into sustained growth is among the most pressing tasks waiting to be accomplished before any general theory of economic development, solidly grounded in comparative historical analysis, becomes possible.

The abstracted translation presented here does less than full justice to the original work in several ways. The long bibliographical essay which constitutes Chapter I, an indispensible tool for the serious research worker, has been reduced to a handful of pages summarizing its essential themes. In Chapters II through VII the comprehensive way in which the available data are set out has inevitably been somewhat impaired by the need to select and abbreviate. Chapter VIII, on the Tonnage Tax, has been left out altogether as being of limited interest to the general reader. On the other hand, a good deal of extra explanatory matter has been added, together with five maps, for the sake of the reader not familiar with the details of Sung history or Sung geography. In footnotes of more than a routine nature this addition is shown by the word '(Transl.)' at the end of the note. Four maps have been added. Map I is based on Hiraoka Takeo, Tōdai no gyōsei chiri (The Administrative Geography of the T'ang Dynasty) (Kyoto: Jimbun kagaku kenkyūjo, 1955) and Matsuda Hisao and Mori Shikazō, ed., Ajia rekishi chizu (Historical Atlas of Asia) (Tokyo: Heibonsha, 1966).

iv

Maps III through V are derived mainly from E. Balazs, 'Une carte
des centres commerciaux de la Chine à la fin du XIe siècle,' in
Annales Economies - Sociétés - Civilisations XII. iv (1957) and
Aoyama Sadao, Tō-Sō jidai no kōtsu to chishi chizu no kenkyū (A Study
of T'ang and Sung Communications, and the Development of
Topographies and Maps) (Tokyo: Yoshikawa kōbunkan, 1963),
especially Map II on page 50.   Following a suggestion made by
Professor Denis Twitchett of the University of Cambridge, the page
on which a direct quotation from a Chinese source begins in the
Japanese edition is noted in parentheses at its conclusion to facilitate
reference to the original words.   As in the previous volume, Chinese
titles of sources mentioned are supplied only once, on the occasion
of first occurrence; they can, however, be easily traced at any
time by referring to the author's name in the appropriate glossary
at the back.   The romanization used is modified Wade-Giles, but
the modern forms of the province names, where these appear, and
'Peking', 'Nanking', 'Canton', 'Kiangnan' and 'Yangtze' are given in
their more familiar Post Office forms.   Years follow the Chinese
lunar, not the Western solar calendar, unless stated otherwise.
There is also a glossary of Chinese terms.

   I should like to acknowledge the very useful comments made
on Chapter II by Mr. Andrew Watson of the University of Glasgow
and on Chapters I, III and IV by Professor G. William Skinner of the
University of Stanford.   Quite especial thanks are due to Professor
Shiba, who not only supplied me at the outset with a list of errata in
the Japanese edition, but also checked the translation when it was
in draft.   Whatever level of accuracy has been attained owes much
to his patient help.

M. E.

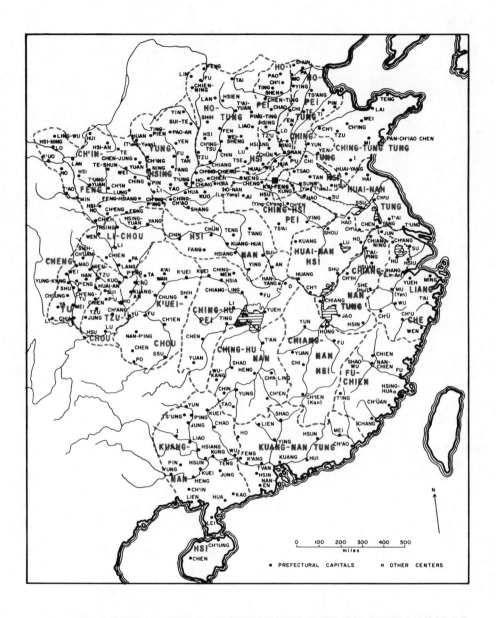

MAP I THE PROVINCES AND PREFECTURES OF CHINA UNDER NORTHERN SUNG

Commerce and Society in Sung China

I. BASIC PROBLEMS

It is generally recognized that the period of transition from the later part of the T'ang dynasty to the Sung dynasty (in other words, the tenth to the thirteenth centuries) constituted a watershed in Chinese history. In the economic sphere, which of course cannot ultimately be considered in isolation from the other aspects of society, this took the form of a number of major changes. The state-controlled land tenure system of 'equitable fields' (chün-t'ien) gave way to private property, most notably in the form of the 'manor' (chuang-yuan)*; and there were corresponding alterations in the structure of taxation. An upsurge in agricultural productivity took place, connected in part with the intensified development of the Kiangnan region.** As a result of these developments, and of improvements in the techniques and organization of water transport, there was an increase in internal and overseas trade, while the volume of money in circulation rose and credit instruments enjoyed a much wider use than previously.

The consequences were multiple. The older system of closed-off officially-controlled city markets, and the legal restrictions which confined merchants and artisans (in theory at least) to specified quarters of cities serving as administrative centers, collapsed; and there was a proliferation of interlinked rural periodic markets, which formed the basis of a national market.*** The T'ang guild (hang) which had essentially amounted to an officially-sanctioned quarter consisting of merchant shops in the same trade, was transformed into something more nearly approaching an autonomous trade association. The structure

---

*Based on tenancy. See D. C. Twitchett, Financial Administration under the T'ang Dynasty (Cambridge University Press: Cambridge, 1963) pp. 18-20.

**The area lying immediately south of the lower course of the Yangtze River. Transl.

***Not of course in the sense that prices were much the same throughout the country, but that regular commercial contacts linked all areas directly or indirectly with each other. Transl.

1

of business organization grew more complex, as all sorts of brokers, wholesalers, and warehousemen appeared, and to some extent the ownership and the management of capital became differentiated. A variety of forms of business combination became common, including the commenda for overseas ventures, partnerships, primitive joint-stock companies, and trading combines composed of a number of co-ordinated units. Cities absorbed a larger proportion of the population than previously, and their character changed. Having previously been based almost solely upon the consumption requirements of the official and military classes, they now became in addition commercial and sometimes industrial centers. From about the middle of the T'ang period the state reacted by instituting superintendencies to tax foreign trade, and by building up a network of internal customs stations. In consequence levies on commerce soon became an important part of state revenue.

The analysis of these phenomena raises certain problems in our understanding of Chinese history in particular and of economic development generally. Why, for example, did the manorial system not decline as the result of the liberating influence (as it is conventionally supposed to be) of money? Tenancy relations after the Northern Sung period seem to have involved a greater rather than a lesser measure of subjection, the reverse of what might reasonably have been expected. Trade and other profit-making activities are not necessarily in themselves forces making for liberation - they must be considered within an overall social context - and while the development of commercial capital undermined the pre-existing economic system, it did not prepare in inevitable fashion the way for the appearance of new powers of production. The volume of trade in medieval China far surpassed that in medieval Europe (where indeed it was far from negligeable), yet the Sung economy did not continue to grow in a 'modern' direction, which leads us to regard with some suspicion the currently accepted historicist or stage theories of development.

As will be apparent in the pages that follows, the Sung economy in its overall character was basically pre-modern. Commercial capital was not, on the whole, invested in the means of production but used to buy land or for money-lending, speculation, the purchase of official position or even simply consumption. Trading profits were typically derived from price differentials between areas which arose in somewhat accidental fashion, and a major function of trade was the provision of temporary relief when local supplies were inadequate.

Sung associations of merchants based on joint capital differed from
the later Chinese partnership (ho-ku) in that individual initiative was
not wholly submerged in collective management. The parallel
existence in Sung times of certain elements of economic 'modernity' is
only an apparent paradox, in the sense that a perhaps excessive
concern with the origins of 'modern' society has caused many scholars
to regard the 'pre-modern' as the negative of or the opposite of
the 'modern', and so to find the origins of modernity in its dissolution
or denial.

It is still too soon for any final judgment to be passed on the
historical character of the Sung economy, and there is need for more
detailed studies of specific aspects. The accumulation of the results
of research over the last few decades do however indicate that the
time has come to attempt to evaluate the significance of the great
development of commerce at this time, and to relate it to other social
changes. What follows is therefore a many-sided enquiry which
touches upon communications, trade, cities, commercial systems,
aspects of industry and other themes in so far as they are relevant
to these primary concerns.

II. THE DEVELOPMENT OF COMMUNICATIONS AND TRANSPORT IN SUNG AND YUAN TIMES

The improvement during the Sung dynasty in the official transportation system, namely that which was concerned with the movement of taxes, officials, troops and documents, is well-known. Of equal importance was the rise of a popular, unofficial system, related to the upsurge in productive forces and the increasing division of labor that characterized this time. This unofficial transport system was to some extent in competition with the official system, but also to some extent dependent for its existence upon it.

1. THE BASIC STRUCTURE OF THE SHIPPING BUSINESS

A shipping business had developed in central and southern China by the period of the Three Kingdoms (3rd century AD) or the Northern and Southern Dynasties (4th to 6th centuries AD) at the latest. This is suggested by the existence of such proverbial sayings as 'Go by boat in the South, take a horse in the North' and 'Use a boat in the South, a tent in the North.' By the T'ang dynasty (AD 618-906) Ts'ui Jung could write:

> Boats gather on every stream in the Empire. To one
> side they reach into Szechwan and the Han River valley;
> they point the way to Fukien and Kwangtung. Through
> the Seven Marshes and Ten Swamps, the Three Rivers
> and Five Lakes, they draw in the Yellow River and the
> Lo, embracing also Huai-an and Hai-chou. Great ships
> in thousands and tens of thousands carry goods back and
> forth. If they once lay unused it would spell ruin for ten
> thousand merchants. If these were ruined, then others
> would have no one on whom to depend for their livelihood.
> Some of them are rogues always ready for a brawl, given
> to gallant deeds and capable of 'beheading dragons' (like
> T'an-t'ai Tzu-yü of yore), or bullies from P'o-yang or
> ruffians from Fu-p'ing, men who have hoards of money
> at home and go out sword in hand. (52)

Li Ch'ao (fl. early 9th century) offered a more concrete picture of regional specialization in the shipping business:

There is no commandery or county in the Southeast in
which communications by water are lacking. Therefore
most of the Empire's profits from trade depend on the
use of boats. The Transport Commissioners transport
more than two million pi culs of rice every year to Kuan-chung,
all of it going there via the T'ung-chi Canal and the Yellow
River. The polers of the Yangtze and the Huai are not
capable of entering the Yellow River, and at dangerous
places such as the Three Gorges in Szechwan, the Three
Gates rapids on the Yellow River, the O-ch'i River (in
Kwangtung) and the Kan-shih shoals (on the Kan River
in Kiangsi) there are locals who act as pole-men. ...
On the Ya ngtze and the Ch'ien-t'ang rivers they take
advantage of the two daily tides for rowing, and shipping
flourishes here more than in Kiangsi. ... There is a
saying among those who live among the rivers and lakes
that 'Water won't carry ten thousand', by which they mean
that large vessels do not exceed 8,000 or 9,000 piculs
capacity. However this may be, between the Ta-li and
the Chen-yuan reign-periods (AD 766-779 to AD 785-804)
there was Aunt Yü's huge boat on board of which people
were born, married and died. Sailing along the creeks
was their equivalent of cultivating their vegetable gardens.
There was a crew of several hundred. They made one
round trip every year from Kiangsi in the South to Huai-
nan in the North, reaping enormous profits. This was
nothing other than 'carrying ten thousand.' Particularly
large numbers of people live on the water in Hung-chou
and O-chou (modern Nan-ch'ang and Wu-han respectively),
amounting to half the population of each country. Large
boats are invariably owned by rich merchants. (52)

Thus, by T'ang times, the natural obstacles which hindered inland
waterway transportation had to some extent been overcome, and there
was a growing differentiation apparent in techniques. Intensive
development in this direction, however, only came with the Sung
dynasty (AD 960-1275).

i. Types of Craft

The advances achieved in Sung and Yuan times are revealed
by the increasing number of different types of boat. The terminology
used by contemporaries classified craft in one of three ways: by

regional specialization, by functional specialization or by peculiarities
of construction. A survey of the documents from these two dynasties
yields terms for at least 35 types of regionally specific craft (by
river system or port of origin), 10 types of sea-going vessel,
21 kinds of functionally specific boats (such as passenger boats,
manure boats, ferry-boats and floating restaurants), 10 varieties of
warship, and 20 categories of craft differentiated according to
structure (including man-powered paddle-wheel boats), besides a
number of other descriptions of a more general nature.

A. Sea-going vessels

Until the T'ang dynasy, long-distance sea-going junks were
operated by foreigners. In Sung times, however, the Chinese
succeeded in overcoming the technical barriers that had hitherto
held them back, and Chinese ships became active in East Asian and
Southeast Asian waters. These vessels mostly came from the
southeastern and southern coasts of China, though some were also
based on the ports of the lower Yangtze region. The relative
unimportance of North China is attested to by Lu I-hao, writing in
the twelfth century:

> In the South, the nature of the wood and the water are
> suited to each other. For this reason Fukien holds the
> first place for sea-going junks, being followed by
> Kwangtung and Kwangsi, and then by Wen-chou and
> Ming-chou. In the North, the nature of the wood and
> the water are not suited to each other. The sea is
> bitterly salt and capable of damaging the wood. Therefore
> boats are incapable of lasting for long after they have
> been launched. They cannot resist the storms either,
> and there are frequent capsizings and drownings. (57)

A detailed description of merchant ships in Hsu Ching's
Illustrated Account of an Embassy to Kao-li in the Hsuan-ho Reign-period,
(AD 1119-1125) (Hsuan-ho feng-shih Kao-li t'u-ching) says that
medium-size junks from Fukien and Liang-Che (present day Chekiang
and southern Kiangsu) were over 100 Chinese feet in length, 30 feet
high and 25 feet in the beam. They carried a cargo of 2,000 piculs
(or approximately 120 tons) and a crew of sixty. The gunwales
consisted of several layers of whole timbers and, in contrast to the

flat deck, the underside of the ship narrowed to a knife-edge. Along the water-line bamboo bags were fixed as fenders and to increase resistance to the waves. The prow and stern were left empty in order to add to buoyancy. Amidships, there were three separate holds. The foremost of these, between the foremast and the mainmast, was undecked and contained the kitchen and the water casks. The lower level served as quarters for the crew. The central hold was divided into four compartments, and was presumably used for cargo. The rear hold was fitted with barred windows from which a view might be had, and served as accommodation. An anchor consisting of a stone held in an anchor-shaped wooden hook was attached to a rattan rope wound on a windlass mounted between two vertical posts on the prow. In storms, two sea-anchors (floating anchors) were used. At the stern were a large and a small rudder, for use in deep and shallow water respectively. In shallow waters two oars were also used over the stern. When entering harbor or passing along channels through shoals propulsion was by means of ten oars worked over the gunwales. The main motive power was, however, provided by sails. There were two masts, the foremast of 80 feet and the mainmast of 100 feet. Canvas sails would be hoisted when there was a following wind; for a wind on the quarter matting sails, which were easier to control, were used. If the breeze was light additional traction would be obtained from topsails on the mainmast.

The outstanding characteristic of these sea-going vessels was their size. The largest of them, according to Chinese sources, could carry 5,000 piculs of cargo and or 500 to 600 persons. Thus, when Mas'ūdī speaks of Chinese ships with 400 to 500 men, Odoric of ships with 700 men, and Ibn Battūtah of ships with 1,000 persons they are not necessarily exaggerating.

Sea-going ships at this time were mostly built of pine-wood. Supplies of this came mainly from Fukien and from Ch'u-chou in present day Chekiang; when these proved insufficient more was imported from Japan. One of the reasons for the double or triple planking of hulls, a practice also alluded to by Marco Polo, was to prevent them being eaten through by 'sea-maggots' (ligia exotica). A point of particular importance was the strength of the rudder and the tiller. According to Chou Ch'ü-fei's Information on What is Beyond the Southern Passes (Ling-wai tai-ta), which was written in 1178:

There are two rare kinds of material to be obtained
in the coastal hills of Ch'in-chou (in present day
Kwangtung). One is called wu-lan wood and is used
for making the rudders of great ships. It is one of the
most remarkable things in the Empire. Ships from
Southeast Asia and the Indo-Islamic world, which
resemble vast buildings and cut deep furrows across the
southern seas, traverse several tens of thousands of li
with hundreds of human lives dependent on a single
rudder. Rudders that are produced elsewhere do not exceed
30 feet in length and are adequate to control a ship of ten
thousand piculs capacity. If they are used to control an
overseas trading ship of several times this size they are
certain to snap in two if a storm is suddenly encountered
on the deep seas. Only rudders produced in Ch'in-chou are
close-grained, sturdy, and almost 50 feet in length. Even
in the fury of a storm they work perfectly without giving,
as though a weight of a thousand chün hung from a single
silken thread while mountain ranges collapsed about it
in rubble. It is in truth for those who cross the seas the
most precious of all things. A pair of such rudders is
worth several hundred strings of a thousand cash in Ch'in-chou.
In P'an-yü (Canton) or Wen-ling (Wen-chou) their value is
ten times this amount. Ten to twenty per cent of purchasers
have to come to the spot because the length of the material
makes it difficult to transport by sea. (59)

The ship-building industry also used great quantities of nails, lime,
silk rags for caulking and oil from the nuts of the t'ung tree (which
served as a wood preservative and was combined with lime to form
a caulking material).

Sea-going vessels commonly had from one to four masts,
although cases are on record of some with as many as twelve.
Two was the usual number. Bamboo matting was often used for sails,
especially by Fukienese craft. Square sails were suspended from
the top of the mast and controlled by a network of sheet-ropes attached
along one side to the individual sections of the sail. It was customary
to rely upon the monsoon winds. According to Liao Kang's Collected
Works of Liao Kao-feng (Kao-feng chi) which was written in the
12th century:

(Sea-going ships) take advantage of the reliability of
the seasonal winds. They go South in the winter and
come North in the summer, never the other way round.
For this reason the ships travel evenly and steadily
without the need for any great attention. Since the
nature of the winds is favorable, they cover a thousand
li (about 300 miles) a day without difficulty. (61)

It was possible to go from Fukien to Korea in 5 to 20 days, and from
Ming-chou (modern Ning-po) to Mi-chou (in southern Shantung)
in a mere three days.

Deep-draught ocean-going sailing ships could not navigate with
ease the shallow Chinese coastal seas with their sandbanks, islands
and tidal currents, or the Huai, Ch'ien-t'ang and lower Yangtze rivers.
Small craft were therefore used instead. Heavy goods from the South
that were destined for Hang-chou were brought north in 'southern
ships' (nan-ch'uan) as far as Yü-yao River in Ming-chou and there,
because of the high tides and sandbars of the Chekiang coast,
trans-shipped into canal boats for passage to Hsi-hsing whence they
were ferried over the Ch'ien-t'ang River to Hang-chou. After AD 1132
they were trans-shipped at Ming-chou instead into special sea-going
shallow-draught oared galleys called 'lake boats' (hu-ch'uan).
A warship with a lake boat's hull constructed here is known to have
had a capacity of 800 hu, being 83 feet long and 20 feet wide, with a
crew of two hundred. Similar craft were also found at other ports
in southern coastal waters.

There were other types of oared craft to be found on these
shallow seas and rivers. They included 'wind-piercers', which were
fishing boats carrying over a hundred persons, and 'flying tiger
warships' with four paddlewheels, each worked by four men, and
eight oars, said to be capable of covering more than three hundred
miles in a day. The use was also known of a leeboard device which
seems to have combined the properties of an outrigger with an
external centerboard. According to The Digest of the Military Classics
(Wu-ching tsung-yao) of 1044:

The 'sea-falcon' is a ship with a low prow and a lofty poop,
shaped like a falcon with a wide front and narrow aft. Floating
boards are fixed to each gunwale, having the shape of a falcon's
wings, and these so assist the boat that even if the wind and
waves rise up in fury it will not capsize. (62)

This piece of equipment was sometimes also known as the 'regulating rudder' (pi-t'o).

Large vessels were far outnumbered by the smaller ones. The AD 1259 gazetteer for Ning-po records the number of ships in that prefecture and in Wen-chou and T'ai-chou of over 10 Chinese feet in the beam as 3,833, and the number of those of less than this width as 15,454.

B. Boats Used on Inland Waterways

From the point of view of the type of boats most prevalent, the Yangtze River may be divided into three sectors. The westernmost, between Chia-chou and Chiang-ling (that is, embracing Szechwan and the gorges), was the domain of Szechwan boats (Shu-chou). The central sector, between Chiang-ling and Chien-k'ang (Nanking) or Chen-chiang, was that of Yangtze River Boats (Chiang-ch'uan). The eastern sector, from Chien-k'ang and Chen-chiang to the sea, that of Sea Junks (hai-po) and Sea Ships (hai-ch'uan). The Yuan dynasty poet Wang Yun, composed the following two verses on the Yangtze River Boats:

Sails

Yellow reeds are woven into foot-wide mats;
Section by section they constitute a sail.
It can be made long or short as is required;
And tightened or slackened as desired.*
Along one side the 'foot-rope' is attached,
Controlling the connected series like a net's main rope.
Northerners use linen sails;
Our custom** is to make them out of reeds.
Greedy for heavy cargoes, the captains of these ships
Hoist their sails high to catch the wind.
Both with the current or against the waves,
The great bird on the prow is given wings.
Seen from far off, coming from distant shores,
They seem a streak of dusky cloud,
Cutting a headlong path through misted isles,

---

*The longest have 27 sections and are over 20 feet wide. (Original note.)

**In the Yangtze valley. Transl.

Heavy with drenching in the Yangtze rains.
A hundred li have passed before the morning's done,
Through effortless use of favouring circumstance.
As evening's anchorage shows in the failing sunlight,
They fold in piles the many-pleated sails.

Oars

A River-Boat is an enormous fish;
The fishtail oars (lu) and rudder are its tail and fins.
Where water is deep and sweeps (chao) inadequate,
A fish-tail oar is fastened at the stern
To join its efforts with the sweeps in front.
This is the most important of the five
Things that are needful for crossing streams.
 . . . . (64)

Sails and the fish-tail oar were thus the most important means of
propulsion. Hauling was also used, however, a long hawser being
attached to the top of the vessel's mast and the mast in turn being
held by stays made fast on the rear gunwales. Lu Yu's Record of a
Journey to Szechwan (Ju Shu chi), written in the later part of the
twelfth century, describes the passage up the Yangtze gorges above
Chiang-ling as follows:

> They took the yard-arm off the mast and installed rowlocks,
> since for the ascent of the gorges only oars and thousand-foot
> hawsers are employed. Sails are no longer set. The
> thousand-foot hawser is made of (strips of) large bamboos
> split (length-wise) into four. It is as thick as a man's arm.
> The boat on which I travelled had a capacity of 1,600 piculs,
> and used in all six oars and two thousand-foot hawsers. (65)

Hauling was also used to drag boats up the dangerous rapids on the
Han River between Ying-chou and Hsiang-yang.

The communications network provided by inland waterways was
most highly developed in the Yangtze Delta. The Wu Boats (Wu-ch'uan)
utilized here were small boats of shallow draught and with flat bottoms,
well-suited to the creeks and irrigation canals. They were generally
punted, less frequently hauled or propelled by oars. The ships which

carried the tribute grain (ts'ao-ch'uan) usually took 8 days to cover the
160 kilometers between Su-chou and Hang-chou.

The Yuan dynasty poet, Yuan Chǔeh, wrote a series of poems
on the various different kinds of boat to be found in the China of his
day. He described how, for example, the boatmen of Wu did not use
anchors but secured their craft by driving a punt-pole into the river-
bottom; and how the Huai Boats (Huai-ch'uan), ' as thin as paper', and
equipped with oars and poles as well as sails, carried heavy loads
of salt and grain. Here, to conclude this section, is part of his poem
on the Yellow River Boats:

> The boats of the Yellow River are like slices of cut melon,
> Covered with iron nails for scraping over the sandy shallows.
> Their towering masts are not secured at the base,
> But guyed on every side by ropes.
> They come like floatingmountains of bundled firewood,
> Scattering before them the boats of Huai and Wu.
> They ply between the North and South to make their living,
> And know but little of the Yangtze River.
> With the wind set fair a thousand sails will be moving at
> different speeds. ...
> In the forefront they rear pigs and donkeys in one pen,
> Availing themselves of the donkey's strength for hauling,
> And laying on the lash unsparingly.
> It is much better than Kiangnan, where men do the work of beasts.
> (67)

ii. Concentration and Specialization in the Shipping Business

The growth of shipping led to an increased production of the
materials needed for the production of boats. By means of this
process even remote and backward areas were often drawn into the
commercial economy. Figures for the construction of the official
inland waterway grain transport boats indicate the main pattern of
concentration assumed by the industry:

Grain Transport Boats Built in or around AD 1021

Ch'ien-chou (S. Kiangsi: Kan-chou)	605
Feng-hsiang Hsieh-ku (W. Shensi)	600
Chi-chou (S. Kiangsi: Chi-an)	525
T'an-chou (Hunan: Ch'ang-sha)	280
Ting-chou (Hunan: Ch'ang-te)	240
Ming-chou (Chekiang: Ning-po)	177
T'ai-chou (Chekiang)	126
Wen-chou (Chekiang)	125
Wu-chou (Chekiang: Chin-hua)	105
Ch'u-chou (Kiangsu: Huai-an)	87
Chia-chou (Szechwan: Chia-ting)	45
Total	2915

All of these were nodal points for inland water transportation and well placed for supplies of wood, iron nails, t'ung oil, lime, hemp and charcoal. A survey of contemporary literature reveals a total of 51 centers of public and private boat-building, all but 4 of them in central or southern China.

Resource endowment differed in the various localities. Kan-chou (Ch'ien-chou), in the heart of a region in which ship-building had been concentrated since T'ang times, seems to have been especially well supplied. According to Chao Shan-kua:

> In the upper reaches of Kiangsi it has long been
> customary for carpenters to gather and establish
> shipyards. They collect pine and juniper, cut medlar
> and catalpa, while their nails are numerous as grains
> in the granary, and their oil overflows into the streams.(75)

Wen-chou was a collecting-point for the pine-wood, varnish, t'ung oil and wax tree oil (Rhus succedanea) produced in its hinterland, and it also exported them. Under the Southern Sung, however, official demand for boats rose so rapidly that timber became in short supply here. The government began to requisition merchant ships and fishing boats for official purposes, and the Shipmasters (ch'uan-hu) who owned most of such craft covered themselves against the threat of financial ruin which this involved by means of the so-called 'system of voluntarily contributing ships' (i-ch'uan fa). Groups of the order of 60 persons would jointly pay for the building of 6 ships and offer half of these to the government. Fukien had good timber and exported pig-iron to

Ming-chou for further working. Kuang-nan suffered from a shortage
of iron nails and t'ung oil, although strong woods for rudders were
a speciality of this region. Hunan, in contrast, produced both
t'ung oil and iron in substantial quantities.

Most of the ship-owners on the south-east coast were landowners, and those who worked their vessels poor fisherfolk or
displaced peasants. Liao Kang, speaking of Fukien, asserted that:

> By and large, very few of those who man the sea-going vessels
> are from households of the upper or middle grades.
> They hold their lives cheap in their search for
> profit. All of them can only just support their wives
> children. (74)

Fan Cheng-ming, who flourished in the last years of the eleventh
century, wrote in his survey of Yo-yang, on the shores of the
Tung-t'ing Lake in northern Hunan:

> The wealth of commoners of the middle grade does not
> exceed 50 strings of cash. Most of them live on boats
> and go up and down the rivers. Almost half of them live
> by fishing. They trade everywhere and are called 'T'an
> households' (T'an-hu). Their fields are, so to speak, the
> middle of the lakes. (75)

These persons were probably the subordinates of well-to-do merchants
who carried on a transport business in conjunction with their other
affairs. Yeh Shih, who lived in later twelfth century, wrote of them
as follows:

> The rivers and lakes are linked together, so that one can go
> everywhere by means of them. When a boat leaves its home
> port there are no obstacles to its planning a journey of ten
> thousand li. Every year the common people use all the grain
> that is surplus to their requirements for seeds and food for
> trading. Large merchants gather what the lesser households
> have. Little boats engage in joint operations with the greater
> vessels as the latter's dependents, going back and forth
> selling grain in order to clear a solid profit. It is a regular
> custom for sons to succeed to their fathers and to grow old
> in their turn facing the winds and waves. (76)

2. THE STRUCTURE OF MANAGEMENT IN THE SHIPPING BUSINESS

The varying techniques used in water transport, the routes followed and even the size of the ships involved, all exerted an effect upon the nature of the labor that was employed. While examining this diversity, we shall be mainly concerned, however, with investigating the foundations of the management of the private shipping business, namely the composition of labor, the manner of its combination and its rewards.

i. Labor on Board Ship

A. Sea-going vessels

Long-distance junks had large crews and engaged in large-scale enterprises. There was therefore a well-developed differentiation of functions among their personnel. Essentially, there were in addition to the ship's owner(s) (ch'uan-chu) and the chief provider(s) of capital (ts'ai-chu or po-shang, i.e. junk merchants), both of whom normally remained on land, and the passengers and merchants on board, four main groups of person. These were (1) Those in charge of mercantile operations generally, fitting out the ship, keeping it in repair, and hiring crew; (2) Officers in charge of accounts or, more generally, purser's duties, of the military arsenal and comparable matters; (3) The captain and senior seamen responsible for the actual sailing of the ship; and (4) The crew. The terminology used to designate these groups was not entirely consistent but it is possible, from the rather fragmentary materials at our disposal, to establish the broad outlines.

According to Chu Yü's Talks From P'ing-chou (P'ing-chou K'o-t'an), written in 1119:

> Large sea-going junks carry several hundred men; small ones rather more than a hundred. Important merchants are made Group Leader (kang-shou), Assistant Group Leader (s) (fu kang-shou) and Purser (tsa-shih). The Superintendency of Foreign Trade (shih-po ssu) gives them vermilion seals (chu-chi) and permits them to inflict the bamboo upon their followers, and, if there are any who die, to confiscate their property. (80)

This may be supplemented by a passage from the section on master mariners in the <u>Enquiry Into the Eastern and Western Oceans</u> (Tung/ Hsi-yang k'ao) written by Chang Hsieh in AD 1618:

> When they venture forth beyond Hai-men (at the mouth of
> the Yangtze) the foam thrown up by the currents blots
> out the skies and the restless billows join with the Milky
> Way. It is impossible any longer to look for a shore, to
> recall villages or to reckon upon the post-routes. The
> Captain and Senior Sailors (<u>chang-nien san-lao</u>) strike the
> rhythm for the rowing-sweeps, and spread the sails.
> They cut through the currents and confront the waves,
> relying for guidance solely upon the mariner's compass.
> ... In each junk, command is in the hands of a Junk Master
> (<u>po-chu</u>). The merchants are all his dependents, like ants
> who have appointed a leader and move together from
> one nest to another. In subordinate positions are the
> Accountant (<u>ts'ai-fu</u>), who is responsible for the financial
> records, and the General Manager (<u>tsung-kuan</u>), who
> controls affairs on board and transmits orders on
> behalf of the Junk Master. There is an Arsenal Comptroller
> (<u>chih-k'u</u>) in charge of military weapons, Mast Watch
> Mates (<u>a-pan</u>) in charge of the masts, a First and Second
> Anchorman (<u>t'ou-ting</u>, <u>erh-ting</u>) in charge of anchors,
> a First and Second Sailrope Mate (<u>ta-liao</u>, <u>erh-liao</u>) in
> charge of the sailropes, and two Helmsmen (<u>t'o-kung</u>) who
> take charge of the helm in alternation. A Chief Mate
> (<u>huo-chang</u>) watches over the compass needle, and when
> the route lies across a wide expanse of ocean, all obey his
> indications. ...* (83)

By the end of the nineteenth century it was usual, at least in Taiwan and parts of Chekiang, Fukien and Kwangtung, for the senior representative of the owner(s) on board, and the executive in charge of business operations, to be called the <u>ch'u-hai</u>, 'he who goes to sea'. His position was comparable to that of a director (<u>tung-shih</u>) in a merchant establishment on land, and his duties were largely similar to those of the Group Leader (<u>kang-shou</u>) of earlier times.

---

*Cp. J. Needham, <u>Science and Civilization in China</u>, Vol. IV. 1 (Cambridge: Cambridge University Press, 1962) pp. 291-292.

A variety of terms were used to designate the captain or chief seaman. According to Wu Tzu-mu, who lived in the later thirteenth century:

> When storms have darkened the heavens, they journey relying on the compass alone. The Chief Mate (huo-chang) has charge of it, and does not dare to make the slightest error.* (81)

Hsu Ching, in his Illustrated Account of an Embassy to Kao-li in the Hsuan-ho Reign-period, recorded that:

> There may be sixty chief polers (kao-shih) and sailors in a sea-going ship. They rely upon the familiarity of the Captain (shou-ling) with the sea-ways, and his skill in judging the weather and human affairs is such that he obtains general confidence. Therefore when a sudden emergency arises, everyone co-operates as if they were a single person and it is possible to come safely through. (82)

Jen Shih-lin, an author of the Yuan dynasty, describes the welcome that awaited junks when they put into port below the Heaven Gate Hill in Hsiang-shan county in Ning-po:

> Before long the shadows on their sails are rising and falling, and the chant of the oarsmen swelling and fading. As they draw up in a straight line below the quayside, the brokers scattered about on the shore shout out enquiries at long range to old acquaintances among the crew. The skippers (san-lao) lean on their masts and make deep bows, while the cargoes are taken off to the markets. ... I have also seen the junks of wealthy men, with masts a hundred feet in height and oars spread out like wings in flight. The senior seaman (chang-nien) keeps the correct direction from the south-pointing carriage (here, clearly, the mariner's compass) seated in the deckhouse, while the members of the crew come on watch and take their rest at the signals of a drum, exactly as in a government office. They make sure that the rudder and anchors are always of good quality, the ropes always finely made, the cargoes always the rare products of strange lands. (82)

---

*Cp. Needham (1962), p. 284.

Besides the information given in the quotation from
Chang Hsieh above, light is thrown on the structure of crews by
a Japanese work of the Edo period, The Local Products of Nagasaki
(Nagasaki Miyage). Ships that came to this port from Fukien,
Chekiang and Kwangtung usually carried a Chief Ship's Master
(cheng ch'uan-chu), Assistant Ship's Master (fu ch'uan-chu), Purser
(ts'ai-fu), General Manager (tsung-kuan), Chief Merchant (?) (k'o-chang),
Ship's Owner (pan-chu), Chief Mate (huo-chang), Helmsman (t'o-kung),
Anchorman (t'ou-ting), Incense Offerer (hsiang-kung) (in charge of the
ship's tutelary deity), Chief Carpenter (ya-kung-t'ou), Carpenter(s)
(ya-kung), Arsenal Comptroller (?) (chih-ku - the Japanese gloss
assigns him 'the duty of looking after the big drum' and the text
elsewhere mentions certain religious duties), Mate in Charge of
Mainsail Ropes (ta-liao), Leading Seamen in Charge of Second and
Third Sails (erh-ch'ien, san-ch'ien), Mast Watch Mate (ya-pan,
probably an error for a-pan), Cook (tsung-p'u), Chief Seaman (lao-ta),
Sailors (kung-she), and Servants (hsiao-ssu). Some vessels also had
a Head Stevedore (ts'ang-k'ou). Much of this specialization probably
occurred in Ming and Ch'ing rather than in Sung times.

Large crews might contain up to several hundred men.
Marco Polo mentions the use of oars which required 4 men to pull
them, and Ibn Battutah ships with 20 oars each of which required
15 to 20 sailors, shouting in unison, to operate it.

B. Coastal Shipping and Inland Waterways Shipping

Small coastal craft often combined fishing with transportation.
Compared with the large sea-going ships, the composition of labor was
relatively simple and undifferentiated. Terms such as 'helmsman'
(shao-kung), 'chief poler' (kao-shih) and 'sailor' (shui-shou) used with
reference to them mostly had a comprehensive and broadly-defined
meaning. There were sometimes the additional categories of Engager
(chao-t'ou) and Anchorman (ting-shou). 'Helmsman' commonly indicated
the captain and 'engager' the chief seaman or chief mate, who
resembled, in his capacity as a supervisor of labor, the chang-nien,
san-lao, huo-chang, and lao-ta referred to in the preceding section.

Inland waterways craft relied more upon poling, fishtailing
and hauling than upon sailing. Their size was relatively small and
labor but little differentiated. The term 'helmsman' was generally
used to indicate the senior sailor on board (in the absence of the
ship's owner) and 'chief poler' might sometimes be given a similar
sense. Normally the chief poler was subordinate to the helmsman.
Government grain-ships in the twelfth century typically had three
such senior sailors on board, either a helmsman and chief polers or
a helmsman, chief poler and engager.

The terms chang-nien (literally 'elder') and san-lao (originally
a Han dynasty term for a lower-level local official), with their somewhat
patriarchal flavor, were also used in some places for the chief
sailors. The T'ang dynasty commentator Yen Shih-ku observed
(a propos of one of Tu Fu's poems) that:

> The men of the Yangtze gorges call the one who holds the
> punt-pole at the prow and spies out the way through the
> water the chang-nien and the main helmsman the san-lo. (92)

Generally speaking, the size of a crew depended on the size
of a vessel and the weight of her cargo.

ii. Labor on Shore

At locks, haulovers and other such places there appeared a
class of porters who specialized in trans-shipping cargoes. This
may be seen from a passage in Li Tao's Continuation of the Comprehensive
Mirror for Aiding Government (Hsu tzu-chih t'ung-chien ch'ang-pien)
for (lunar) 1089:

> The Ch'ing River (which then linked Wu-chou (present day
> Huai-an) with a lake N.E. of K'ai-feng and thence with the
> Gulf of Po-hai) is joined to all the routes leading to
> Chiang-Che and Huai-nan. Boats transport commodities
> back and forth along it. At the two lakes in Hsu-chou, the
> Lu-liang and the Pai-pu, with their currents, their shallows
> and their dangerous places, their boatmen, oxen, donkeys,
> trackers (ch'ien-hu) and trans-shippers (p'an-po-jen), all sorts
> of obstructions are encountered, and damage done to the vessels,
> and so merchants do not go that way. (94)

According to the <u>Draft Sung Digest</u> (Sung hui-yao chi-kao):

> Going upstream from Han-k'ou to Ying-chou (on the Han
> River) there are still but few rapids and submerged rocks;
> but from Ying-chou and Hsiang-yang upwards there are
> the dangers of the thirty-six rapids. When a convoy
> (<u>kang</u>) has brought its cargoes this far, it is necessary to
> load them into several hundred smaller craft, a practice
> which is called 'trans-shipping past the rapids' (<u>p'an-t'an</u>).
> The boats are all hauled upstream with thousand-foot
> hawsers made of bamboo. (94)

Sometimes the goods had to be portaged. Thus Fan Ch'eng-ta,
in his <u>Record of the Boats of Wu</u> (Wu-ch'uan lu) states with regard to
the Pai-kou Gorges of Kuei-chou (W. Hupeh) in 1177 that:

> When one reaches the New Rapids, which have the worst
> repute of any of the Three Gorges, if one wishes to avoid
> either ascending or descending them one must trans-ship
> (<u>p'an-po</u>) and go by land, negotiating the rapids with an
> empty boat. There are many inhabitants on both banks
> called Rapids Men (<u>t'an-tzu</u>) who make their living solely
> by transporting goods past the rapids. (94)

In the great cities there were porters who could be hired
by the day. According to the section on rice shops in the <u>Meng-liang
lu</u> ('Dreaming of Splendors in the Midst of Deprivation'), Wu Tzu-mu's
description of the Southern Sung capital of Lin-an:

> There are moreover Labor Hirers (<u>lin-hu</u>) who provide
> men to unload the sacks. The carriers and porters
> likewise have bosses who control them; and each boat
> has its Receiver of Cargo (?) (<u>shou-tsai chou-hu</u>). Although
> the arrangements for transport at the rice markets are
> complicated, there is never any squabbling. Therefore the
> shopkeepers do not waste any unnecessary energy and the
> rice comes directly to their shops. * (95)

---

* Cp. E. Balazs, <u>Chinese Civilization and Bureaucracy</u> (New Haven:
Yale University Press, 1964), p. 92.

These labor contractors also provided their services when grain from the official granaries had to be moved to its recipients.

When necessary boats were hauled by men, often trackers who specialized in this task, or by animals. Towing-paths had therefore to be constructed along the banks of the major rivers. Where there were no such paths, tug-boats might be used, a practice recorded by Lu Yu in his Record of a Journey into Szechwan. According to Jōjin, the Japanese monk who came to China in AD 1072, at certain haulovers water-buffaloes were used to turn capstans by means of which the boats were pulled through.

iii. The Recruitment of Officers and Crew

Much of the shipping business was carried on by family groups. The following verses by Kao Chu, a wandering scholar of the twelfth century, give a general impression of the life which such people led:

> They load all their household possessions into a light boat
> And ply back and forth along the Yangtze as the spring passes
> into autumn.
> Three generations, fathers and sons, live by the tiller in
> the stern,
> Knowledge from all the four quarters meets at Sha-shih
> (W. Hupeh).
> Old men rise with the first light to determine the direction
> of the wind;
> Young wives perform their morning toilette with the waters
> as a mirror.
> They rejoice in the roving life
> And a living earned from travel to distant parts. (98)

The Yuan dynasty poet Yuan Chüeh paints a similar picture in his lines on the boats of Wu:

> The boats of Wu are oval, like turtles with tucked-in heads.
> Upon them families sail all year without returning.
> The thatched hut, the old plot of land, have long since vanished.
> Once they have gone North they are free from hunger.
> . . . .

Throughout each morning they know the toils of travel,
But for the entire year they are spared the pain of parting
                                    from their families.
Just eight years old, the eldest son skips about nimbly,
While his younger brother learns to treat a sailboat as
                                    terra firma.

. . . .

They do not understand the use of the anchor to secure their boats;
At the day's end their curved poles* point to the heavens.
The captains marry womenfolk from one another's families.
Only in Huai-nan do they abduct the fisher-girls,
Sending word back to their villages that they should not harbor a
                                    grudge about it. (99)

Sometimes family-operated transport ships would be available for
hire by the day. This is suggested by the remarks of Ts'ai Hsiang,
who flourished in the first half of the eleventh century, on the boats
of Fu-chou in Fukien, a place of which he was once the prefect:

> In the house-boats of Fu-t'ang (present-day Fu-ch'ing) there
> are entire families living in a single vessel. In the hot
> weather and the cold, whether eating, drinking, suffering from
> sickness or getting married, they never leave it. How
> constricted are their lives! Yet they come and go as they
> please, and support themselves by taking wages for work
> on the water. (99)

These families of boatmen were often of peasant origin, having been
driven by poverty or debt into abandoning agriculture. Lines in
the form of a boat-song from a thirteenth-century work, Fang Hui's
Continuation of the Collected Works From T'ung River (T'ung-chiang
hsu-chi), symbolize what was probably the common fate of many small
farmers in Kiangnan:

> They lived at Hsieh-t'ang, next door to a wealthy family.
> When times were hard and rice was dear, they fell in debt to
>   these neighbors.
> So they took to shipping, being unable to return,
> Penniless folk piloting a small boat.
> It cost four thousand and five hundred cash to charter it at
>   Wei-t'ang, **

---

*Used as 'stick-in-the mud' anchors. Transl.
**In Chia-shan county in Chekiang. Transl.

And five hundred more as the shipping broker's commission,
A thousand for repairs to the rudder, one thousand three
                                  hundred for rice,
And for three days no receipts at all.

It takes twenty thousand cash to repay a debt of ten,
And creditors insist on several times more.
The officials are bound to jail any family which goes back,
Besides charging further for the lodging of its women-folk.

Southward bound to Hang-chou and northwards to Ch'u-chou,
By the Three Rivers and Eight Dykes the waters flow unbroken.
The hauling-board and punting-pole - these are their rice-bowl.
They do not have the bitter toil of working with the hoe.

They earn meager wages for moving heavy cargoes.
The father hauls, the son shoves with the pole.
With five thousand catties of beeswax and three thousand of lacquer
They have to do their travelling by night.

From prow to stern the sound of singing resounds.
Between Su-chou and Hsiu-chou, Hu-chou and Hang-chou all of
                                   them are brothers.
If quarrels arise they either call each other to the attack or
                                 shout to break it up,
And they are pitiless to rogues and thieves. (100)

When the family circle was insufficient to supply the
necessary labor, the principle of a common area of origin might serve
as a basis for further recruitment. Lu Yu's Record of a Journey to
Szechwan contains the following entry for 1170 concerning a boat
belonging to Chao Ch'ing, a man who is known to have come from
Chia-chou:

There was a certain Wang Pai-i who was a native of Chia-chou.
He had previously been hired to serve as the engager (chao-t'ou)
on a boat. The engager is the chief of the mates (san-lao chih
chang) and is employed at a somewhat higher wage. Whenever
there is a sacrifice to the gods he receives twice as much of the
sacrificial meat as do ordinary persons. Later on Chao Ch'ing,
who owned the boat, employed his acquaintance Ch'eng Hsiao-pa

as engager instead, which meant that Wang Pai-i lost his job.
He fell into a state of depression and did not go away but
subsequently went insane and threw himself into the river.   (99)

When relatively large numbers of boatmen were required, some
form of labor contracting was probably widely used. Thus the
Draft Sung Digest observed for 1170 that:

> As to the polers required for one boat travelling North,
> these are all recruited by the helmsman (chou-shao) before
> the undertaking starts. Most of them are vagrant, rootless
> men. (98)

For shipping that was under government control certain
special conditions applied. Thus when the state hired a ship the
helmsman/captain was normally given Hiring Cash (ku-ch'ien),
Porterage Cash (shui-chiao ch'ien) and Wastage Tickets (hao-ch'üan)
to cover the costs of fitting out the vessels and engaging a crew.
When the government forcibly hired ships at Wen-chou, an imposition
that was often ruinous for those who suffered from it, it used the
method described as follows in Lou Yao's Collection of the Kung-K'uei
Master (Kung-k'uei chi):

> Helmsmen for ten ships are conscripted in rotation from those
> boat owners (ch'uan-hu) in Yung-chia county who own
> agricultural land. The sailors employed in each boat are
> also conscripted in random fashion from among the poor folk
> in the county who live along the coast. All this class of
> person live by fishing and greatly dread having to do this
> task. (102)

In Yuan times, a merchant engaged in maritime trade (hai-shang) had to
report to the authorities the name of the group leader, arsenal
comptroller, purser, Captain (pu-ling), helmsman and anchorman
whom he had hired.

Although Sung population figures are not entirely trustworthy,
being mostly too low and almost certainly omitting many of those
who had no fixed residence, it would seem that in some counties
on the south-east coast up to one-third of the population lived on

board ship, and that in the prefecture of Ming-chou (Ning-po),
Wen-chou and T'ai-chou alone something like 200,000 persons were
engaged, either whole-time or part-time in the water transport
business. In some of the inland parts of Chekiang, where trade
and transport had brought new economic vigor to previously backward
and hilly areas, the situation was probably very nearly comparable.

iv. Wages

        Available information on wages is almost solely concerned
with ships and boats hired by the government. Thus we know that
in 1179, in the nine coastal counties of Fukien, the government paid
captains who held no official rank at a daily rate of 250 copper cash
and two and a half pints (0.025 of a picul) of rice. A helmsman
on such sea-going vessels received a daily wage of 150 cash and
two and a half pints of rice, while engagers, anchormen and
ordinary sailors got 100 cash and two and a half pints of rice. On
the day on which the hire commenced there would be a feast
(k'ao-she) and the captain would be furnished with funds for repairing
his ship. Each helmsman would get 15 strings of a thousand cash
each, the engagers and anchormen 10 strings each and sailors 5 strings
each. The captain was held responsible for the costs of outfitting the
ship. Such practices were probably much the same as those followed
when ships were hired by private persons.

        The system used by the government for inland waterways
boats is revealed by a memorial cited by the Sung Draft Digest
for 1073:

        'Before the transportation in convoy starts they have to
        repair and fit out the boats and for this purpose twenty per
        cent of the wages which the state pays for the hiring of the
        crew are issued in advance. When the wages are provided
        later only the remaining eighty per cent is given. Investigation
        has shown that the convoys do not receive a large sum in this
        way and that the helmsmen are compelled to borrow considerable
        quantities of money at interest and to purchase on credit
        at high prices such items as bedding. Because this causes them
        to run short of cash, they engage too few members of crew and
        pilfer the official goods (which they are carrying). It is
        requested that the sum paid out in advance should be thirty
        per cent.' It was so done. (105)

The most important point to be noticed here is that wages were not generally paid directly by the hirer to those whom he hired but passed through the hands of an intermediary. What limited evidence there is suggests that, as with sea-going vessels, inland waterways boats also used differential wage-rates to different categories of boatman.

3. THE CHARACTERISTICS OF MANAGEMENT

Generally speaking, when the transport business is but little developed, the person who requires transport arranges it for himself. Thus transport is extremely closely linked with commerce and trade. Water transportation under the Sung dynasty was no exception to this rule. The basic character of its management had still not left behind the stage in which transportation is in a merchant's own ships. Nonetheless, the rising demand for transportation, the increase in the quantities of goods transported and distances covered, and the decisive advance made in the techniques of transportation meant that the business progressed beyond being merely the carriage of the carrier's own products and became commercialized. The forms of management became accordingly differentiated. The owners of ships sometimes managed their affairs through employed intermediaries, were entrusted by others with goods for sale and purchase, and transported goods for others on the basis of contracts of carriage. Sometimes, too, persons who did not own the means of transportation would either hire ships or charter ships and crews. In connection with all these practices, namely hiring, chartering, carriage contracts, and the loading and sale of goods, the activities of Shipping Brokers (ch'uan-hang) and comparable persons became for the first time a generalized phenomenon.

i. The Forms of Ownership

A. Management by the Ship's Owner

    a. Direct Management

Already in T'ang times most of the owners of large ships were merchants. The situation was broadly comparable in Sung times but those who owned ships also included members of the imperial household, civil and military officials, Buddhist and Taoist monasteries and

temples, owners of manors, powerful local families both with and
without official status, well-to-do peasants, ordinary peasants,
poor fishermen, and persons who lived on the water. Members
of the imperial family, religious establishments, and merchants
connected with the state tea and salt monopolies escaped the
unexpected requisitioning of their boats by the government and were
exempted from the payment of the taxes on trade, tonnage cash
(li-sheng ch'ien) and supplementary trade tax (t'ou-tzu ch'ien),
- rights which conferred on them a privileged commercial position.
There were also, however, numerous wealthy merchants without
such privileges, many of whom owned their own ship(s), travelled
on board and managed their own affairs in person.

     The combination of the joint ownership of ships and goods
by a group of merchants with the direct management of affairs was
also known. An example of this may be found in a commemorative
inscription of the later eleventh century in Ch'in Kuan's Works of Ch'in
Huai-hai (Huai-hai chi):

> The (Ch'ing-shan) Master's personal name was Chao-ch'ing
> and his style was Hsien-chih. His surname in secular
> life had been Lin. He was from Chin-chiang in Ch'üan-chou.
> When he was young he was unrestrained and of a wilful
> disposition. He joined up with several persons from the same
> locality as himself and they went trading, sailing the seaways
> from Kwangtung and Fukien up to Shantung, coming and
> going across the seas for more than ten years. He became
> extremely rich. In the Huang-yu reign-period (1049-1053),
> he became by imperial favor a monk. His father and mother
> had previously promised him to be a monk when he was a
> boy, and his name had been registered at the K'ai-yuan Temple
> in Chang-chou. He now suddenly abandoned all his business
> pursuits, gave his wealth to his business partners (t'ung-ch'an)
> so that they might take care of his family, and entered the
> monastery penniless. He shaved off his beard and his hair,
> and observed all the abstentions, much to the wonderment
> of the local people. (110)

Temporary partnerships, in contrast to this one, which seems to have
been permanent, were formed by merchants and sailors for trade with
Korea, Japan, the East Indies and Southeast Asia. The partners

(t'ung-pan, huo-pan) would go in the same boat and share out any profits. Discipline at sea and the control of the joint assets would be entrusted to a Group Leader (kang-shou) or Chief Merchant on Board (chu-po ta-ku).

The small family business, however, remained the core of inland and coastal shipping.

b. Indirect Management

Wealthy merchants who engaged in maritime trade would often hire a managerial agent (hsing-ch'ien) to manage their ventures for them, in a fashion analogous to the ch'u-hai ('he who goes to sea') of later times. Merchants like Fo Lien, a Moslem from Southeast Asia who owned 80 sea-going vessels, clearly had either to use agents or to hire out their ships. In at least one instance a Yuan dynasty law code distingusihed between the financial backer (ts'ai-chu or po-shang), the owner(s) of the ship (ch'uan-chu) and the person immediately in charge of an overseas trading venture (kang-shou) when considering the allocation of punishment for misconduct. Collective ownership was involved in the 'system of voluntarily contributing ships' (i-ch'uan fa) found at Ming-chou, Wen-chou and T'ai-chou and referred to on page 13 above. This system must also have necessitated the use of managerial agents, both for the ships which the consortium retained for its own use and for those with which it provided the government, each of the latter being placed under a Public Business Manager (kan-pan kung-shih).

At least in large-scale operations, therefore, there was some division of functions and of financial and operational risk-taking.

B. Hiring and Chartering

The T'ang Law code (T'ang-lu shu-i) refers to the hiring of boats, and the Sung Draft Digest mentions 'boats for hire' as being, like pawnshops, wholesale stores with warehouses, lodging-houses, stores, and oxen for renting, as one of the standard categories used for the assessment of family wealth for taxation purposes. How general the hiring of boats had become by this period is suggested by a cautionary tale recounted in a letter written in the twelfth century by Yang Wan-li to the famous statesman Yü Yun-wen (Pin-fu) and included in the former's Collection from the Studio of Sincerity (Ch'eng-chai chi):

There was a rich man in a certain place. He owned ten
thousand ch'ing of agricultural land and his goods filled a
thousand ships. He grew rich not by his own activities but
by making use of others to act for him. One day someone
said to him: 'You have understood, Sir, how to amass
wealth, but you do not know how to utilize it. Your ten
thousand ch'ing of land bring in a mere five thousand
(strings of cash) each year; your thousand ships of goods
a mere five hundred (strings of cash). This means that
you, as the owner, are not getting all the profits because
you share them with outsiders (k'o).' The rich man forthwith
personally took over the farming of all his fields and the
trading engaged in by his boats. Within three years he was
poverty-stricken. Why was it that, formerly, he had
shared and yet been wealthy, and, latterly, had kept
everything to himself and yet become poor? His income
had been extensive and was now restricted. His outgoings
had previously been slight and were now ruinous. How
can one take away from others all the profits of the Empire
and appropriate them oneself? This is simply because people
exchange with each other and merchants exchange with
merchants. (114)

The most familiar instance of the chartering of boats together
with their crews is the'harmonious hiring' (ho-ku) of commoners' boats
by the government for the transport of the tax grain. As the Sung
government became aware of the relative inefficiency of transport
by government-owned vessels in comparison with those owned by
commoners, the early policy of offical self-sufficiency gave way to
a greatly extended use of 'harmonious hiring'. Although the system
was based upon contracts involving three parties, namely the state,
the commoner concerned and a shipping broker, yet because it
amounted to forcible hiring and the government was in a position to
force down the price paid and to impose severe conditions regarding
indemnification by the carrier in the event of accidents or damage to
cargo, those in the shipping business generally tended to shun these
engagements. There were, however, many powerful local persons and
merchants with liquid capital who were attracted by the right of ships
so hired to carry a specified amount of private cargo in addition to
their official cargo, and by the bestowal of official titles by way of

reward, and even by the freedom from anxiety about finding a cargo; and so the tax grain transport system gradually shifted towards reliance on 'harmonious hiring'. There is no doubt that this official practice was the reflection of an antecedent and continuing non-official practice. On at least one occasion (in 1111) official rates were explicitly based on those prevailing in the private sector. Cases of non-official chartering will be given in a subsequent section.

C. The Carriage of Personal Goods By Shipmasters and Crews

Fixed quantities of personal goods were carried by shipmasters and crews on most vessels, whether these were under the direct management of the owners or on hire or charter. This was also the case on official boats, initially illegally but later generally with government permission. The Draft Sung Digest gives an instance as early as 970 of officials in charge of the conveyance of salt, silk and currency at Ch'eng-tu in Szechwan, and also the commoners and soldiers working on the ships, 'illicitly carrying goods and contraband salt for clandestine sale.' In (lunar) 1025 crews on official craft on small waterways carrying grain and salt were allowed to fill half the vessel with their own goods. By the twelfth century boats chartered by 'harmonious hiring' were being conceded a generous quantity of personal goods and government craft being permitted from ten to twenty per cent. If private goods were not carried, crews had the right to proportionately greater pay.

Sea-going ships carried an even higher percentage of private goods than inland waterway craft. According to Liao Kang when official duties brought him to Chang-chou in Fukien:

> When ships are officially hired it is necessary to give a favorable price, and, as before, fill 60 per cent of the vessel's capacity with official goods, conceding the other 40 per cent to the crew for sales on their own account. Since they are paid but meager wages they have to make a good profit from these activities if their willing involvement is to be obtained. (116)

It was probably not permissible for rare goods, such as certain spices, to be carried in this way.

In the 'Miscellany on Travel' in his <u>Extensive Record of the</u> <u>Forest of Affairs</u> (<u>Shih-lin kuang-chi</u>) Ch'en Yuan-ching remarked regarding the hiring of vessels:

> When in the course of one's travels one encounters
> convenient rivers, who would grudge the hire of a
> boat? It is necessary, however, to make enquiries as
> to the state of the waterways. If they are free of rapids
> or narrows one should bring the matter to a conclusion
> by going to a broker who is the master of a shop or
> lodging-house (<u>tien-chu ya-chia</u>), striking a bargain,
> drawing up a contract of hire and paying out the initial
> cash or paper money. One should not pay out a large
> sum, however, for it is to be feared that bridges, fords,
> marshes or ice may stop the advance of the boat and that
> one may have to proceed by land as before. It is essential
> that, as the boat goes along, one should not let the
> helmsman (captain) carry his own goods or passengers
> in excess of the number stipulated. (117)

Contracts which survive from the early Ming period likewise forbid the carriage of private goods; but it would seem reasonable to believe that, in view of the untrustworthy nature of shipmasters and their crews, this practice would have been an effective safety-valve, which diminished the risk of the boat, passengers or goods being lost or damaged through either accident or malice.

ii. Investment and Management

The Sung period saw the separation of financing and entrepreneurship in ocean shipping, and also the appearance of the collective ownership of ships. Both the <u>commenda</u> and the <u>societas</u> <u>maris</u> were found. In the former, a wealthy person or merchant (<u>ts'ai-chu, hai-shang</u>) entrusted money or goods to another merchant (<u>kang-shou</u>) who made use of them. This practice ran parallel to ordinary commercial money-lending whereby a lender (<u>ts'ai-chu,</u> <u>ts'ai-tung, yeh-chu</u>) advanced money to an entrepreneur (<u>hsing-ch'ien</u>) or 'manager' (<u>kan-jen, ching-chi-jen, ching-shang</u>) for repayment with interest at a time contractually specified, being differentiated from it only in so far as the emphasis was on profit-sharing rather than on lending at a fixed rate of interest.

Hsu Meng-hsin's twelfth-century <u>Collected Materials on Relations with the Northern Tribes</u> (<u>San-ch'ao pei-meng hui-pien</u>) contains a passage for 1137 which suggests the commonness of investment in shipping:

> There are numerous commercial transactions at the capital conducted by merchants from every part of the country, and the city is therefore reputed for its wealth and population. Most of those who possess capital engage in stockpiling and storage (<u>t'ing-t'a</u>), pawnbroking (<u>chieh-chih</u>) or trading in ships. How could they permit their accumulated wealth to lie idle, or buy gold for hoarding at home? (118)

An example of a <u>societas maris</u>, which differed from the <u>commenda</u> in that the capital employed was at least partly supplied by merchants who participated directly in the conduct of the venture, is to be found in Ch'in Chiu-shao's <u>Mathematical Treatise in Nine Sections</u> (<u>Shu-shu chiu-chang</u>), completed in 1247:

> Problem: Assume that there is a sea-going junk which has been to the customs station and cleared off its obligations. Apart from the goods to be paid to the owner of the ship (<u>chu-chia</u>) there remain 5,088 ounces of <u>aquilaria agallocha</u> (heart of Cambodian lign-aloes, garu-wood), 10,430 packets of 40 catties each of black pepper, and 212 pairs of elephant tusks. These have been brought by A, B, C, and D as the result of their trading with joint capital (<u>ho-pen</u>). A announces to the government that A's capital consisted of 200 ounces of gold, 4 bales of salt, 10 <u>tao</u> of paper money, B's capital consisted of 800 ounces of silver, 3 bales of salt, and 88 <u>tao</u> of paper money, C's capital was 1,670 ounces of silver and 15 <u>tao</u> of ordination certificates (<u>tu-tieh</u>), and D's capital was 52 <u>tao</u> of ordination certificates and 58 ounces 8 <u>shu</u> of gold. The total value of the foregoing is estimated to be 424,000 strings of cash. A has borrowed B's paper money, B has borrowed C's silver, C has borrowed D's ordination certificates and D has borrowed A's gold. * The goods so borrowed are now all returned to their original owners, and establish the ratio for an equitable distribution of the commodities first

---

*So that each now disposed of assets equal in value? Trans.

> mentioned. It is desired to know what the original value
> of the gold, silver, bales of salt and ordination certificates
> were, and how much aloes, pepper and ivory each man
> should have received. (118)

Although this is a mathematical problem, it reveals the nature of a
temporary partnership in which the profits were shared out in
proportion to the sum invested by each partner.

Pao Hui, writing during the Southern Sung dynasty about
the flow of copper cash out of China, mentions the willingness of
relatively poor people to invest small sums of money in the sea-going
ventures of others:

> The households of the middle and lower grades who live
> along the sea-coast are not able to cause any large outflow
> of cash but harm is caused by 'leakage through entrusting',
> a phenomenon which has been little noticed. Its cause is that
> all the people along the sea-coast are on intimate terms with
> the merchants who engage in overseas trade, either because
> they are fellow-countrymen or personal acquaintances.
> 'Leakage through entrusting' occurs when the former give
> the latter money to take with them on their ships for the
> purchase and return conveyance of foreign goods. They invest
> from 10 to 100 strings of cash and regularly make profits
> of several hundred per cent. The foolish people only understand
> gain. Why should they have any scruples about doing this? (119)

Besides collective ownership of ships and collective chartering
of ships, there were also commercial networks in which small
businesses, while retaining their entrepreneurial initiative, were
brought under the umbrella of larger concerns. The passage by Yeh
Shih cited on page 14 above is an illustration of this. There were also
the beginnings of joint-stock capital. This is apparent from a passage
in the Draft Sung Digest for 1142 which draws a distinction between
three different types of mercantile association:

> Merchants are forbidden to trade privately in tea and to cross
> the Huai River secretly in order to engage in private commercial
> exchange with merchants from the (Chin Tartar) North. Members
> of associations of partners (chiu-ho huo-pan), joint-capital

partnerships (lien-ts'ai ho-pen) or associations of members
of the same trade without joint capital (fei lien-ts'ai ho-pen erh
chiu-chi t'ung-hang), who lay information against smuggling
shall not be regarded as committing any offense. (120)

In the second of these a primitive form of joint-stock company may
be discerned.

iii. Contracts of Carriage

A. Freight Charges

For boats chartered by the government under the 'harmonious
hiring' system, freight rates were calculated on the basis of weight and
distance. Thus in 1061 payment was 100 cash for 100 catties carried
100 li. In 1157, for boats hired by the state from powerful local people
and merchants, 'under 300 cash were paid as porterage cash (shui-chiao-
ch'ien) for every picul carried 3,000 li.' In a work by a Mongol writer
of the Yuan dynasty, Sha-k'o-shih's Comprehensive Discussion of the
Defenses of the Yellow River (Ho-fang t'ung-i), the following
calculation is offered:

> Supposing that there are 15,350 bundles of twigs and
> straw which have to be taken somewhere, and that it is
> agreed after discussion that porterage cash for carrying
> 100 catties 100 li will be 240 cash. ... (121)

The Gazetteer of Su-chou Prefecture (Su-chou fu-chih) for the Hung-wu
reign (1368-1398), speaking of the official grain transport from
Kiangnan to North China by sea during the preceding dynasty, says:

> In 1284 it was determined that the government should
> pay porterage fees; and the order was given that wealthy
> families who lived along the coast should undertake the
> building of ships themselves, hire helmsmen and sailors
> and transport the grain, porterage fees to be 8.5 ounces
> (of silver) per picul, on the basis of the rates for 10 catties
> over 100 li. (121)

Since official hiring was sometimes explicitly done 'at the prices prevailing among the people,' it is likely that this system of calculating charges was also used in the private sector.

Sha-l'o-shih gives the daily mileage which boats on the Yellow River could expect to accomplish in a day as follows:

Upstream:	Heavily-laden boats	35 li
	Lightly-laden boats	50 li
Downstream:	Heavily-laden boats	100 li
	Lightly-laden boats	200 li

and it is clear that weight, direction and the nature of the waterways to be travelled all affected costs. He also has this to say about the way in which capacity was measured:

If you use a vessel of 300 hu capacity, it will be able to carry 150 bales (k'uai) and 18 persons as steersman and crew. It will be 45 feet in length and, apart from the flooding compartments (shui-ts'ang)* fore and aft, which take up to 15 feet, there will be 30 feet remaining, each foot of which takes 10 hu, each hu being 60 catties. (122)

Partial payment of charges was usually made in advance, both on private and government craft, as is suggested by the passage from Ch'en Yuan-ching quoted on page 31 above, and known under such names as 'initial deposit of cash or paper money' (shang-ch'i ch'ien hui), 'silver paid before hiring' (hsien-chieh shang-ch'i yin) or 'deposit cash' (ting-ch'ien). The balance was paid after safe arrival at one's destination.

B. Contracts of Hire

The establishment of its commercial independence by part of the transport industry gave rise to the use of contracts of carriage. They were probably further necessitated by the need to check the malpractices, such as disputes over fares and the theft of cargoes, which were prevalent among boatmen at this time. At the end of the

---

*It is hard to believe that these were necessary on inland waterways, and this term may refer to something else. Transl.

eleventh century the government had to lay down a fixed tariff of
charges at Fu-chou (in Fukien) as part of an attempt to curb widespread intimidation and robbery of passengers.

By Sung times these contracts had developed to the point
where some degree of standardization of form had been achieved.
A story told by Chang Pang-chi (fl. 12th century) in his Random
Jottings from the Literary Manor (Mo-chuang man-lu) is suggestive
in this regard:

> Ts'ui Kung-tu, whose style was Po-i, was proceeding to
> Hsuan-chou   (present-day Ning-kuo in Anhwei) to take
> up the post of prefect there. While travelling along the
> Yangtze at night he saw another boat silently following
> his. The next evening, when his boat had found a harbor
> and anchored, this other boat which he had seen was likewise
> right in against the bank. Ts'ui was suspicious and sent
> people to have a look at it. They found it empty. Inside
> there were bloodstains, and in the stern they picked up a
> length of black rope with a document wound around it.
> When Ts'ui examined it he saw that it was a contract for the
> hire of the boat (ku-chou ch'i). Thus he was able to learn
> the names of the people and the brokers and guarantors in-
> volved. On reaching the prefectural capital he ordered
> his police officers to have them arrested, and all of them
> were apprehended. What had happened was that the master
> of the boat had murdered the merchants who had hired his
> boat, stolen their goods and abandoned the boat. He (and
> his accomplices) were subsequently executed. Do not the
> ghosts of the dead remember their wrongs and submit their
> plaints? (124)

A model form for such a contract appears in a Yuan dynasty
collection of documents reprinted early in the fourteenth century. The
original version probably dates from the latter part of the preceding
century, and ultimately derives from epistolary forms used in the
T'ang and Sung.

Form for a Contract for the Hire of a Boat

Shipmaster (ch'uan-hu)....of.....in.....county in.....
  prefecture
The Foregoing....., having now been guaranteed by shipping
broker (ch'uan-ya).....of.....canton in .....district,

undertakes to convey.....piculs of baggage belonging to
official....of....., and to proceed to.....where it will be
unloaded. As a result of the discussions between the three
parties, it has been decided that paper money worth.....
strings of cash will be paid for the hire of the boatmen, of
which .....strings are to paid as a deposit and the remainder
to be handed over in full after arrival at the destination and
unloading. Once the goods have been loaded they must be
looked after carefully and (the boatmen) shall not dare to let
them get wet either through seepage from above or leakage
from below. If they are damaged, then restitution of like
for like shall be willingly made without recourse to the
lawcourts. A respectfully made contract.
.....year, ...month, ...day.

> Shipmaster................., seal.....
> Shipping broker............., seal..... (124)

A Ming dynasty model contract preserved in a similar collection, like
the five other known Ming specimens of this genre, all of which date
from the Wan-li reign (1573-1619), is basically similar to the above.
The only differences of note are that the shipmaster is held responsible
for any trans-shipping past rapids or shallows, the broker is called
a guarantor (pao-jen), and if the goods are negligently treated the
shipmaster has to make restitution 'according to the selling price
prevailing in the locality.'

There is important background information on the shipping
business in the late Ming encyclopedia of matters of everyday use-
fulness, The Correct Source of a Myriad Practical Usages from the
San-t'ai Hall (San-t'ai wan-yung cheng-tsung), particularly the section
on shipmasters:

When one is hiring a ship it is necessary to entrust a broker
with the task of determining whether or not the other party
is to be trusted. On all accounts you should avoid hiring on
your own in the hope of so gaining some small profit. Even
the old criminals and big rogues of the rivers and lakes still
have difficulty in escaping the boatmen's wiles. How much
more is this the case for honest persons! On ships which
have just recently been launched or purchased there will be
details that are still in confusion. Old and slovenly ships
are insufficiently sleek and clean. Boats with rough or
decrepit crews should be but little hired. When one examines
a boat one must make an estimate of the quantity of cargo

which it is capable of carrying, and see whether the caulking
of the seams is soft or firm, and only then complete the
transaction. The proverb says, 'Hiring a boat is like making
small purchases; one stresses good faith.' When one is
loading food-grains one should be on one's guard against
the particularly bad seams in the stern hold, the 'horse-
door beam' and the 'eye-beam'. The two holds on the 'tween-
decks should also enter one's calculations. One should do
likewise for unloading. While loading is proceeding it is
necessary to keep a watchful eye on the water line so that
the boatmen's greedy spirit is afforded no easy chance for
satisfaction, to keep a record of the sub-total in each of
the holds and not to permit them to be loaded in a confused
fashion. When one has gone halfway they sometimes make
false seals and give short measure, or purposely wet and
dry (grain), or mix the various kinds together. Helmsmen
and sailors have a corrupt practice for every type of cargo
and any number of sly frauds. If they are taking on a cargo
of your sesame, rape or grain, it is necessary to seal the
holes in the seams with paper paste. If of hemp-seed
cakes, they will break up pairs of cakes and refashion them
into three (and take the third). They will substitute small
salted pigs for large ones. They drill holes in kegs of oil
and use wedges of hibiscus wood as spigots to draw the oil
off, a practice which they call and explain away as 'drying
out'. They even thrust in needles to make holes so that they
may obtain the oil, inserting hogs' bristles the ends of which
they then burn off in order to close the holes. They employ
a pair of bamboo batons to pinch hold of the center of (a roll
of) cotton cloth and so draw it out. For rice packed in sacks
they insert at an angle a reed tube down which the rice flows.
They loosen the heading of (blocks of) paper and extract
whole quires. They loosen the bindings on bundles of fish
and pilfer one from each. They set to work on raw cotton
when it is being loaded and unloaded, something about which
one can do nothing (?). They purposely shift government
monopoly salt about, looking for an opportunity to steal it,
so that there is no bag which escapes being pilfered. As to
miscellaneous goods and pharmaceutical materials, they act
when they see a chance. Sometimes it even happens that the
goods which they have stolen are worth twice as much as the
ship, and in such cases they will drill through the latter and

scuttle it, and then run off leaving it behind. There are constantly instances of boats which never reach their destination.
If one has paid them in advance and they unload less than the
original quantity of cargo, this will cause them to practise
such non-violent deceptions as shamming innocence and
being unwilling to make restitution in full, or swearing oaths,
begging for mercy and offering goods of inferior quality as
replacements. It is hard to enumerate all the harmful
things these rascals do to shipping. When faced with con-
triving hearts and deceptive schemes, the most important
thing is to be on one's guard. When the contract is concluded
one should avoid giving an inadequate gratuity. If any payment is made in the course of the journey, this should be
because one has sold some of the goods. Any surplus cash
must be concealed. 'Careless hiding induces men to steal',
as the ancients aptly observed. Even if a shipmaster should
prove to be a guileless servant, how can one be sure of it?
(126)

No doubt the regularity with which cargoes were stolen was the product
of social conditions, notably the circumstances under which the boatmen had left farming, and their dependence upon the merchants and
brokers for a living.

Once transport had advanced some way beyond the stage where
owners of goods had to provide for their own transport, there was a
need for brokers as intermediaries between customers and trans-
porters. A carrier who was either the subordinate of a shipping broker,
or who relied upon his services, could be sure of getting passengers
and cargoes and of selling any goods which he had brought. Through
the mediation of a broker, the owner of goods could be certain of
their safe arrival. The passage from Jen Shih-lin about the ships
entering Ning-po, quoted on page 17 above, continues:

> ....Afterwards (the skippers) come ashore and go with a
> self-satisfied swagger into the houses of the market brokers
> (shih-k'uai). They hold hurried consultations, talking at a
> great rate and with no regard for niceties. The following day
> they bludgeon a sheep and pour out a libation to the gods. A
> drum is struck to summon people to market and every day
> pedlars come to trade in keen competitive fashion. (128)

The passages from Fang Hui, on page 22 above, and from Ch'en

Yuan-ching, on page 31 above, both refer to the activities of shipping brokers. The extent of the control which they managed to exert is suggested by a memorial of 1312:

> The rise in prices at the capital in recent years has been caused by the shipping brokers established in various places. They give dishonest treatment to the merchant at the piers and possess control over the shipmasters (ch'uan-hu). In consequence the latter have been delayed and goods have not been circulating. (128)

Shipping brokers were also responsible for making good any losses suffered by a merchant who hired a boat. According to the section on brokers in the T'ung-chih t'iao-ko, a Yuan dynasty law code:

> In 1294 the Grand Secretariat successfully proposed that henceforth all those who hired boats for travel on rivers should do so through shipmasters (kuan-ch'uan) and brokers (fan-t'ou jen). A three-sided agreement should be concluded and a clear contract drawn up. The shipmaster's true name and local registration should be entered. Such unclear phrases as 'has no registration' or 'shipmaster of Ch'ang-ho (the Milky Way)' should not be written. Once a guarantee covering the carriage of goods has been given, the broker who has originally given this guarantee shall also be punished if there is any negligence or loss. He shall also keep a register in which are clearly entered the names of merchants, the place to which they are going to transact their business, and the shipmaster who is being guaranteed, and this shall be submitted, sealed by him, to the local authorities for their examination. (128)

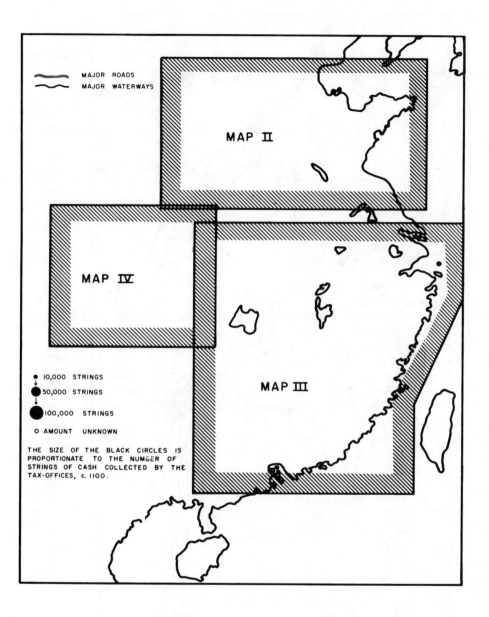

GUIDE TO MAPS II, III, IV.

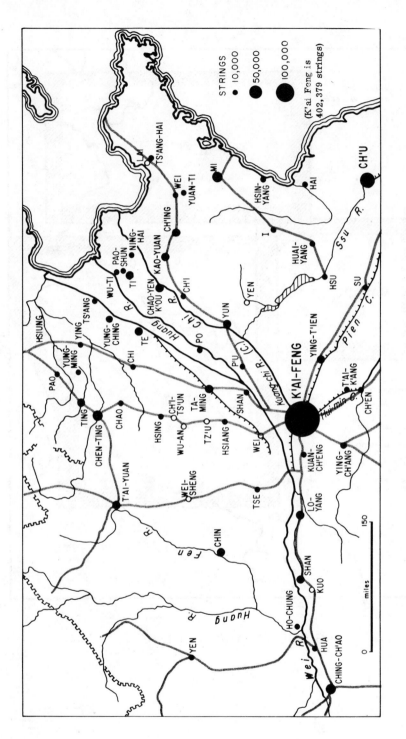

MAP II TRADE AND TRANSPORT IN NORTH CHINA AROUND
1100

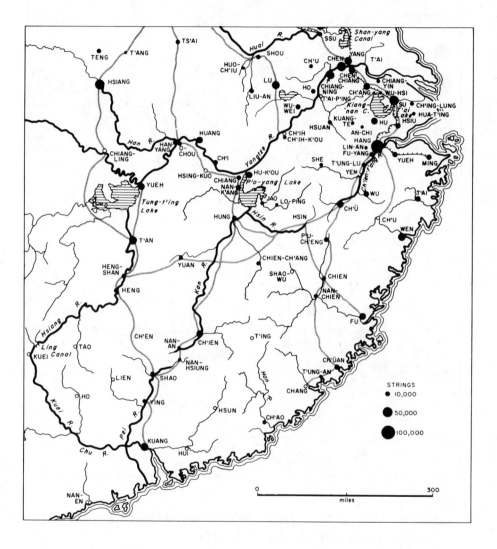

MAP III TRADE AND TRANSPORT IN SOUTH CHINA AROUND
        1100

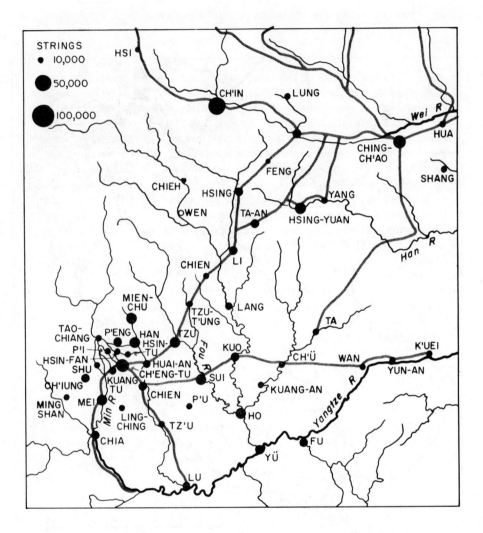

MAP IV TRADE AND TRANSPORT IN SZECHWAN AND THE
NORTHWEST AROUND 1100

III. THE FORMATION OF A NATIONWIDE MARKET DURING THE SUNG DYNASTY

In the course of the later part of the T'ang dynasty and the Sung dynasty a nationwide market was formed in China. This was the consequence of the upsurge in agricultural productivity, the growth of regional specialization in the production of commodities upon the basis of underlying natural and geographical differences, and the development of transport and communications. The revenues of the early Sung government were largely drawn from the taxation of agriculture although, where appropriate, paper, lacquer, wax, silk or mineral products were permitted as means of tax payment. After the middle of the Northern Sung period, however, the state drew an increasing proportion of its revenue from trade, and acquired articles needed for official and military use through large-scale purchases. Growing urbanization also meant a swelling demand for agricultural and related products by city residents in addition to officials and wealthy commoners. Sung government policy did not attempt to safe-guard government income by keeping peasants from participation in trade. Rather it aimed at protecting commerce as a factor which made a useful supplementary contribution to the system. In conse-quence, agriculture was exposed to the influences of commerce, and cash crops were grown for the market.

Only limited information is available on the products which circulated in T'ang times. Writings by Yuan Chen, Liu Yü-hsi, * Tu Mu and Po Chü-i suggest that the most important were probably salt, tea, high-quality silks, timber, horses, slaves, precious metals and stones, and rare animals. They remained important under the Sung, as may be seen from a remark of Li Hsin, who flourished in the latter part of the eleventh century:

> Merchants who trade across the seas either value pearls and jade or else rhinoceros horn and tortoiseshell. Merchants who trade overland either value salt and iron or else tea. (135)

---

*Of which excellent English translations, based on the work of Ishida Mikinosuke, may be found in D. Twitchett, 'Merchant, Trade and Government in Late T'ang,' Asia Minor (N. S.) XIV, i, pp. 81-85, and id. , 'The T'ang Market System,' Asia Minor (N. S.) XII, ii, pp. 229-230.

At the same time, however, there was a great increase in the number
and the variety of commodities in commercial circulation, and the
part played by articles of everyday use became much more significant.

An outline of the products of the main areas of China may be
found in the description given to the Chin Tartars by Fang Hsin-ju
when he was serving as the ambassador of the Southern Sung. It is
reproduced in Yeh Shao-weng's Experiences of Four Reigns (Ssu-ch'ao
wen-chien lu):

> Riches such as ivory, rhinoceros horn, pearls and jade
> are all produced in the two Kuang provinces. The unending
> vistas of tea-shrubs and the mulberry trees in both
> Chiang-tung and Chiang-hsi seem to be a sea on land.
> Huai-nan-tung and Huai-nan-hsi are the chief areas
> producing salt-brine and copper. As to the fourteen
> prefectures of Che-hsi, you know, Chief of Chiefs, that
> 'if Su-chou and Hu-chou have a good harvest then the
> whole empire has a sufficiency,' but it is also true that,
> because of the multiplying population, the new lands being
> brought under cultivation, reed-swamps and thickets being
> opened up each year and the dyked fields spreading ever
> wider, even if they do not enjoy a good harvest they still
> obtain enough to sustain them for several years. Che-tung
> is rich in salt and fish, the treasures of the sea and
> the resources of the hills. Although these are consumed
> by many persons yet they live without penury. The capital
> of Min (Fukien) is itself a great city of the Southeast,
> controlling six prefectures and engrossing what is produced
> in the Yangtze and the Huai regions besides. (136)

In somewhat comparable fashion Chang Ju-yü's Further Bibliographical
Inquiries from the Mountain Hall (Shan-t'ang ch'un-shu k'ao-so hsu-chi),
which was compiled early in the thirteenth century, describes the
economic preponderance of southern China over northern China by
this time:

> Since our dynasty (the Southern Sung) possesses southern
> China, south of the Great River (Yangtze) and Chien-ko
> (in northern Szechwan) all is calm and controlled.
> Furthermore, Pa, Shu and the northern bank of the Yangtze

join to form an outer screen. Compared with the
twenty-three circuits of the Yuan-feng reign (1078-1085)
as regards registered population and amount of cultivated
land, (southern China) constitutes two-thirds of the
empire. With respect to geographical extent and wealth
it constitutes three quarters. The northwest corner was
formerly three quarters of the empire; now it is but one
quarter. In ancient times Confucian scholarship flourished
in Tsou and Lu (Shantung). Today it does so in Min and
Yueh(Fukien and Kwangtung). Once, skill in the textile
industry lay in Ch'ing and Ch'i (Shantung and Hopeh).
Now Pa and Shu (Szechwan) are reputed for it. The North
in the past profited from dates and millet, neither of
which southern China has had at any time. Nowadays the
South enjoys abundant profits from perfumes and teas,
neither of which has ever existed in the North. The North
benefits from its hares, the South from its fish. None of
these things has been possessed by both North and South,
but the northern specialities yield only a slender profit,
while the southern specialities give rich returns. Thus
although the population which lives to the south of the
Great River and of Chien-ko only occupies a part of all
China, yet it has two thirds of its total wealth. It is the
Yangtze and the Huai rivers that are well-known today
for the benefits of water transport. There is no question
of the rivers within the northern passes (being more used).
It is Hai-yen (in northern Chekiang) which is renowned
today for the profits from its salt-pools. The empire
depends upon it and it sends salt to deficitary areas.
At the present time the profits of both land and sea
to be found first and foremost in Chiang-Che (the Yangtze
delta and the surrounding region). There is no question of
the Northwest (being better off). The use of irrigation
is today more developed around Lake T'ai than anywhere
else in the empire. Neither the Yellow River nor the
Wei River may be considered comparable. (136)

A number of regional products, notably certain raw materials and
textiles, achieved a nation-wide reputation.

There were three main economic regions: the North and
the South, which were separated by the Huai River, and Szechwan.
Of the trade between the first two The Continuation of the Comprehensive
Mirror for Aiding Government says, with reference to the town of
Pan-ch'iao in Mi-chou (southern Shantung) in 1088:

> Merchants from Kuang-nan, Fukien, Huai-nan and the
> Liang-Che come to this town in sea-going junks to sell
> such dutiable goods as spices and drugs. Merchants from
> the circuits of Ching-tung, Hopeh and Ho-tung come
> bringing copper cash, silk thread, silk floss, silk gauze
> and thin silk, and do an extremely thriving trade with them.
> When merchants who deal in overseas goods come, however,
> they all have frankincense, ivory, rhinoceros horn and
> such precious things. Although these are without exception
> prohibited* yet such is the eagerness of petty persons for
> profits that they will scale the mountains and sail the seas,
> devising a hundred clever schemes, so that it is quite
> impossible to prevent some inflow of these articles by means
> of deception and concealment. ... The trade of Ming-chou
> and Hang-chou is limited to one circuit, but Pan-ch'iao
> has the commerce of merchants from the several circuits
> in the Northwest. Its silk thread, floss, double-thread
> silk cloth and silk are also commodities desired by
> barbarian merchants. From this one can see that it is the
> place to which North and South hasten to meet for trade. (138)

During the Southern Sung there was a flourishing North-South trade
(official, private, and illegal) with the Chin Tartars. The main
articles exported by the South were tea, rice, sugar, porcelain,
lacquerware, silk goods, hemp and ramie cloth, bamboo and cane
goods, cotton, writing materials and books, precious materials
(tortoise-shell, ivory, rhinoceros horn, steel, shells of the
ch'u-pi turtle, coral, agate and frankincense),military supplies
(bows and crossbows, wood and bamboo, shafts for spears and arrows,
fish-glue, white wax, ox-hides, leather saddleflaps and soles for
shoes, pig-iron and wrought-iron, sheep, deerskins, hare furs,
dogs' pelts, horse-hides, sulphur, nitre, lygodium japonicum and t'ung
oil), copper cash, plow-oxen, green ginger and dried orange peel.

---

*To private traders, by an ordinance of 982. Transl.

In exchange the Chin provided northern pearls, silks, northern medicines
(such as ginseng and liquorice root), sheepskins, horses, saffron
and lithospermum officinale (a dye-plant). It is clear that, on
balance, the flow of goods was mainly from the South to the North.

Szechwan was relatively independent in economic terms,
and goods produced there had their own characteristic area of
circulation centered upon Ch'eng-tu. The most important items
were tea, silk and hemp goods, medicines, writing materials and
books, fruits and sugar. Imports into Szechwan consisted mainly of
salt, horses, medicines and porcelain. Every spring and autumn
Medicine Fairs (yao-shih) were held at Ch'eng-tu and a wide range
of northern and southern goods, as well as Szechwanese goods,
were exchanged there.

International trade was carried on with Liao (the Khitan
empire in Southern Manchuria) from which the Sung imported silver,
hemp cloth, sheep, horses and slaves, and with Japan, from which
the main imports were gold, gold dust, pearls, seed-pearls (for
medicinal uses), mercury, antlers, China root (fu-ling), sulphur,
shells, tatami matting, various woods, artistic handicraft work,
copper vessels and weapons. To Southeast Asia the Sung, and later
the Yuan, exported gold, silver, gold and silver ornaments, copper,
copper goods and copper cash, pewter, iron blocks, strips and
wire, iron pots and needles, mercury, celadon and white porcelain,
glazed earthenware dishes, coarse china bowls, earthenware jars,
lacquerware, light closely-woven multi-colored silks, silk thread
from north and south China, blue and white printed linen, hemp
cloth, sulphur, nitre, t'ung oil, bamboo baskets, wooden combs,
straw mats, paper, grains, refined sugar, woods and books.
Southeast Asia in return sent China spices, cotton, bird and animals,
fruits, beeswax, tortoiseshell, ivory, rhinoceros horn and pearls.

Certain places in China developed specialized industries.
Su-chou, Hu-chou and Wen-chou were known for their lacquer;
Yueh-chou (Shao-hsing) and Ch'u-chou (in Chekiang) for their
porcelain; Chen-chou for its pewter and candlesticks; Chieh-k'ang
(Nanking), Yueh-chou, Ming-chou (Ning-po) and T'ai-chou for their
copperware; Ch'ang-sha for silver goods; Ming-chou for straw mats
and iron pots; Fu-chou for sugar; Ch'uan-chou for combs of
tortoise-shell and wood, and for cotton.   This local specialization

in handicrafts, and also the cultivation of the agricultural materials necessary for them, led to a growing trade in daily necessities, especially grain. In what follows, the production and circulation of various products will be examined individually.

1. NATURAL AGRICULTURAL PRODUCTS

i. Rice

        Rice had an extensive commercial market in the Sung dynasty. Many different qualities were put on the market and differentiated by specific names. Circulation was not, however, entirely unrestricted. The government sometimes controlled the prices and the inter-regional flow of rice, particularly when the presence of famine made it necessary to check profiteering and the regional export of local stocks. International export was banned by the 'interdict on outflow overseas' and, during the period of confrontation between the Southern Sung and the Chin, rice was forbidden to leave the strategic frontier area of Huai-nan for China south of the Yangtze, lest this diminish vital military resources. The long-distance movement of rice developed partly in opposition to and partly in dependence upon such extra-economic pressures.

A. The Production and Circulation of Rice

        The great advances in agricultural productivity achieved since the middle of the T'ang dynasty, the improvements in the techniques of cultivation, and the changes in the structure of agricultural organization have been described by many previous writers. In particular, superior hydraulic control, the use of drought-resistant Champa rice, the double-cropping of rice with rice and of rice with wheat, better agricultural tools, the wider use of fertilizers, and the dissemination of knowledge by means of agricultural treatises led to more intensive farming and this, together with the opening up of much new land, contributed both to the expansion of the market which will be described in the pages that follow, and to a greater output of rice.

There were great regional disparities in agricultural practice.
Thus, during the Southern Sung, rice farming in the Yangtze
delta was much superior to that found elsewhere. Wei Ching, who
lived in K'un-shan in the later twelfth century, observed that:

> According to my investigations, when our state was
> at peace (i. e. during the Northern Sung period), most of
> the grain transported by water to the capital came from
> the Southeast, and the greater part of that from Chiang-Che
> (the Yangtze delta). Since the restoration of the dynasty's
> fortunes (i. e. the Southern Sung period), the location of
> the metropolitan area in Che-hsi (northern Chekiang)
> has meant an especial reliance upon this region. There
> are plentiful harvests, the benefits of which extend into
> the neighboring circuits, for the level fields are fertile
> and the boundary dykes run on in unbroken line. (145)

In Su-chou there were estate-owners with several hundreds of thousands,
or even a million, piculs in their storehouses. Further south,
however, the land grew poorer. Lü Tsu-ch'ien, who lived in the
latter part of the twelfth century, wrote of mountainous Yen-chou
(Chien-te):

> Leaving on one side the rice of high gluten content (no-mi),
> the tax rice paid in each year by all six counties only
> amounts to 8,751 piculs of rice of moderate gluten content
> (keng-mi), or less than the quantity harvested by one rich
> commoner household in Hu-chou or Hsiu-chou. (145)

Wang Po wrote in the thirteenth century about Wu-chou (Chin-hua):

> A household regarded as rich in Chin-hua would not be
> the equivalent to the lowest grade of poor household in
> Chiang-nan-hsi or Che-hsi. (145)

In a similar vein, Fang Ta-tsung observed of Hsing-hua prefecture
in Fukien:

> Important families do not have much food-grain, unlike
> those of Chiang-Che who can count their (hulled) rice
> in thousands or tons of thousands of piculs. There are

many families at the present time with two or three
hundred piculs, and half of this will, moreover, be
husks. Persons with small properties are particularly
to be pitied. (145)

Wu Yung, in a proclamation for the encouragement of agriculture
and therefore no doubt exaggerating somewhat, addressed the
prefecture of Lung-hsing (Nan-ch'ang) in the thirteenth century
as follows:

According to the treatise on geography in the History of
the Sui Dynasty, the customs of Yü-chang (Nan-ch'ang)
somewhat resemble those of Wu (the Yangtze delta), the
men being diligent at husbandry and the women toiling
at spinning. By this it is meant that the fields are opened
for cultivation, that silkworms and mulberries give good
returns, and that the common people are all attached to
agriculture and suffer from neither cold nor hunger.
When your Prefect came from Wu and, on entering this
area, made enquiries about the local customs, he discovered
that this was not the case. The soil is rich in Wu and rice
gives two harvests in one year. Silkworms can be brought
to maturity eight times in one year. But in Yü-chang,
girdled with streams and lakes, with many lake-fields
and few hill-fields, there is only one rice harvest and the
silkworms mature but twice. In Wu the people open up
the waste lands and swampy depressions for the cultivation
of rice of moderate gluten content, and they also plant
vegetables, wheat, hemp and beans. When they cultivate
they do not neglect their dykes; when they reap they do not
overlook the boundaries between the fields. But in Yü-chang
they grow mostly Champa rice of low gluten content,
either the 80-day, the 100-day or the 120-day variety,
from any of which a harvest may be had in a few months.
In the remaining three seasons they abandon husbandry and
work at nothing. Everywhere there is unused land and roaming
people. Thus the farmers of Wu are distinguished for
their application, and so the proverb says, 'A harvest in
Su-chou and Hu-chou and the empire has enough.' This is the
outcome of hard work. The peasants of Yü-chang rely only
upon the benevolence of Nature ('Heaven') and so the proverb
says, 'No good crops for nine years out of ten, but one good
harvest gives ten times as much as usual.' This is the outcome
of laziness. Hard work makes people rich; laziness makes
them poor. (146)

Wang Yen, who lived in the twelfth century, wrote of Hupeh:

> For the most part, the fields in Hupeh are different from
> those in Chaing, Che and Min (i. e. the East and Southeast).
> Although they have some land not suitable for irrigation
> they grow neither hemp nor mulberries upon it; they do
> not rear silkworms, nor do they spin; but rely for their
> entire year's livelihood upon their (rice-) fields. Because
> the land is so sparsely people they do not have to bestow
> any great effort upon their farming. They sow without
> planting out or weeding. If perchance they have weeded,
> they do not apply manure, so seeds and grainsprouts grow
> up together. Thus they cultivate vast areas but have poor
> harvests. In a good year they can just support themselves.
> If once there is a crop failure, then the people are seized
> with panic. Thus it is not comparable to Chiang, Che
> and Min. ... In these latter areas there are many persons
> capable of farming, but little cultivable land. Everyone
> exerts himself to the utmost and the yield per mou is
> generally double that of the fields in Hupeh. Moreover,
> they harvest in the autumn and sell in the off-crop seasons;
> and so they make several times as much money as their
> counterparts in Hupeh. Besides working hard at agriculture,
> they invariably raise silkworms and spin. Thus the people
> can support the heavy taxes which they pay; but this could
> not be regarded as generally applicable. (146)

Ch'en Fu-liang declared in a proclamation for the encouragement of
agriculture in Kuei-yang (southern Hunan) that:

> The soil in Min and Che (i. e. the southeast coast) is
> exceedingly poor. It therefore needs to be hoed and
> harrowed several times and to receive applications of
> manure and irrigation water before good fields can be
> obtained. In this area, however, no one expects to have
> to put one manure, and hoeing and harrowing are perfunctorily
> done. The rice and wheat which has been planted flourishes
> of its own accord. From this one can see that the soil is
> richer than in Min and Che. But, in Min and Che, the best
> fields yield three piculs of rice per mou, and the next best
> two piculs. Harvests here never reach such figures. It
> must be that yields are low because of inadequate effort. (147)

Certain considerations emerge from the foregoing materials. The flow of rice from areas of high productivity to areas of low productivity will not in itself explain the commercialization of rice in the full sense of the term, that is to say something more than a marketed surplus produced incidentally to the effort to satisfy the producer's own needs. Production intended from the beginning for the market was rather the result of a need for money to pay taxes and of the demand for rice which came from regions specializing in the cultivation of other crops or in handicrafts. Fang Ta-tsung, writing in the thirteenth century, had this to say about Hsing-hua prefecture in Fukien:

> The four upper prefectures (namely Chien-ning, Nan-chien, Shao-wu and T'ing-chou) are the most productive of rice in Fukien, yet they have forbidden the cultivation of rice of a high gluten content (shu), the manufacture of wine (lit. 'yeast') from it, the growing of oranges, and the excavation of ponds for the rearing of fish. The reason for this ban is the desire that no inch of land should be uncultivated, and no grain of rice uneaten. If regions which produce a surplus of rice take such precautions, how much more should those whose harvests cannot supply half of their needs! Today the fields of Hsing-hua county have been taken over by rice with a high gluten content (for wine-making) and there are I know not how many thousands of piculs carried each year into the county capital. The fields of Hsien-yu county have been consumed by sugar-cane, and there are I know not how many tens of thousands of jars transported each year to Huai-nan and the Liang-Che. There can be no doubt but that sugar-cane is an obstacle in the way of (rice-) fields. (148)

The Shun-hsi Reign-period Gazetteer for Hsin-an (Shun-hsi Hsin-an chih) tells how, by the later twelfth century, Hui-chou (Hsin-an) depended on rice from Chiang-nan-hsi:

> The hills produce fine timber which is every year bound into rafts. Those who go down the Che (i. e. Ch'ien-t'ang) River obtain great wealth. ... The Ch'i-men River flows into the P'o-yang Lake. People take tea, lacquer, paper and wood along it to Chiang-nan-hsi, upon which they depend for their supply of rice. (148)

There was probably a growing number of such areas into which rice
had to be imported because of concentration on specialized types
of production.

Under the Northern Sung the main grain consumed by the
people of Kiangnan was presumably rice. Under the Southern Sung
there was some double-cropping of wheat or barley with rice, but
the increasing variety of types of rice is suggestive of the commercialization of the latter. Fan Ch'eng-ta's poem 'The Toil of Farming'
names some of the kinds found around Su-chou:

> In Wu the soil is black and fertile,
> In Wu the rice has the freshness of jade,
> 'Long-waist' is as thin as gourd-seeds,
> 'Level-head' as lustrous as pearls.
> 'Red Lotus' is superior to the tiao-hu of ancient times,
> 'Fragrance' has the perfume of autumnal orchids.
> Some are ancient Chinese rices,
> Some come from Champa;
> But it is the early rice of low gluten content and the late-
> ripening indica
> Which pour forth steam from the steaming-pots.
>
> They do not grudge tending the rice in the spring
> But fear the payment of taxes in the autumn.
> The evil officials act like sparrows or rats,
> And the thieving clerks like locusts or caterpillars.
> They take extra with their enlarged measures,
> They profit by accepting strings of cash at a discount.
> Two chung are needed to make one measure.
> People cannot avoid being flogged to make them pay up,
> And are further oppressed with private debts.
> No smoke rises from the abandoned homesteads.
> Never once in their lives have they tasted
> Rice clean and bright as the cloudstone.
> Those who eat it are always the idle (officials and city people);
> The mouths of those who grow it are forever watering. (150)

Although some early-ripening Champa rice was paid in as tax rice or
bought for its granaries by the government, as a general rule tax
rice was supposed to be unhulled rice of moderate gluten content,
because it lasted much longer. According to Shu Lin, who flourished
in the middle of the Southern Sung:

If one examines how things are at the present time, hulled
rice goes rotten in the store in four or five years, but stored
unhulled rice will keep eight or nine years without harm. There
are, moreover, different qualities of unhulled rice. There is
greater and lesser rice, the former being what we term 'rice
of moderate gluten content'. It has large grains and an
awn, and can only be grown on rich soils. Lesser rice is
what we call ' Champa rice', or 'shan-ho' rice'. It has small
grains and no awn, and can be grown on either rich or poor
soils. From unhulled rice of moderate gluten content but
little hulled rice is obtained. It is expensive and, apart
from being used for the payment of taxes, is only eaten by
upper-class families. From unhulled lesser rice much
hulled rice can be obtained. It is cheap and is eaten by all
households from those owning a modest amount of property
on downwards. (151)

Some peasants had, therefore, to purchase their tax rice. Liu Ch'ang
wrote in the mid-eleventh century:

They do not grudge toiling to farm the high dry lands;
The late harvest slowly spreads across a hundred mou.
How should they know that paying taxes in rice is like paying
    in money?
Only rice-cultivation may be trusted, growing millet yields
    nothing.
When they take their millet to market to exchange it for money
They find that rice is soaring while millet is cheap.
They do not shirk exchanging ten chung for a picul of the latter.
After three seasons of painful farming they are amazed to find
    themselves penniless. (151)

Early-ripening Champa rice was the most common food and
the variety mainly eaten in the cities also. It therefore constituted the
greater part of the rice put on the market. Price differentials in
1173 for government purchases were as follows: low-quality moderate-
gluten rice cost 2700 cash per picul, middle-quality Champa cost
2,600 cash per picul, and low-quality Champa cost 2,300 cash per picul.

Rice was consumed not only in the area south of the line formed
by the Ch'in-ling mountains and the Huai River but also in the capital

at K'ai-feng and in other northern cities. Troops along the northern frontier ate a certain quantity of rice from Kiangnan although soldiers of northern origin did not always care much for it. 'Official rice' was that eaten by the Emperor, the imperial family, the bureaucrats and the army. It was also used for such purposes as famine relief. The rice of high gluten content used in the wine monopoly may equally be regarded as official rice. Old rice which had remained too long in the government granaries, and was known as 'stale rice' or 'granary rice', was sold off to the lower classes to make way for new stocks. Under the Northern Sung there were over 20,000 salaried higher officials; in the middle of the thirteenth century over 24,000. Under the Northern Sung there were up to 1,250,000 soldiers in the central army, and around 400,000 at the beginning of the Southern Sung.

The greater part of the official rice was levied as a tax in kind. About twenty per cent of it was retained by the local authorities and the rest forwarded to the capital or specified military areas. The remainder was purchased with promissory notes for official cash, tea or spices, either from peasants directly or else from rice merchants. Under the Northern Sung the annual rice tax quota from Kiangnan (Szechwan, Fukien and Kuang-nan did not send rice) was about six million piculs; two million piculs were purchased by the government; and on the northern frontier several million piculs of grain, not exclusively rice, were also bought. Under the Southern Sung about 3,320,000 piculs were levied (not of course from Huai-nan) and from one million to four million piculs purchased.

Lin-an (Hang-chou) consumed about 1.5 million piculs of official rice each year. About 800,000 piculs of this were tax grain; the remainder was bought by the government from merchants. The commoners of Lin-an consumed in addition from 3,000 to 4,000 piculs a day, or between 1,100,000 and 1,400,000 piculs annually. Thus those in the government service and private persons together depended on merchants for from 1,800,000 to 2,100,000 piculs annually. Chien-k'ang (Nanking) consumed between 500,000 and 800,000 piculs of military rice a year, obtained partly from taxes and partly through purchase; while the rice eaten by commoners amounted to over 700,000 piculs annually. Thus it probably relied on merchants for of the order of a million piculs a year. The Hu-kuang military command, whose headquarters were at O-chou (Wu ch'ang) distributed 1,307,000 piculs of rice annually, all of it bought from merchants. It would thus appear that the activities of rice merchants were based on the capital, the great cities and the major military centers.

There were great differences between the various prefectures, departments and commands as regards their degree of dependence upon rice merchants. Some were wholly dependent; some relied on them for supplementary supplies; some needed them only in bad years or times of natural disaster. The pattern of circulation seems to have been as follows:

a. Che-hsi

According to Wang Yen's Literary Works from Shuang-ch'i (Shuang-ch'i wen-chi):

> In the Liang-Che the departments of Hu-chou, Su-chou and Hsiu-chou have the reputation of being rice-producing areas. In a year when the harvest has been good, boats and carts will usually set out in all directions. (159)

Other prefectures were less fortunate. The Gazetteer for P'i-ling compiled in the Hsien-shun reign-period (1265-1274) observed:

> Che-yu prefectures are noted for the richness of their soils. Only P'i-ling (Ch'ang-chou) has land of uneven height, and it needs an extremely good harvest if the people are to have enough. (159)

Of Yen-chou Fang Feng-chen wrote in a preface to the local gazetteer that is included in his Dragon Peak Collection (Chiao-feng chi):

> All the rice for allocation in the granaries of the military authorities is obtained from neighboring prefectures, and the common people's daily purchases of rice come from the merchant boats from Ch'ü-chou, Wu-chou, Su-chou and Hu-chou. Compared with the other prefectures of Che-yu, its rank is the lowest of the low. (159)

An account of famine relief in Chien-to county (then in Yen-chou prefecture) in the Complete Works of Mr. Hou-ts'un (Hou-ts'un hsien-sheng ta ch'uan-chi) by the thirteenth-century writer Liu K'o-chuang says:

There were floods in the spring of 1266 in Chiang-Che and drought in the summer. At this time the famished inhabitants of the prefectures and counties even chewed grasses and twigs for food. Ch'ü-chou and Yen-chou were the worst hit. Previously they had relied on buying grain from the capital, but the Court closed the waterways at this point and the officials wrung their hands, having no idea what to do. (160)

The twelfth-century statesmen Lü Tsu-ch'ien wrote of this prefecture in a memorial:

Even if there is a good harvest they still do not have enough to eat. They depend for their survival upon the transport and sale of grain by merchants. If there is no rain for ten days and the streams run dry and merchants' ships cannot come through, then the price of rice rises abruptly, and great and small will make a clamor, just as in a year of dearth. (160)

The capital at Lin-an relied upon merchants bringing rice from Su-chou, Hu-chou, Ch'ang-chou, Hsiu-chou and even Huai-nan and Kuang-nan. A proclamation for the encouragement of agriculture by Ch'eng Pi, included in his Collection From the Ming River (Ming-shui chi) says of it:

The land is overpopulated, and the poor soil yields a meagre harvest. Taking the county as a whole, they only have supplies for half the year. For the other half they all depend on sales by merchants. (160)

b. Che-tung

Chu Hsi noted in a memorial on Shao-hsing prefecture that:

Shao-hsing is overpopulated and produces insufficient rice for its needs. Even when the harvest is good it is supplied from neighboring prefectures. It is not like Che-hsi, where rice is plentiful. (160)

Of Ming-chou the <u>Ning-po Gazetteer</u> (<u>Ssu-ming chih</u>) for the Pao-ch'ing reign-period (1225-1227) says:

> The year's harvest is not insufficient to supply the people
> of the region but the great families hoard or purchase
> much of it, and the humble folk all rely on rice from
> Che-tung and Che-hsi. In bad years upper classes and
> lower classes alike are fearful, orders urging the people
> to share with each other have no effect, and the
> department even gets rice from Kuang-nan to relieve
> the famine. (160)

Of Wen-chou a memorial written jointly by Ma Kuang-tsu and Wu Yung and reproduced in the latter's <u>Collection From the Crane Forest</u> (<u>Ho-lin chi</u>) says:

> Wen-chou and Ch'u-chou are neighbors. In normal times
> the flour of Ch'u-chou comes down (the Ou River) and is
> sold as something lacking in Wen-chou, while Wen Chou's
> rice goes upstream to relieve the lack of it in Ch'u-chou. (160)

Much of this rice was in fact first imported by sea into Wen-chou. The same memorial says elsewhere:

> The prefecture has sea communications, and merchant
> junks come to and go from it. So long as steps can be taken
> to induce them to come there is no problem about the rice
> boats not gathering and sailing (upstream). ... (160)

A memorial submitted in 1173 stated:

> This year's harvest in the prefectures of Che-tung has been
> harmed by drought. The two departments of Wen-chou and
> T'ai-chou have recently had bad harvests every year and
> have been entirely dependent on the transport of rice by
> sea from Che-hsi, which has enabled them, however imperfectly,
> to have supplies. We have heard as the result of our
> enquiries that in the counties along the seacoast which are
> under the jurisdiction of P'ing-chiang (Su-chou) and Hsiu-chou
> in Che-hsi it has recently been entirely merchants from other
> prefectures who have been carrying away the rice, and

that they are not normally permitted to proceed by sea.
For this reason purchasers of rice have been few and the
places affected by shortage have been greatly harmed.   (161)

Hsin-chou and Ch'ü-chou also often had to rely on rice from Su-chou
and Hu-chou.

c. Fukien

With the increase in population which took place under the
Southern Sung, coastal Fukien was frequently oppressed with famines.
According to Chou Pi-ta, who flourished in the later twelfth century,
'The land of Min is cramped and the fields few. Every year they
rely on rice from Kuang-nan and are always concerned lest the
merchant ships may not arrive on time.' Several other writers of
this period echoed this theme. Thus Chen Te-hsiu noted that,
'Fu-chou, Hsing-hua and Ch'uan-chou have poor soils and even with
the best harvest only have rice for half a year. They especially
rely on merchants from the North and South transporting and selling
it for their supplies.' Kuang-nan was the main source but Yeh Meng-te's
proposal that the movement of grain ships from Che-hsi to Fukien
should be temporarily halted in order to deny food to Chu Ming, the
pirate leader who flourished early in the twelfth century, shows
that northern ships were also of importance. The inland prefectures,
Chien-ning, Nan-chien, Shao-wu and T'ing-chou, were usually
self-sufficient but imported rice from Kuang-nan and elsewhere in
times of crisis.

d. Kuang-nan

As mentioned above, a large amount of Kuang-nan rice was
exported to the Liang-Che and Fukien. In 1130, according to the
Sung Digest (Sung hui-yao):

It was stated in a decree that the price of rice in Che-hsi
had become extremely dear. Although there were southern
ships (nan-ch'uan, i.e. ships from Kuang-nan) bringing
cargoes to the coastal prefectures, a great number of them
were being intercepted by the rice brokers, who were

buying rice with outsize measures at low prices so that
they could illegally hold it back and release it for sale
at high prices. It was ordered that, as before, strict
measures should be taken in Wen-chou, T'ai-chou, Ming-chou
and Yueh-chou to check this. (162)

The Kuang-nan of this period was still underdeveloped as compared
with Fukien and the Liang-Che. According to Chou Ch'ü-fei's
Information on What is Beyond the Southern Passes:

The farmers of Ch'in-chou are careless. When they work
the soil with an ox they merely break up the clods, and
when the time comes for sowing they go to the fields and
broadcast the grain. They do not transplant seedlings.
There is no more wasteful use of seed than this. After
they have planted it, they neither hoe it nor irrigate it,
but place their reliance on the forces of Nature. (162)

A memorial of 1198 cited in the Sung Digest observed that, 'The lands
of the two Kuang cover several thousands of li. Many of the best
fields have been criminally appropriated by powerful rogues to such
an extent that they do not have the means of cultivating them.'
Li Tseng-po was of the opinion that 'The people of Kuang-nan
cultivate what they need for their own personal consumption and
suffer from the lack of reserve stock.'

The main rice-producing areas were Kuang-chou, Hui-chou,
Ch'ao-chou, Ying-te, Hsun-chou and Hsiang-chou. Wang Hsiang-chih's
thirteenth-century Geography of the Empire (Yü-ti chi-sheng) states
of the last-mentioned:

It has much fertile land. Its 'Long-waist' and 'Jade Kernel'
rice are the best in the South. Neighboring prefectures also
obtain much of their supplies from it. (163)

Kuang-nan rice had the reputation of rotting rapidly in storage, but it
was cheap and suitable for such purposes as famine relief. Except
when the price was pushed up by unusual outside demand, it cost
3 to 4 cash per pint (sheng) as against 20 to 30 cash in Chiang-Che.
It was also exported abroad. In 1288, for example, it was officially
reported that:

The officials and commoners of Kuang-chou who purchase
rice in the country willages in hundreds, thousands or even
tens of thousands of measures frequently transport it
overseas to Champa and other foreign lands, where they
sell it, in the hope of realizing substantial profits. (163)

Nor was Kuang-nan unique in this. Che-hsi and Huai-nan also did so.
According to a passage in the Sung Digest for 1217:

Criminals and powerful households in such coastal counties
as Hua-t'ing, Hai-yen, Ch'ing-lung, Ku-ching and also
Chiang-yin, Chen-chiang, T'ung-chou and T'ai acquire
large stocks of rice which they sell to foreigners. Each
sea-going junk contains not less than one to two thousand
measures. They go both North and South, making profits
of several hundred per cent. (164)

e. Chiang-nan-tung

The city of Chien-k'ang (Nanking) consumed large amounts
of rice and was the central market at which the merchants from the
upper reaches of the Yangtze congregated. Liu Tsai, who flourished
in the early part of the thirteenth century, observed that:

Chin-ling (i.e. Nanking) is the ancient seat of emperors and
a place where goods and people gather. There are many
consumers, few producers. Every year they rely upon
purchases of rice from merchants. The Yangtze River
presents a natural hazard and if the boats fail to come on
time the price rises suddenly. (164)

Other writers also noted Chien-k'ang's dependence upon commerce for
its supplies of daily necessities such as rice, wheat, firewood, coal,
wine and tea. The Chien-k'ang Gazetteer (Chien-k'ang chih) quotes
Yueh K'o, one-time Judicial Officer for Transport in Chiang-nan-tung,
to the affect that:

As regards the nine prefectures under the jurisdiction of
this office: in the secondary capital at Chien-k'ang there is
a dense population. Because it is located on the lower
reaches of the Yangtze and because of the distance of both

land and water routes, the price of rice is normally higher
here than in the other prefectures. Second in this respect
is Hui-chou, set among the passes, with numerous mountains
and but few cultivable fields. Kuang-te consists of stony
hillocks and is entirely inaccessible to water transport.
T'ai-p'ing and Ning-kuo have upland and dyked fields in
equal proportions, and because of these differences in
elevation suffer either from floods or drought, so that
it is difficult to obtain a full harvest. Although Ch'ih-chou
and Nan-k'ang have water communications they customarily
have few reserves. Only Jao-chou and Hsin-chou (the present
Kuang-hsin) have long produced (enough) rice, but since the
streams are swollen in the summer and those with rice to
sell are greedy for a profit, they transport too much downstream,
and if they have not put by quite enough for their own needs
for the year then, since the streams run dry in autumn and
winter, even if there is rice available to supply them, there
is no means to bring it upstream. (164)

According to one Yuan author Jao-chou depended on Kuang-hsin and
Yü-chang (Nan-ch'ang) for grains, silk thread and hemp. As indicated
on page 54   above, Hui-chou obtained much of its rice from Chiang-nan-hsi
in return for tea, lacquer, paper and timber. Hsin-chou also sometimes
obtained rice from Su-chou and Hu-chou in Che-hsi. Of Ch'ih-chou
Yuan Shuo-yu wrote in a memorial, preserved in his Collection from
Tung-t'ang (Tung-t'ang chi):

Land in this prefecture is limited and the people are poor.
Even when there has been a good harvest the inhabitants
must rely for rice to eat upon the merchant boats from the
upper Yangtze which come down-river and sell it near the
city, if they are to have enough.   (165)

Sometimes, he noted, the authorities in Hupeh and Kiangsi prevented
the rice boats from coming.

f. Chiang-(nan-)hsi

Chiang-hsi at this time was second only to the Liang-Che in
its wealth and in the quota of taxes for which it was responsible. In
respect of taxes actually collected it surpassed the Liang-che. The
tax rice levied and rice officially purchased by the General Commissariat

Offices* (tsung-ling so, tsung-so) on the central and lower Yangtze was
largely provided by Chiang-hsi. The major rice-producing areas
were Lung-hsing (present day Chiu-chiang) and Chi-chou (present
day Chi-an). Chu Mu in his Triumphant Vision of the World (Fang-yu
sheng-lan) says of the former prefecture:

> Its fields are suited to rice of moderate and high gluten
> content. Its tax grain is taken to the Capital and is the
> most (of any prefecture) in the Empire. (165)

Chi-chou was probably even more important. Rice grown there was
already being exported to Hupeh in T'ang times. A despatch written
to a fellow-official by Li Cheng-min in the first half of the twelfth
century, and preserved in his Collection from Ta-yin Mountain
(Ta-yin chi), says:

> The prefecture of Chiang-hsi have from ancient times
> had a reputation for their prosperity. The little region
> of Lu-ling (i.e. Chi-chou) is especially noted for its rich
> plains, where across a thousand fertile li of land the rice
> waves in endless clouds. It pays 400,000 piculs as tax,**
> and the rivers disappear beneath the fleets of boats. It
> is the foundation of the Court, and the common people rely
> upon it for their well-being. (165)

Owing to the dearth of historical materials the nature of the circulation
of rice in Chiang-hsi is unclear, but it seems likely that a certain
quantity must have made its way into Chiang-nan-tung.

---

*There were four of these in early Southern Sung, along the frontier
with the Chin: Huai-tung, Huai-hsi, Hu-kuang and Ssu-ch'uan.
They had charge of levying taxes in the prefectures under their
jurisdiction and supplying the troops with necessities. They also
participated in military administration generally. Transl.

**According to the Sung Digest Chi-chou paid 370,000 piculs in 1173.
Wang Hsiang-chih was of the opinion that Chi-chou paid the heaviest
tax of any Chiang-hsi prefecture (cf. however Chu Mu on p. 65 above).

g. Hunan and Hupeh

O-chou (present-day Wu-ch'ang) was the site of the Hu-kuang
General Commissariat Office and the central market of this area.
A memorial written by Ts'ai Kan, who flourished in the latter half
of the twelfth century, describes the movements of merchants from
Hunan and Hupeh (as these provinces were constituted in Sung times)
in the following manner:

> Merchants from Ch'ang-te, T'an-chou (Ch'ang-sha), Heng-chou
> (Heng-yang), and Li-chou who sell rice go to the official
> rice-purchasing yard (at O-chou) to dispose of it. (At any
> one time) there are usually ten thousand piculs piled up
> on the bank. (166)

Wang Yen's Literary Works from Shuang-ch'i outlines the general
pattern:

> O-chu (i.e. O-chou) is the most important place in the
> Hu-kuang. This is because to the south of it there lie
> T'an-chou, Hang-chou, Yung-chou, Shao-chou (present-day
> Pao-ch'ing) and to the west of it there lie Ting-chou
> (present-day Ch'ang-te), Li-chou, Chiang-ling, An-chou
> (present-day Te-an), Fu-chou (present-day Mien-yang)
> and Hsiang-yang, all of whose merchants come to trade
> at O-chu. (166)

Elsewhere Wang Yen also observes:

> When the merchants' rice-boats come upriver they generally
> gather at O-chu. When they go downriver they must first
> pass through the counties of Hua-jung or Pa-ling (in Yueh-chou).
> This county (i.e. Lin-hsiang in Yo-chou) can only rely on
> grain being brought on foot from T'ung-ch'eng county
> (in O-chou). ... Unless the harvest has been bad then
> merchants go trading from Hunan into Ting-chou and Li-chou
> (then in Hupeh), their boats being as numerous as the
> clouds. If the rivers are in flood they have to go through
> Hua-jung, but if the water-level is low they must set out
> from Pa-ling. (166)

Although Ch'ang-sha had previously been well-off for grain, by
the middle of the twelfth century it had to obtain extra supplies
from Ting-chou and also from Kuang-nan via the Ling Canal, which
linked Kuei-yang with the Hunan water network. Tao-chou in the
southern part of the province was however commercially undeveloped.
One of its prefects wrote of it in 1160:

> This is the smallest prefecture in Hunan. It covers
> less than 600 li and its population does not amount to
> 40,000 households. Boats and carts do not come here.
> There is no intercourse with merchants. (167)

According to Ch'en Fu-liang's Literary Works from the Study of
Arrestation (Chih-chai wen-chi):

> Kuei-yang is a hilly area and depends every year for its
> rice on Ch'en-chou. Whenever the purchase of rice in
> Ch'en-chou is forbidden, the people of Kuei-yang are placed
> in a difficult situation. ... When there is famine in
> Ch'en the people move to Kuei-yang, and when Kuei-yang
> has a famine the people move to Ch'en-chou. (167)

From the foregoing outline of the circulation of rice in the
various provinces it is apparent that Lin-an (Hang-chou), Chien-k'ang
(Nanking) and O-chou (Wu-ch'ang) were central regional markets
serving a large-scale long-distance trade freely carried on by
merchants. It is also clear that at the periphery of the commercialized
system there remained a number of localized, discrete and
self-sufficient marketing systems.

B. The Structure of the Rice Market

When peasants carried their own grain to market this was
called 'carrying on foot' (pu-tan) or 'carrying on the back' (fu-tan).
When rice was temporarily stored in the granaries of landlords and
wealthy peasants, such persons were known as 'rice owners' (mi-chu),
'storehouse owners' (t'a-chia) or 'stockists' (t'ing-t'a chia). This
rice and peasant rice would be brought up by 'rice boats' (mi-ch'uan)
or 'rice merchants' (mi-k'o) for transport to a market. Here,
together with rice brought personally by the peasant cultivator, it

would be purchased by 'rice brokers' (<u>mi ya-jen</u>, or <u>mi-hang</u>), finally reaching the consumer through a 'rice shop' (<u>mi-p'u</u>), which might not infrequently be run by a broker concurrently with his other business. It was of the foregoing elements that the structure of the rice market was composed, and they are examined in turn in what follows.

a. Carriage to Market by the Peasant Producer

Wang Yen wrote in a letter:

> As a rule all of those who act as brokers in the market
> of Lin-chiang (in Kiangsi) are poor persons. Even if
> a hundred piculs were offered for sale they would not
> have the capital with which to buy such a quantity. Every
> day it is only humble folk who carry their grain in on foot
> to the markets and squat down among the brokers to sell
> it. Other humble persons generally bring cash and buy
> rice in pints or pecks. For this reason, when rice is
> cheap, those who bring it in on their backs are anxious
> lest they may be unable to sell it, and when rice is dear,
> those who purchase it by the day suffer from a lack of
> food. (168)

Chu Hsi **also** mentioned **the** practice:

> In every county the people in the country villages carry
> in their rice for sale at the market, but many are intercepted
> by deceitful rice-brokers, who undertake to do it for them.
> In their shops the latter mix the rice with water, inflate
> the price and sell it with small measures, making a fat
> profit. (168)

A further mention of peasant marketing occurs in a poem by the eleventh-century writer Lu Nan-kung, and is preserved in his <u>Collection from the Well-watered Garden</u> (<u>Kuan-yuan chi</u>):

A copper cash is heavy as the hills,
But a peck of grain's not worth a pile of shit.
I used to hear good harvests brought good fortune.
Now I know that they occasion misery.
My neighbors to the East have rice that's silver-white,
My neighbors to the West have sheaves as big as drums.
They've been repeatedly to market and as often had to
                              carry it home again.
There's no purchaser even at a reasonable reduced price. (169)

Sales of this sort were probably not all that numerous, and may
be regarded as a sort of subsidiary commerce carried on by
peasants.

b. Rice-owners, Storehouse Owners and Rich Persons

Persons with sufficient means to assemble substantial
stockpiles of grain played an important part in the structure of the
rice market. Thus Wei Ching wrote in a letter:

> Government purchase of rice for the purposes of price
> maintenance is essentially a good system, but if it is
> done too early or too late in the year it becomes per contra
> an abuse. It should be done at the end of the eighth month
> and the beginning of the ninth, when the peasants have rice
> and urgently need to repay their debts. Rich households
> welcome it as a time of low prices. If the authorities can
> eliminate this they will maintain equitable prices,
> to the advantage of public and private interests alike.
> After the tenth month the threshing-floors are quite empty,
> all that the poor people have having been priced away
> from them and made its way to the great families. The
> people have no more rice. (170)

Liao Kang echoed this view:

> If purchases of rice (for price maintenance) are delayed, the
> rice will have been brought up beforehand by the storehouse
> owners, and even if one wishes to buy at an increased
> price there will be no rice to be had from the common
> people. (170)

In Ou-yang Shou-tao's thirteenth-century <u>Literary Collection from the Study of Gentleness</u> (Sun-chai wen-chi) there is a discussion of a shortage of food in Chi-chou (of which he was a native) and the manner in which the authorities higher up the Kan River had prohibited the export of rice from their territories:

> I have heard that these counties are exercising an extremely
> strict control. They do not punish the rice-owners but,
> in the first place, the helmsmen-captains of the boats,
> so that crew and captains are afraid of being punished and
> do not dare to undertake to carry cargoes. (170)

From this it would appear that stockpilers of rice would hire boats to take them to market. On occasions these rich persons seem also to have been able to control the prices in the rice shops.

A good description of a typical rich local stockpiler is given in Hung Mai's work <u>The Records of I Chien</u> (I Chien chih), a collection of strange and uncanny incidents which took its name from a fabled recorder of marvels in antiquity:

> In the southeast part of Ch'ang-shu county in P'ing-chiang
> prefecture (Su-chou) there is a place called Chih-t'ang.
> It is more than a hundred <u>li</u> from the county capital. There
> was a rich commoner there named Chang San-pa who
> founded his family's fortune by his clever contriving. After
> the premature death of his eldest son in 1165 he had a salt
> merchant come from O-chou to stay in his house. ... Eight
> years later he died. His second son, who was known as
> Wu-san Chiang-shih, did not h eed the warnings given him
> by his father and elder brother, but became an adept at
> underhand dealing, taking profit wherever he saw it.
> In 1174 there was a merchant who drew up a contract with
> him for the purchase of 500 piculs of rice. The price had
> already been settled when he demanded an extra 20 cash
> per pack. The merchants would not agree to this and so
> forfeited the deposit which he had paid on the conclusion
> of the agreement. The merchant was distressed but had no
> remedy, so he simply raised his hand to his forehead and
> called upon Heaven. It was the thirteenth day of the fifth
> month and the sky was clear and without a cloud. In the

afternoon, however, a strong wind arose suddenly in the
Northwest. ... The cash and grain stored in Chang's
strongrooms and granaries could be counted in tens of
thousands but they were all swept away without one being
left behind. The great mansion where he lived was plucked
up and put down several li away. Trees an arm's length
in circumference were completely uprooted. The money
and silks locked up in his pawnshop went whirling about
in mid-air, and I have no idea where they came down.
The thirteen different sizes of grain-measure which he
regularly used were all deposited in a row outside his
gate as if to let people know. Just as Mr. Chiang-shih
stood dumbfounded a tree fell beside him and broke his arm.
His neighbor, Mr. Hsing, lost his clothes and a thousand
strings of cash. In the evening of the same day a further
storm arose at the county capital. Mr. Wang lost eight
thousand strings of cash and Mr. Tu a thousand. (171)

The main objective of these people was to hoard rice for sale
during that part of the year when rice prices were high. Thus Chu
Hsi observed of Nan-k'ang command (in Kiangsi):

There was harm done by drought this year in the area
under the jurisdiction of this command. I have
discovered from my enquiries that when merchants
from other prefectures came to sell rice here and
reached the ports of the counties of Hsing-tzu and
Tu-ch'ang, powerful families monopsonistically
purchased the entire quantity with the object of waiting
until grain prices rise next year, when they will be
able to make a good profit from their stocks. They
did not let the poor people buy any. (171)

On another occasion he expressed a somewhat contrary attitude:

When the rice boats draw up to the shore they wish to
sell but the lower-class households only purchase a
peck at a time; and thus in the last analysis it is hard
to get goods and money exchanged, and delays and
impediments are unavoidable. A proclamation should
be issued to the upper-class households to the effect

that they should buy up this rice at an appropriate time.
This will not only enable them to give hlep in the future
when famine threatens but also be a profit, will it not,
to those who stockpile reserves. (171)

Owners of rice reserves and rice shops often seem to have collaborated
in times of dearth to keep prices high.

c. Rice Boats and Rice Merchants

The terms 'rice boat' and 'rice merchant' were practically
synonymous, but many merchants also conducted a transport
business and carried other goods besides grain. Rice merchants
bought rice from the granaries of the well-to-do farmers, or else
directly from the peasants, and sold it to brokers and rice-shops
in distant markets, making their profits mainly from interregional
price differentials. The scale of management and the transactions
involved were large, as may be deduced from the size of the
grainships, and it would seem that, when the size of their resources
permitted it, merchants might set up networks of branch shops.

Lu Chiu-yuan (the philosopher) wrote in a letter about
Chin-chi county in Fu-chou (in Kiangsi) that:

At the present time the peasant farmers are all poor.
At harvest-time most of them do not have the facilities
for storing their grain and need as a matter of urgency
to sell it in order to make provision for their other
needs, and to repay their taxes and debts. If we do
not find a means of (officially) purchasing it then the
price will inevitably be low, and the grain will slip
away into the boats of the rice merchants and the
granaries of the rich. (172)

An epitaph written by Lou Yao on Wang Cheng-kung and included
in his Collection of the Kung-k'uei Master (Kung-k'uei chi) contains
the following passage:

In 1194 he became prefect of Ch'i-chou (in present-day Hupeh).
Since the abolition of illegal coinage many of the Huai people
were in want, and few of them had storage facilities. If
there were heavy rains then the markets might come to a halt
and (government) purchase become impossible. ... He also
noted that a good harvest would enable the people to be
self-sufficient except for the fact that great merchants
would come prior to this time with other goods for sale and
then, the moment that the grain came on the market, make
a great profit from it. (172)

In another epitaph contained in the same work Lou Yao also mentions
how when Chang Chung-tzu was prefect of Fu-chou (in Hupeh) in the
closing years of the twelfth century:

Water accumulated in the lowlying land and there was only
one good harvest every three or four years. Every year
rich merchants would first lend salt and tea to the people
and then in the autumn they would take away the people's
rice loaded in their huge flat-bottomed boats. (173)

The passage by Yeh Shih, quoted on page 14 above, shows that there
was a mercantile organization with several levels in the rice trade,
level depending on the amount of capital of which a merchant disposed.

Shen Kua's Dream-pool Essays (Meng-ch'i pi-t'an) of 1086,
in describing the installation of a better lock at Chen-chou, mention
that thereafter private grain ships travelling on the northern part of
the Sung Grand Canal could carry cargoes of up to 1,600 piculs.
Evidence from other sources reveals grain-ships of 600 to 1,000 piculs
at Lin-an (Hang-chou), of 1,000 piculs at Wu-hu (in Anhwei), of 300
piculs at Jao-chou (in present-day Kiangsi), of 1,000 piculs at Wu-hu
(in Anhwei), of 1,000 piculs on the Ling Canal which linked the waterways
of Hunan and Kwangtung, and of 2,500 piculs at Chiang-ling on the
Yangtze. At O-chou (Wu-ch'ang) there are even said to have been
boats of 10,000 piculs' capacity and more. Sea-going rice junks ranged
from several hundred to two thousand piculs capacity. The size of
these vessels is in itself, as indicated above, a proof of the large
scale of transactions in the grain trade.

Regional price differentials probably afforded the main source of profit. So much at least may be deduced from a brief remark in Hung Mai's Records of I Chien:

> The people of Chien-ch'ang county in Nan-k'ang (Kiangsi) devoutly believe in the great magical powers of the Violet Lady Spirit*, for she always informs them of profits to be made from forthcoming events. Sometimes she will tell them that tea will be expensive down the river, and so suitable for dealing in; or else that there will be a shortage of rice in some place or another, to which a cargo of it should be taken. They invariably do as she says and make substantial profits. (174)

In most cases rice boats combined their operations with a transport business.

d. Rice Brokers

Rice brokers occupied an intermediate position between rice merchants and retail rice shops, either as agents who facilitated a deal or as holders of stocks. Chu Hsi observed, 'In normal circumstances [as opposed to emergencies and natural disasters], when merchants sell rice, they would not ever venture to do it except through a broker.' In many cases rice-brokers also operated retail outlets. This appears from Wang Chih-tao's comment in his Writings from Hsiang-shan:

> When the common folk go into the markets to sell grain, the shopkeepers take a brokerage fee (ya-ch'ien) of from 10 to 20 cash for every tenth of a picul under the designation 'sales and purchases.' (176)

---

* On whom see E. T. C. Werner, A Dictionary of Chinese Mythology (New York: Julian Press, 1961) p. 535.

This would have amounted to between 5 and 10 per cent of the price.
Brokers also served as measures and determined price-levels.
The Gazetteer for Chien-k'ang County for the Ching-ting reign-period
(1260-1264) noted that in this area 'Several hundreds of thousands
of lives depend on the uncertain boats, while the power to raise or
lower the price of rice has fallen into the hands of the brokers. '
On the whole brokers enjoyed a more or less monopolistic position
buttressed by official support, but there is evidence that on occasion
they had to face competition from rich local families.   That brokers
could also sometimes operate on a small scale and with limited
capital is shown by the passage from Wang Yen quoted on page
above.

e. Rice Shops

There were numerous small shopkeepers in addition to those
brokers who were also in the retail business.   Something of their nature
may be seen from Ou-yang Shou-tao's remark that, 'What prompts
shopkeepers to sell rice isthe desire to make a profit.   They are
basically vagrant people, not persons who first had rice of their own
from their own homesteads. '

In the larger cities there was a high degree of organization,
as may be seen from Wu Tzu-mu's description of Lin-an (Hang-chou):

> As to the rice that is sold every day in the markets - if we
> leave to one side the palaces and the government offices,
> the mansions and the houses of the wealthy, and the employees
> in the departments of state who receive salaries (partly in
> rice), the ordinary folk in the city and its suburbs consume
> not less than one to two thousand piculs daily, * all of which
> they must obtain from the rice shops.   The prefecture
> depends upon rice brought by merchants from Su-chou,
> Hu-chou, Hsiu-chou(present-day Chia-hsing), the Huai valley
> and Kuang-nan.   This comes to the Hu-chou Market, the
> Rice Market Bridge and the Black Bridge.   In each case the
> brokers of the rice guild receive the merchants who have
> brought it for sale. ...   Furthermore, the rice shop proprietors

---

*Three thousand piculs to be correct.

within and without the city walls each arrange the price at
the market in consultation solely with the head of the guild,
after which the rice is directly despatched to their various
shops for sale. The rice shop owners agree on the day
upon which they will pay for the rice; and small brokers
from the rice market come round in person to each shop
to supervise the retailing. There is also a market
consisting of thirty to forty firms on South Street below
Hay Bridge outside the newly-opened city gate. They
receive (wholesale) merchants, distribute to shops, and
sell to merchants from the hill regions. It is quite
different from the city markets. * (177)

An account of the efficient transport arrangements for the Hang-chou
rice market has already been quoted on page 20 above.

The section on 'Quarrels Over Money' in the Collection of
Lucid Decisions by Celebrated Judges (Ming-Kung shu-p'an ch'ing-ming chi),
a Southern Sung anthology of famous legal opinions, contains the following
judgment pronounced by a prefect in a case involving the establishment
of a small rice shop:

I have examined the county magistrate's records concerning
this matter: '... . According to the deposition made by
Li Jun-tsu, he opened a small rice shop in premises rented
from Fan Ya. Towards the end of 1235 Fan Ya gave him
on credit some 50 piculs of rice to sell, and they made a
verbal agreement that the price to be paid for these would
be 50 strings of cash. In the third month of the following
year the period of the loan was extended and interest added,
and he was compelled to write a note of hand for 170 strings
of cash. -- As regards this point, it cannot really have
been the case that interest more than doubling the 50 strings
of cash for the rice should have been added after a few
months, and it is even more difficult to believe the statement
that he was compelled to write the note of hand. Even if
some things in this world are neither in accord with right
principles nor follow human sentiment, yet how could he

---

*Compare the translation on pages 91-92 of Balazs (1964).

have allowed someone else to force him to do something to
which he did not willingly consent? ... He says that
thereafter he cleared off the debt by installments but Fan Ya
having told him that the note of hand mentioned above
had suddenly disappeared, he had later negligently omitted
to go and get it. -- As regards this point, even if he could
not get his original bond back after he had returned the
money, why didn't he demand a receipt as evidence which
would put the matter beyond question? ... According to
Li Jun-tsu's testimony he had served as a tutor [or secretary*]
in Fan Ya's house for three years, a relationship which
creates an incomparably deep sense of mutual obligation
(jen-ch'ing). (Discord had arisen between them) only because
the women of the two families had had some slight disagreement,
and because when he himself had gone to Hsiao-hu to pay
his respects to his parents a crowd of Fan Ya's concubines
had shamefully abused his wife Ch'en so that she had been
obliged to leave. -- Isn't this assertion ridiculous!
If we bring these six doubtful points together for further
scrutiny, so as to obtain a comprehensive view of the
situation, what evaluation are we to make? Now the
note of hand written by Li Jun-tsu and produced by Fan Ya
says: 'From the first month of 1236, a further extension.
A further 3 strings of cash are to be added to the 168 strings.'
Moreover Li Jun-tsu's deposition states that in 1228, 1229
and 1231 he was resident in Fan Ya's household as a tutor
[or secretary*] and that in 1234 he leased premises from
Fan Ya in which to open a rice shop. Now, that he was
a tutor [or secretary] for up to three years is solid evidence
of the depth of mutual obligation. It was on account of this
that Li Jun-tsu could suggest that Fan Ya lend him a little
money as the capital needed to start the shop, and that Fan Ya
could not refuse him. After Fan Ya had made the loan he
became apprehensive that if the money were lent for a long
period it might not be returned. So in 1236 he demanded a
contract and Li Jun-tsu made out a note of hand for 171 strings
of cash. Although it is impossible to ascertain if part of
this sum was interest added in consideration of the extension
on the loan, since he wrote it himself, there is no more to be said.

---

*The Chinese terms used are ch'u-kuan in the first instance, and
shou-kuan in the two following instances. Transl.

Li Jun-tsu is not out of his right mind and if he asserts
that he wrote it this way because Fan Ya compelled him
to do so, I do not believe it. ... On the day when he was
being examined Fan Ya adhered to the view that Li Jun-tsu
had been merely his store-keeper (k'an-k'u) and from time
to time quarrelled with him in a harsh tone of voice with
the intention of showing that he was the manager and Li the
store-keeper, and making me realize that there was a
difference in status between them. But seeing that formerly
Li was a resident tutor (kuan-pin), and Fan his employer
and host, a relationship in which mutual satisfaction creates
a great depth of reciprocal obligation, it is quite wrong for
Fan to regard him as a store-keeper even if he has borrowed
a little money and not yet returned it. When Li Jun-tsu
and Fan Ya were on terms of intimacy, the former borrowed
money and goods from the latter with which to set up a shop.
Later, because of a quarrel, Li wished to roll up his mat
and abscond. When Fan Ya learnt of this he had him
intercepted. There is no more to it than this and it is
absurd to call it robbery [as had been alleged by Li's wife] .'
This is the county magistrate's report, and he desires
me to render a decision. I must now request the county
magistrate to summon the two parties once again to court.
He shall compel Li Jun-tsu to take steps to repay Fan Ya,
though not necessarily the entire sum, this being what is
known in vulgar parlance as 'the seller showing generosity
to the buyer'. How much more is this applicable in consideration
of the instruction which Fan Ya's son, Fan Chi, has received
from Li Jun-tsu! If Fan Ya can abate part of his claims on
Li Jun-tsu this would also be an act of unostentatious charity. (180)

This interesting judgment reveals the mechanism by which persons
of modest means might acquire the capital needed for a rice shop.
It also suggests how the status relationship between a former master
and a former tutor (or store-keeper) might persist, even after the
termination of the employment, and make itself felt in a relationship
of economic dependence. Although independent shops with substantial
capital presumably also existed at this time, there were probably
many small establishments of the sort run by Li Jun-tsu.

C. The Distinctive Characteristics of the Rice Market during the
Southern Sung

The main features of the Southern Sung rice market are
represented schematically in Figure I below:

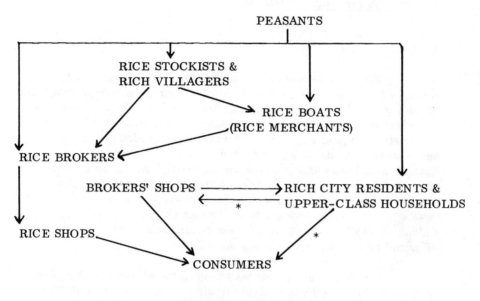

Figure I   Structure of the Southern Sung Rice Market
(*indicates an exceptional relationship)

It is clear both that the circulation of rice through this system
presupposed a national market in the sense of regional interdependence
on a nationwide scale, and also that the market was to some extent
imperfect in view of the profits made by the exploitation of regional
price differentials. The varying state of transportation also meant
the coexistence of areas in close contact with this national market
system and of those which were relatively closed off from it.
For this reason and for others, such as the greatly varying productive
capacity of different regions, the society of this time must be
analyzed in pluralistic rather than in unitary terms.

Finally, it is important to note the many-sided nature of many businesses, the number of persons who engaged in trade as a subsidiary rather than a main occupation, and the particular strength of the influence and control exercised by the brokers.

ii. Other Agricultural Products

A. Oils

Oils and fats were used for cooking, for lighting, for cosmetics, in the construction of ships, the manufacture of weapons, lacquer goods and inks, in building, and as lubricants and rust preventatives. They were indispensable both in everyday life and in industry. Writers on city life invariably regarded oil as a basic necessity, and it regularly figured on the somewhat varying lists of 'articles in daily use among the people' exempted from the payment of internal customs duties which were issued from time to time by the Sung government. The consumption of oil undoubtedly rose with increasing urbanization. During the lantern-viewing in Ch'eng-tu on the fifteenth of the first month some 5,000 catties of oil would be consumed in a single night.

A wide variety of oils was used in the different parts of the country.* Some indication of this is afforded by a passage in Chuang Ch'o's Miscellany (Chi-le pien):

> Oil is used everywhere for eating and burning, but the
> best variety is that made from sesamum seeds (hu-ma),
> commonly called the 'oil-hemp' (chih-ma). It is said
> to have eight perverse characteristics: When the weather
> is rainy or overcast, the crop is poor, but when it is
> very dry there is an abundant harvest. Its blossoms droop
> downwards, while its fruits reach upwards. When the
> seeds are roasted and pressed, they yield raw oil. When
> carts are greased with it, they run smoothly, but awls and
> needles (smeared with it) become rough. In Ho-tung, however,

---

*There is a comprehensive table on pp. 186-7 of the original work.

people eat hemp oil, which has an offensive smell and,
like perilla seed oil, is suitable for use in the manufacture
of rain-garments. In Shensi, they also consume oils made
from almonds, red and blue hibiscus seeds, and rape-turnip
seeds, besides using them in their lamps. Tsu T'ing
[a statesman of the sixth century] lost his sight through
the smoke of rape-turnip seed oil in his eyes, but in recent
times I have not heard of anyone suffering in this way.
In Shantung they also use an oil made from burweed seeds
(xanthium strumarium) which is useful for curing colds.
There is not much sesamum oil in Chiang-Hu. Oil from the
t'ung tree is much used in lamps but its thick and filthy
smoke is especially to be shunned where objects such as
pictures and statues are concerned. Clothes stained with
it can only be cleaned with winter melon. It has a clear
color and a sweet taste, but anyone who eats it by mistake
will suffer from vomiting and diarrhoea. Drinking either
wine or tea will purge it, for southern wine contains a good
quantity of lime. There have been cases of women anointing
their hair with it in error. It congealed into a lump, and
every method resorted to in the effort to remove it proved
unsuccessful, until at length the hair fell out. There is
also p'ang-p'i seed oil from the same lindera strychnifolia
whose root is used as a drug. Villagers use it in candle
form for lighting but its smoke has a particularly unpleasant
smell and for this reason it is little used in cities. Oil from
the wax tree resembles fat and can be poured so as to form
candles. It is used everywhere in Kuang-nan, and is also
found in Ch'u-chou and Wu-chou. In Ying-chou they also
eat fish oil, which has a somewhat rank odor. When there
was a great dearth in Ching-hsi (Honan and Hupeh) during
the Hsuan-ho reign-period (1119-1125) and people were
eating each other, brains were refined into an edible oil
which enjoyed a wide sale, it being quite impossible to taste
the difference. (195)

The Complete Domestic Compendium (Chü-chia pi-yung shih-lei
ch'üan-chi) also observed:

For reading books by the light of a reading lamp it is
necessary to burn hemp oil because it produces no smoke
and does not harm the eyes. It has, however, the unfortunate
propensity of easily drying up, and three ounces of t'ung
oil should be mixed with every catty, after which it will
be unlikely to go dry and rats will also be driven away.
If oil from the rape-turnip, poppy or red hibiscus is used,
then three ounces of t'ung oil should be mixed with each
catty and a little salt placed in the bowl of the lamp. This
will economize on oil. If the sides of the bowl are rubbed
with green ginger, this will prevent the formation of sediment
or vapors. If some sapan wood is simmered in the middle
of the lamp, there will be no ashes when the wick burns dry. (187)

Sesamum oil was produced in most parts of China, with the
exception of wet, lowlying areas. The pressed husks of the seeds
were also used as a fertilizer. Wang Chen, in his Treatise on Agriculture
(Nung-shu) of 1313 gives the first description of the process of
manufacture: roasting the seeds in pans, pounding them and crushing
them with rollers, steaming them in caldrone and pressing them in
a wooden press.

Hemp seed oil was also widely used, both in North China and
in Kiangnan. The small-scale production of peasants was probably
often co-ordinated by middlemen, as the following passage from
Hung Mai's Records of I Chien suggests:

Hu Nieh-ssu, a commoner from Yung-feng in Lo-p'ing
(in the prefecture of Jao-chou in present-day Kiangsi),
set up an inn at Ta-mei-ling. In the winter of 1165 a
merchant from I-yang county (in Hsin-chou) came on his
own with his sacks to lodge there. When night had fallen,
he bought some wine, invited Hu to join him for a drink,
and made enquiries about the price of hemp. Hu responded
with a return round of drinks and the merchant, having
become intoxicated, pulled out two lumps of silver and gave
them to him, saying: 'May I trouble you to undertake a
commission for me tomorrow? Buy me some hemp seeds
and press the oil from them so that I can take it home with
me to sell.' Hu said delightedly: 'Nothing could be easier!
It can be done in a morning. ...' (188)

It is conceivable that this passage refers to sesamum, but it may
be provisionally taken as indicating ordinary hemp.

Perilla was sometimes grown along the edges of fields by the
roadside in order to prevent cattle from trampling on the grain.
Its seeds yielded oil for lighting and various other purposes,
notably, mixing with lacquer to give the latter added strength and
oiling silk.

Rape-turnip seed oil was used in Shensi for lighting and food.

Rape-seed oil was produced in the Han River Valley and along
the coasts of northern Chekiang and southern Kiangsu.

T'ung oil was manufactured for sale in parts of Kiangnan,
in Hunan, and even in Fukien. It was used in shipbuilding, and is
probably the 'oil' referred to in the quotation from Chao Shan-kua
on page 13 above. Smoke from burning t'ung oil was used to make
a kind of ink, and it was sometimes used in the manufacture of lacquer
in the same way as perilla seed oil. Because of its usefullness in the
production of weapons, it was forbidden to export it to the Chin Tartars
under the Southern Sung. In Yuan times however it seems to have
been exported to Cambodia.

Wax-tree oil made better candles than beeswax, and could
also be used as a dye for hair. It was produced in Kuang-nan,
Chekiang, Kiangsi and Szechwan. A passage from the National
Gazetteer (I-t'ung chih) for the Yuan dynasty compiled by Yueh Lin
describes the production and sale of wax-tree oil:

> Wax-tree oil is produced in Yü-kuan from the nuts of the
> black wax-tree. Candles manufactured from it burn with a
> bright and clear flame. There are three grades: a hard
> variety made from the oil of the outer coating which is
> capable of surviving the summer's heat, a less good variety
> made of soft oil, and oil made from the pith, which is
> burnt in lamps and sold everywhere. ... (192)

Tsai Piao-yuan,who lived in Ning-po in Yuan times, also mentions
the 'wax-tree (oil) merchants' of that region.

Fish oil was also consumed in certain area.

Besides ordinary Beeswax, which was yellow, there were
two different types of White Wax, one a refined form of beeswax, and
the other the deposits of the white wax insect (flata limbata). The
high price commanded by the latter made rearing these insects a
profitable sideline for peasants. Wax of one kind or another was
widely produced in hilly regions throughout China, and it was also
imported from Southeast Asia. A reference to the domestic trade
in wax appears in the quotation from Fan Hui on page 23 above.
Certain places were also noted for the manufacture of wax candles.
Even among the upper classes these were regarded as luxury items,
as emerges from two anecdotes related by Ou-yang Hsiu:

> The patterened wax candles of Teng-chou (in present-day
> Honan) are renowned throughout the Empire. Even at
> the Capital they are not capable of making them. There
> is a tradition that the technique originated with Mr.
> K'ou Lai, who was once prefect of Teng-chou. Ever since
> his youth he had enjoyed riches and honors, and he never
> burned oil lamps. He was particularly fond of night-time
> banquets and drinking-bouts. Even in his bedroom he would
> kepp candles burning until dawn. Whenever he vacated an
> official post and his successor moved into his offices, he
> would often find the floor of the privy covered with a mound
> of candle-drippings. Mr. Ch'i was frugal and uncorrupted.
> He never burned official candles while he was in office.
> When conversing with his visitors he would use only a
> single oil lamp, sputtering and on the point of extinction. (196)

B. Vegetables

Vegetables were often grown commercially as subsidiary
foodstuffs for the growing urban population, and also as raw materials
for handicraft industry.

In his Miscellany from the Hall of the Two Elders (Erh-lao-t'ang
tsa-chih) Chou Pi-ta had this to say about Hang-chou when it was the
capital of the Southern Sung:

There is a proverbial saying that 'Vegetables come by the
East Gate, water by the West Gate, firewood by the South
Gate, and rice by the North Gate.' There are no inhabitants
outside the East Gate, but vegetable gardens everywhere one
looks. At the West Gate the water from the lake is drawn
into the city and then distributed to the various quarters and
markets by means of small boats. The firewood of Yen-chou
and Fu-yang are gathered at Chiang-hsia and come in by the
South Gate. Rice from Su-chou and Hu-chou comes in through
the northern customs barrier. (197)

There were special vegetable-growing areas outside most cities, such
as Ting-chia Island, some 300 li across, which was devoted solely to
the cultivation of radishes for the Nanking market, or the 20 villages
outside the modest county city of Ts'ai-hsia in Shou-chou (in Anhwei)
which produced melons for consumption there.

A number of famous local specialities, especially certain
kinds of ginger, melons, mushrooms and bamboo shoots, travelled to
markets far away from where they originated. Certain dye-plants were
also cultivated commercially, notably the red hibiscus, madder,
indigo, and lithospermum officinale, which yielded a purple dye.
In his 'Song on the Weaving of Brocade' the Yuan litterateur Liu Shen
wrote of dyes from places in Szechwan province:

Brocade woven in Szechwan is prized the Empire over;
In every family women workers set up brocade looms.
A myriad measures of cosmetic yellow come from P'eng-lai;
The red madder of Wei-ch'uan grows in a thousand fields. (200)

In the Northern Sung period the manufacture of official silks at
K'ai-feng necessitated the annual purchase of tens of thousands of
catties of red hibiscus and of lithospermum from the common people,
and the latter was therefore much cultivated by peasants near the
capital. In Southern Sung times it was also widely grown in Kiangnan.

Peasants' surplus vegetables found a commercial outlet in
local markets, as is indicated by these verses composed by Shu
Yueh-hsiang on T'ai-chou prefecture in present-day Chekiang:

In the remote hamlets the women sigh
At the small returns from the sale of vegetables -
Turnips smoother than mother's milk,
And globes plump as lambkins.

With sacks across their shoulders and cash stowed in their belts
They go to town to buy their meat.
Vegetables are far more profitable than paddy;
They can buy rice, and have no fear of hunger. (201)

Wang Chieh, an eminent offical of the early fourteenth century, had
some interesting things to say about the production and sale of
vegetables in the section on gardens and orchards in his ' Basic
Principles for the Improvement of Customs':

Grains satisfy our hunger. Vegetables add flavor. Both are
indispensable in the daily lives of the people. ... Now,
although the farmers toil at agriculture and sericulture they
ought also to cultivate vegetables on the waste ground around
their homes. This will save them money and provide them
with goods for sale. Leeks, moreover, simply have to be
planted to grow, taking little effort and having a fine
savor, which makes them particularly suitable for
large-scale planting. Other vegetables, such as melons,
aubergines, onions and garlics, should be cultivated as
convenient. If there are few of them, they will serve for
home consumption; if they are plentiful, they can be sold.
If there is a surplus of land the labor available to work it,
then taro, rape-turnips and lucerne should be grown as well,
for they yield a very heavy harvest and not only serve as a
supplement to the diet but can also stave off famine and help
people through bad years. (202)

Equally revealing of the degree to which vegetable production might
be commercialized is the following passage from the supplement to
Shen Kua's Dream-pool Essays:

Chang Yung, the President of the Ministry (of Personnel),
had previously been the county magistrate of Ch'ung-yang
in O-chou. Ch'ung-yang had much unused land, for the
people did not work at farming or sericulture, but made

their living solely by the cultivation of tea. Chang ordered
them to cut down their tea plantations and induced them to
grow mulberry trees and hemp. After this time the number
of tea plantations gradually diminished, and mulberry trees
amd hemp flourished notably well between O-chou and
Yueh-chou. When the official tea system was altered in
the Chia-yu reign-period (1056-1063) the people of Hu-Hsiang
(i.e. Hunan) suffered from the tea tax. Only Ch'ung-yang
had a very low tea tax, and when the people of this county
looked at the other counties they remembered the kindness
shown to them by Chang and set up a temple to him in
gratitude.

There had also been persons who had come into the markets
to buy their vegetables. To them Chang issued the following
proclamation:

People who live in the county city have no land to cultivate
and pursue other occupations. For them, it is permissible
to buy vegetables. You villagers all have land. Why are you
not growing them for yourselves instead of wasting cash on
the purchase of expensive vegetables?

He had those who tried to do so bambooed and driven away.
After this everybody laid out gardens, and down to the present
day turnips are known as 'Magistrate Chang's vegetables'. . (202)

C. Fruits

The cultivation of fruits had a highly commercialized character.
They were even sold to peasants in the small local markets. This
may be illustrated by some verses composed by Hsiang An-shih, an
official of the Southern Sung:

> The market at dawn –
> Fruits in profusion.
> Boxes that brim with loquats, plums
> With one red spot on each
> And apricots all yellow.
> The greengages wait for the summer's warmth,
> Quinces evoke the frosts.
> The busy peddlers deal
> With everything in season. (203)

The production of fruit for distant urban markets was also well
developed. Yen-chou, Wu-chou, Ch'ÜChou and Hui-chou regularly
provided the Southern Sung capital at Hang-chou with fresh and dried
fruits, as well as with firewood, charcoal and timber.

Lychees were a speciality of Kuang-nan, Fukien and Szechwan.
Together with oranges they were the most highly esteemed fruit
commercially available. The range of their sale is indicated by a
passage in Ts'ai Hsiang's Manual of the Lychee (Li-chih p'u):

> The most lychees are grown in Fu-chou. They stretch
> along the plains and the uncultivated lands, being
> particularly abundant to the west of the Hung-t'ang River.
> To the north of the prefectural seat the hill slopes are
> covered with dense groves of trees. When the summer
> rains begin to clear away and the evening sun is shining,
> not even the greatest painter could depict the dark red
> skins of the fruit and their verdant leaves sparkling fresh
> and clear for miles on end. No account can do justice to
> this sight. When the branches are first putting forth their
> blossoms, merchants make estimates of the crop grove by
> grove, and on this basis draw up contracts (with the peasants).
> They can tell if the coming harvest is going to be
> plentiful or meager. All the fruit, regardless of its
> color or complexion, is preserved in red salt (i.e. steeped
> in the brine of pickles plums dyed a red color with the rose
> of China) and taken by land or water to the Capital. Some
> of it goes abroad to the northern barbarians and to the
> Hsi-hsia. Some goes in ships to the East and to the South,
> to Korea, to Japan, to the Liu-ch'iu Islands and to Persia.
> Everyone appreciates lychees and handsome profits may be
> made from them. For this reason merchants are trading
> ever more extensively in them while fewer and fewer country
> folk are growing them. Although the annual output is an
> incalculable number of tens or hundreds of thousands, very
> few peasants are in a position to overeat as a result. This
> is because they sell on a grove by grove basis. (210)

It would seem, however, that lychees were mostly grown in the gardens
of officials, rich persons, and institutions such as Buddhist and Taoist
monasteries. Besides brine, sguar and honey were also used as
preservatives.

Oranges of various sorts were grown in most parts of southern China. It was generally agreed that the finest of all were grown in the eastern and western Tung-t'ing hills in Lake T'ai. This area was also one of the most specialized, depending for its entire grain supply upon merchants. An eleventh-century official, Ch'en Shun-yü, has left a long annotated poem describing orange cultivation here in detail, the main points of which may be summarized as follows. The orchards were in the hands of well-to-do families who did not count their holdings in terms of trees but of mou. Seedlings were purchased in Su-chou, Hsiu-chou or Hu-chou, those from the last-mentioned place being the best. The trees were grown on stone terraces and surrounded with thorn hedges. Wells were dug beside the trees to keep them properly moist and owners would spend large sums in times of drought employing carriers to fill them wit h water from the lake. Insects in the bark were killed with small pointed implements, and dense foliage on the sunny side was cut back so as to allow the fruit to receive more sunlight. Branches so overburdened with fruit that they threatened to snap were propped up. After the oranges had been picked they had to be 'sweated' under straw for a few days before they could be packed for market. A basket of a 100 catties weight would fetch anything from 600 to 1,500 cash. Oranges which had fallen off early were used for the manufacture of dried orange peel, and it was estimated that the area put from 5,000 to 6,000 ch'eng (a unit of about 15 lb weight) of this commodity on the market each year. The smallest oranges were preserved by being repeatedly smoked in special cellars dug into the hillsides. (212-213)

Some twenty-seven different varieties of orange were produced at Wen-chou, and when they were not sold fresh they were preserved by steeping in brine or honey. Of the oranges of Kuo-chou in Szechwan Fen Shan observed that, 'They are much cultivated and yield a greater profit than the gardenia (which provides a yellow dye) or the madder-plant.' In the 'upper prefecture' of Fukien orange-growing had to be forbidden because of the shortage of farmland, as is indicated by the quotation from Fang Ta-tsung on page 54 above. Oranges were also widely grown in Kuang-nan, where their cultivation was sophisticated, at least in comparison with the relatively slapdash methods used in agriculture at this time. According to Chuang Ch'o's Miscellany:

There is little land in Kuang-nan that is suitable for farming, and the people grow a lot of oranges in order to make some money. They have constant trouble from grubs which eat the fruit and damage it. Only if there are ants in a tree is it impossible for these grubs to survive. The owners of the orchards therefore buy ants from others, and consequently there are people who collect ants in order to sell them. They fill the bladder of a pig or a sheep with fat, stretch its aperature wide open, and place it besides an ants' nest. Once all the ants have gone inside it, they take it away. These are called 'ants for the cultivation of oranges.' (214)

Generally speaking, the Sung period was marked by the establishment of specialized areas of orange-production serving a national market.

A large variety of other fruits wa also grown for the market. In Lin-an (Hang-chou) there are known to have been guilds (t'uan, hang) both of fruit merchants and of orange merchants, and it seems likely that the circulation of fruit largely rested in their hands.

D. Sugar

According to the late Professor Katō Shigeshi, sugar-cane first appeared in South China towards the end of the Warring States period (3rd century BC), and spread slowly northwards until by the time of the Northern and Southern Dynasties (5th and 6th centuries AD) it had reached the southern parts of Kiangsu and Anhwei. In T'ang and Sung times it was also cultivated in Szechwan and in Fukien, which was later to become pre-eminent in the sugar industry. Initially the cane was simply chewed and the juice imbibed. It was only gradually that the practice of extracting the juice by crushing the cane, refining the syrup and reducing it to powder form became common. These techniques, which probably came, like the plant itself, from Indo-China, were known in Kuang-chou (Canton) by the Liang Dynasty (AD 502-556), and in Szechwan and along the southeast coast by T'ang times. Granulated sugar and lump sugar were also manufactured.

In the cities of Sung times, particularly the capital, large amounts of sugar were consumed and there were itinerant vendors who walked the streets with supplies of it in earthenware jars. In the villages of Wu, sugar was eaten as a delicacy at the New Year.

These trends stimulated an expansion of sugar-cane cultivation in the villages of the main producing areas, as may be seen from the quotation from Fang Ta-tsung given on page 54 above. Merchants came from as far away as Pan-ch'iao in Shantung to purchase Fukien sugar. Wang Hsiang-chih's Geography of the Empire mentions how in T'eng-chou in Kwangsi, 'The local people all grow sugar-cane along the rivers, and there are forests of it as far as the eye can see.' Wang Shao's Manual of White Sugar (T'ang-shuang p'u), written in the twelfth century, describes how in his native prefecture of Sui-ning in Szechwan as many as forty per cent of the peasants in some areas might be engaged in growing cane. Oxen were used to work the crushing rollers and the finished sugars, of which there were a wide variety, were transported in jars packed with lime, probably to prevent spoilage by damp. It took eighteen months from the planting of the cane until the sale of the product and sugar must therefore have been to some extent a speculative business.

E. Timber

Timber had been an important item of interregional trade since very early times. Certain woods are listed in the Book of Documents as tribute from some of the nine ancient provinces of China. Ssu-ma Ch'ien refers to profits made from tiber and bamboo in the Han dynasty, and T'ang writers also mention these commodities as a source of large commercial returns.

In the Sung dynasty the government needed wood for buildings, for city walls, hydraulic projects and ship-building. This was obtained through taxation, through excise levies of ten to twenty per cent at downstream timber markets, and through direct purchases either here or at the upstream logging centers. Among the common people the principal uses of timber were for houses, coffins, ships, wood and lacquer vessels, and of course for fuel, either in the form of firewood or of charcoal. Transport was a major item in the cost of timber, as is suggested by a remark in Hung Mai's Records of I Chien:

> There are abundant forests in Hsia-chou (in Hupeh) but most of them are a long way away from rivers. One could well afford to buy the timber but would immediately be faced with the difficulty of hauling it to these latter. (220)

There was a great expansion in the consumption of wood in Sung times, with the result that profits were made not only from logging and transport, which was nothing new, but also from the commercial cultivation of trees, which was.

There was much lavish spending on houses by the well-to-do, and an instinct for aping the fashions prevalent among social and political leaders, as may be seen from another story in the Record of I Chien:

> Ts'ui Yü-chih, styled Chü-p'o, became Prime Minister
> under the Emperor Li-tsung. When he returned to Szechwan
> he built himself a mansion of extraordinary elegance.
> It was copied by a powerful local merchant family called Li.
> They hired the very same artisans who had put up Ts'ui's
> house and followed the design in every particular with the
> result that there was not the slightest difference between
> the two. (232)

At the other end of the social scale, the dwellings of peasants were probably often built from the timbers of old houses that had been demolished. This may be deduced from a supplementary decree passed in the T'ien-sheng reign-period (1023-1031) which stated, in part, that:

> All those selling old house timbers, firewood, hay, rice,
> flour, and wood and iron for farm tools shall be exempt
> from the payment of customs duties. (222)

For the more elaborate of the buildings put up by the government an extraordinary variety of special woods was assembled from all over the country. Thus for a Taoist temple constructed in K'ai-feng at the beginning of the eleventh century pinewood was brought from Ch'in-chou (Kansu), Lung-chou, Ch'i-chou, and T'ung-chou (Shensi), cedar wood from Lan-chou, Shih-chou and Fen-chou (Shansi), catalpa wood, camphor-tree wood and oak wood from T'an-chou, Heng-chou, Tao-chou, Yung-chou and Ting-chou (Hunan) and Chi-chou (Kiangsi), zelkova tree wood and camphor-tree wood from Yung-chou and Li-chou (Hunan) and Ch'u-chou (Chekiang), cryptomeria from T'an-chou, Ch'en-chou (Hunan), Ming-chou and Yueh-chou (Chekiang), and pagoda-tree wood (sophora) from Huang-chou (Hupeh) and Meng-chou and Tse-chou (Shansi). During the Southern Sung period Kuang-nan, southern Anhwei and Fukien also became important as suppliers of timber.

Some idea of the amount of timber (and iron) needed for
boat-building may be obtained from Sha-k'o-shih's estimate in Yuan
times that for every 100 piculs' capacity some 223 planks and 3,685
nails were required. The woods most commonly used for boats were
pine, camphor-tree (nan) and cryptomeria (shan), which was the best.
According to the Cheng-ho reign edition (1116) of T'ang Shen-wei's
Herbal (in Readiness for Emergencies) Drawn from the Classics and
Histories, and Verified According to Category (Cheng-ho ching-shih
cheng-lei (pei-chi) pen-ts'ao):

> The notes of Kuo P'o* says: The cryptomeria resembles
> the pine. It grows in Kiangnan and is suitable for making
> boats and coffins. Pillars made from it do not rot when
> buried in the ground, and people also regularly use it
> for buckets since it is little affected by water. (223)

As mentioned on page 8 above, Ch'in-chou in present-day Kwangtung
was famous for its wu-lan wood, which made the best rudders for
large ships. Other woods also used for this purpose were the Ch'in-chou
t'ieh-leng ('iron-beam') and the ch'a of Hui-chou (in Anhwei).

The boat-construction industry grew up at places where
a supply of the necessary materials could be assured. Usually this
came from the immediate hinterland, as in the case of Ming-chou
and Wen-chou: less frequently from some distance, as in the case
of Chien-k'ang (Nanking) which obtained its wood from Hunan and
Kiangsi. Official boat-yards relied on timber purchased from
merchants, and the lack of it sometimes limited output and made it
necessary to requisition private vessels for service.

The importance attached by the Chinese to the ceremony of
burial also meant that there was a constant demand for wood for
good quality coffins. According to Hsu Hsuan, a statesman of the
later tenth century:

> Hsu Yen-ch'eng, a military official, made a regular business
> of dealing in timber. In 927 he went to Jui-k'ou in Hsin-chou
> (in Kiangsi). There was no wood to be bought, so he anchored
> his boat and waited for it. ... After he had been there for
> a day or two there arrived a large quantity of cryptomeria

---

*Who lived in the Chin dynasty.

wood, of good quality and available at a cheap price.
He was making his farewells, business dealings having
been brought to a conclusion, when the young man (who
had been his opposite number) brought out four more
pieces of cryptomeria and said to him: 'I sold the other
wood to you. This is a gift. It ought to fetch a good price
if you go to Wu (southern Kiangsu). Hsu went first to
the Ch'in-huai river (in Chiang-ning county in Kiangsu)
at a time when the ruler of Wu-Yueh had just died, and
planks of cryptomeria were being collected to make a
particularly distinctive coffin. He obtained several hundreds
of thousands of cash, after which he bought costly presents,
which he took to Jui-k'ou in order to repay the young man.
He did business with him once again, and went back and
forth three times in all, making a substantial profit. (225)

The best wood of all for coffins was fragrant wood (hsiang-mu),
as may be seen from the following story of filial impiety recounted
by Hung Mai:

The father and mother of Wang San-shih, a commoner from
Hsiao-ch'eng village in P'o-yang, had bought in readiness
for their own deaths two coffins made of fragrant wood.
Wang substituted coffins of Hsin-chou cryptomeria, and then
sold these too in their turn, replacing them with coffins
of chu(-yü) wood. When his mother died he further wished
to keep the chu(-yü) wood for his own use, and simply
bought a pinewood coffin to bury her in. (226)

Coffin-wood, mostly pine, cryptomeria and juniper, was also imported
from Japan. According to a memorial submitted by Pao Hui, an
official of the Southern Sung dynasty:

The Japanese boats only bring such useless things as
planks of wood and shellfish to our customs yards. They
return home with our copper cash gained in exchange. This
is as if they had bartered mud for our real metal, or stones
for our lovely jades. It is not hard to see who has the best
of the bargain! The shellfish merely provide for banquets.
It is not as if we should be without the grain to support life
if we were to do without them. I am unaware of any urgent
function fulfilled by wood planks. Even if we were to do
without them, it would not be as if we had no coffin-wood with

which to pay our parting respects to the dead. Would it
not be right to prohibit the import of these items? Sulphur
on the other hand supplies a military need. We should
permit trade in it and levy a tax on it. (226)

Urban demand for wood fuel may be seen from a remark
in Chuang Ch'o's <u>Miscellany:</u>

> When formerly the capital was at K'ai-feng (under the Northern
> Sung) its several millions of families relied entirely upon
> coal; not a single one of them burned firewood. * At present
> the (Southern Sung) Court is stationed in Wu-Yueh. The
> extent of the forest-covered hills is not adequate for the
> gathering of fuel. In the course of time even the gorgeous
> flowers, the beautiful bamboos and the pines and catalpa
> trees that grew upon the burial-mounds have all become
> bare earth. (227)

This demand meant that in the environs of cities the forests were
commercialy exploited. Chu Chi-fang alludes to this in some
verses on 'Carrying Firewood':

> Climbing up to the white mists with one's matchet at one's waist,
> One is saddened to find that the tall pines have not grown a
> full span of years.
> Near to the city every hill is somebody's property,
> And it is hard to reach the distant ranges and the higher slopes. (227)

The Yü-chang hills of Lung-ch'üan county in Ch'u-chou
(in Chekiang) and Hui-chou were famous for their wooden furniture,
and merchants from Kuang-ling (in Kiangsu) sold more than a hundred
varieties of finely-made cedar-wood furniture in Chieh-k'ang (Nanking).

Lumber was usually collected at a logging yard, bound there
into rafts and floated downstream to the timber and firewood yards of
a central market where it would be sold. Taxes and transport
constituted the greater part of the price, as is clear from the entry
for January 3** 1173 in Fan Ch'eng-ta's <u>Ts'an-luan lu</u>, a journal of a
three months' journey from Lin-an to Kuei-lin in Kwangsi:

---

*Because of the exhaustion of supplies. Transl.
** January 18 in the Western calendar.

96

> We anchored at Yen-chou, and then passed through the
> floating bridge on the river there. ... The official
> controls at this bridge are extremely strict. Rafts of
> cryptomeria wood from She-p'u (at the juncture of the
> Hsin-an and the Lien-ch'i rivers in southern Anhwei)
> all pile up below the bridge. The essential objective pursued
> is to tax them heavily, which is a source of great distress
> to the merchants, who are sometimes delayed for several
> months before they are able to proceed. I learned a certain
> amount about this when I was an official in She county
> (in Hui-chou). The hills of Hsiu-ning are well-suited to
> the cryptomeria, and few of the local people cultivate
> fields, most of them making their living by growing cryptomeria
> trees. The cryptomeria also grows easily and it is
> difficult, therefore, to exhaust the supplies of it. When
> it is brought out of the hills the price is extremely cheap.
> When it reaches the prefectural capital it has already been
> taxed without limit. By the time it arrives at Yen-chou
> say: 'Our prefecture has no large source of earnings. Without
> the cryptomeria wood from She county there would be no
> prefecture.' In view of this statement, will there ever come
> a time when the afflictions of the merchants are eased?
> For, when a log comes from the hills, it is sometimes
> not worth a hundred cash; but when it reaches the (lower
> course of the) Chien River (i.e. the Che River) it is sold
> for two thousand cash. This is entirely the result of
> heavy taxes and expenses incurred by merchant because of
> the long time involved. (228)

Timber from the Chekiang hills also went down the Ch'i-men River into
Kiangsi.

> Fang Hui, in his Continuation of the Collected Works from
> T'ung River, described some of the uses to which the cryptomeria
> wood of Wu-yuan county in Hui-chou was put:

> The land is suited to the cryptomeria; the hills
> From crests to hollows are full of nothing else.
> A cryptomeria twenty years of age
> Provides enough for a boy and a girl to wed.

The twigs provide them with a garden fence;
The bark makes roofing; and the planks
Make pens for pigs and cowsheds for their cattle.
They bind them into rafts upon the River Che
And sell them downstream for no little price. (229)

Ch'ü-chou in Chekiang was also a center of timber production. Much
of the wood was shipped out through Wen-chou by sea. Yuan Ts'ai,
who was a native of the latter prefecture, has left an account of how
the sale of cryptomeria enabled families there to meet the costs of
their daughter's marriage portions:

Families of moderate means must take careful thought
in every matter. If a son is born to them, they teach
him a trade so that he can make a living. All this is the
outcome of forethought. When they bring up a daughter,
they must likewise prepare in advance her dresses,
bedclothes and trousseau, so that when the time comes
to send her off to be married they have no further expenditures.
... These days when a girl is born there are some people
who plant a large number of cryptomeria trees. When
the girl has grown up, they sell the wood to provide for the
expenses of her marriage. In this way, when a daughter is
of an age for marriage she will not fail to find a husband
in time. (230)

In Fukien there was a brisk circulation of the woods needed
for building ships. Timber from the counties of Lo-yuan, Ning-te
and Lien-chang was made into rafts and sailed for North and South
along the coasts. When Ch'en Mi was magistrate of An-ch'i county
in Ch'üan-chou he issued a rhymed proclamation urging the inhabitants
to engage in forestry:

The waste hills here aspire to reach the skies,
Their soil as rich as flour, grass thick as felt.
In the right season plant pine and cryptomeria seeds,
And reap your reward a mere ten years hence.
....
There's no good reason not to grow them,
But most men lack the foresight to plan ten years ahead.
It fills me with regret to see
Bare hills everywhere I look. (230)

By the Ming period, however, much timber appears to have been grown in this and neighboring counties.

Wood grown in Kuang-nan was sometimes even sold in Indo-China, and there was a long-distance trade in a number of special woods, such as <u>cercis chihensis</u> for beams and <u>wu-lan</u> wood for rudders. There was also an important timber trade in Kiangsi and Hunan.

F. Cattle and Fish

Cattle were most abundant in central and southern China. There were three main varieties, namely 'yellow cattle', 'black cattle' and water-buffalo. The two former were rather more common towards the North and the latter towards the South. Cattle were used both as draft animals and for meat. Their horns, hide and glue wer e utilized for the manufacture of military weapons and other items. The export of cattle either to barbarian non-Chinese or to foreign states was forbidden; and whenever there was an epidemic of cattle plague, all dealings were prohibited. Official permission was required by anyone engaging in slaughtering. Under the Southern Sung, all horns, hides and glue had to be sold to the government though this had not invariably been the case earlier. Furthermore, government-owned oxen were hired out in return for the payment of 'ox rent' (<u>niu-tsu</u>), and an 'ox tax ' (<u>nin-shui</u>) was levied on sales of draft-oxen except when previously waste lands were being opened up to cultivation, in which case the tax would be suspended and subsidies given to those maintaining oxen.

Oxen were raised in Huai-nan, Ching-hu (Hunan and Hupeh) for sale in North China. The Southern Sung banned the sale of plow-oxen to the Chin Tartars, but there was a large-scale smuggling trade. Smugglers from Chiang-chou (in present-day Honan) are said to have been selling from 70,000 to 80,000 beasts a year in the middle of the twelfth century. A report made in 1168 by Shih Cheng-chih, Governor of Chiang-nan-tung (Northeast Kiangsi and Southern Anhwei) likewise suggests the size of the illegal traffic:

Numerous merchants drive herds of oxen through Ho-chou
(on the North bank of the Yangtze), the smallest of
them containing more than ten animals. They are
en route from Kiangsi to sell them in Hao-chou,
Shou-chou and Kuang-chou, especially the last mentioned,
all of these being places on the frontier. (234)

There was also an illicit trade in hides and horns. A vivid picture
of cattle merchants in Yuan times is given by Yang Wei-chen in his
Old Airs by the Gentlemen of the Iron Cliff (T'ieh-yai hsien-sheng ku
yueh-fu):

Merchants selling oxen and merchants selling water-buffalo
Drive their beasts across the Huai on the long road ahead.
Days by the Huai are panting hot, yellow the Huai moon.
The old merchants cherish their herds with anxious care.
The Huai farmers' grain is on the threshing-floor,
And government orders are out for hides and horns,
So they fear for their oxen. Didn't you see last night
The thousands of mares and stallions requisitioned by the troops
And driven away just like a flock of sheep? (235)

Sometimes the cattle trade seems to have degenerated into a form of
semi-brigandage. In 1212, according to Ch'en K'ung-shih, the
official in charge of fiscal supervision and salt affairs in Kwangsi:

A tax on the sale of cattle has been collected for a long time
by the prefectural authorities of Kuang-nan. Just recently
it has been suspended as the result of a request made by the
fiscal supervisory officials. Once the people of Kan-chou
and Chi-chou (in Southern Kiangsi) have finished their
farmwork for the year, they always form groups allied
together and go South to deal in cattle. They call this
'doing a winter'. To begin with they take a small quantity
of their local cloth to barter for their purchases; but after
they have bought a few oxen they will amalgamate into groups
of over a hundred and wherever they go every beast belonging
to someone else will be pressed into their herd. When the
southerners are weak and few in number, they have to watch
helplessly without making any protest; when they are strong
and numerous, the two sides come to blows. Some of them

have been caught and killed by the authorities, being dealt
with according to the laws. In other words, few of them
are cattle-traders and most of them are brigands. Since
I came to Kwangsi recently, it has often been said to me
that people from Hunan and Hupeh are in the habit of coming
to Kwangsi to trade in cattle and cause harm, and that since
the memorial which brought about the abolition of the tax
those coming have been more numerous and the harm done
greater. (235)

Kan-chou in southern Kiangsi and Kuei-lin in northern Kwangsi, each
being situated on one of the two arterial North-South routes, were also
the scene of much illicit commercial activity in tea and salt, both
government monopoly products. Hu Ch'üan, a statesman who
flourished in the middle of the twelfth century, further noted that:

> The men of Chi-chou make their living by (illegal) wine
> manufacture. Those of Ch'ien-chou (i. e., Kan-chou) make
> theirs by the (illegal) slaughtering of cattle. These
> activities have been subject from times past to strict
> controls, but orders from the government have not
> been able to make the prohibition effective. (236)

In spite of Buddhist taboos, it seems that meat-eating was widespread
and the price of meat rising. Thus a number of small-scale
disreputable butchers, slaughtering and selling in covert fashion,
were to be found scattered in the corners of rural markets and
around the outskirts of villages.

The rearing of fish in ponds built in the wet, low-lying places
along the banks of lakes and rivers was a profitable subsidiary
occupation. It was practised chiefly in Chekiang, Fukien, and Kiangsi.
In the area around the P'o-yang Lake in the latter province there
were even fish hatcheries which specialized in supplying peasants with
baby fish. According to the More Miscellaneous Information from
Kuei-hsin District (Kuei-hsin tsa-shih pieh-chi) written by Chou Mi
around the beginning of the fourteenth century:

> In Chiang-chou (modern Chiu-chiang) and other places,
> young fish are reared along the riverbanks. When summer
> comes the landlords all sell them for a profit. Dealers
> gather from far around. Most of them go to Chien-ch'ang

(Nan-ch'eng county in Kiangsi) and a lesser number to
Fu-chou (in Fukien), Chien-chou (Chien-ning), Ch'ü-chou
and Wu-chou (Chin-hua). The method which they use
is to make out of bamboo splints vessels which resemble
buckets, and to paste varnished paper around the inside.
The baby fish which they keep in them are as minute as the
tip of a needle, and there is such a mass of them that it is
impossible to count them. They are not covered with
any great amount of water but when they are taken by a
land route new water has to be poured in every time they come
to an embankment or a dyke, which is several times each
day. They also use small baskets, constructed in the same
fashion and placed on top, to complete the containers.
They have besides funnels which have rounded mouths and
taper towards the bottom which they use for putting (water)
into the vessels. Surplus water is take out with a small
teabowl. They also pick out and get rid of any fish that are
larger than average and have black scales. If this is not done
they will harm the others. This is why they remove them.
They hasten all through the daylight hours, nor can they rest
at night. If they want to snatch a short nap they will make one
of their number specially responsible for shaking the
containers from time to time. The reason for this is that
if the water is in an unsettled state the fish will swim about
as vigorosly as they would in a river or in a lake. On the
other hand, if this is not done and the water becomes still,
the fish will die. This may be regarded as a further source
of toil. When they reach their homes they place a large
piece of canvas in a wide stream, the four corners being
held up by lengths of bamboo. The four edges of the canvas
rise a little more than a foot above the surface of the water.
All the baby fish are relased into this canvas trap, and when
they see the ripples moving in the wind they turn with the
current and disport themselves happily. They are reared
for half a month or a month, during which time they grow
larger by imperceptible degrees. They are then sold.
Some people say that when one starts to rear them, one
should feed them on bran fried in oil, after which they will
not give birth to any young. (237)

This account is in the main corroborated, with minor point of difference, by the Chia-t'ai reign-period (1201-1204) Gazetteer for Kuei-chi Prefecture:

> South of Chu-chi county in Kuei-chi (present-day Shao-hsing in Chekiang), many of the great families excavate ponds and make a business of rearing fish. Every year at the beginning of spring there appear vendors of baby fish from Chiang-chou. The great families purchase fish in tons of thousands and release them into their ponds. When the fish are minute, they feed them on rice-flour; when they are somewhat larger, on distillery dregs; and finally on hay. The next year they sell them to meet their land tax, which may run to some tens or hundreds of strings of cash. The fish are for the most part merely tench, bream, carp, leueiscus idella and mullet. The extent of the ponds in several tens of mou or more. (238)

A reference by Fang Ta-tsung to a ban imposed at one time on fish-ponds in the four 'upper' prefectures of Fukien may be found on page above. Hsing-hua-chün, one of the four 'lower' prefectures along the coast, was famed for the specialized production of baby fish. Fish were produced in Hu-chou for sale at the Southern Sung capital. Well-known varieties also came from other places in the Yangtze delta region, such as P'ing-wang, Sung-chiang and I-feng-ch'iao. The capital at Hang-chou boasted a Fresh Fish Guild, a Fish Guild, a Crab Guild, a Dried Salt Fish Guild, and also a Goldfish Sellers' Guild.

Finally, some mention should be made of other animals. In Northern Sung times, several tons of thousands of sheep were purchased for government consumption every year both in Shensi and, above all, at the markets for Sino-barbarian trade with the Hsi-hsia and the Khitan. Since the losses of animals on route were heavy, supplies were assured after 1070 partly by making payments in advance to a number of butchers and partly by rearing sheep (usually some 3,000) in pens in the capital prefecture. At the Ch'ung-te Temple in Szechwan, in front of which several hundreds of butchers are said to have resided, up to 40,000 sheep were slaughtered each year in sacrifice. Pigs, deer and ducks were also sometimes raised for sale in large numbers. Thus Chang Shih, a farmer of Wu-yuan county in Hui-chou, kept a flock of ducks who provided him with additional income by producing from 4,000 to 5,000 eggs for the market every year; and there are frequent references to the sale of geese, chickens and ducks at local markets.

2. HANDICRAFT PRODUCTS

i. Paper

The origins of paper-making can be traced back to the end of the Former Han dynasty. Major technical improvements were probably made by Ts'ai Lun around the beginning of the second century AD, fish-nets and other materials such as paper-mulberry bark, hemp scraps and old rags being substituted for silk fibers as the basic ingredients. After this paper-making spread throughout the country, and paper replaced bamboo, wood and silk as the main writing material. The cultivation ofthe paper-mulberry tree, and the manufacture and sale of paper, are described in Chia Ssu-chieh's Arts Essential to the Common People (Ch'i-min yao-shu), written between AD 533 and 544, and from this it may be deduced that these occupations were widely practised in the mountain villagers by this time.

The T'ang dynasty saw the production in many parts of the country of a multitude of fine special papers, mostly rather heavy and destined for use by officials and members of the upper classes. As yet there was no market based on everyday needs and catering for a full differentiated range of tastes. In the Sung period, however, the paper industry took a great leap forward. After this time the production and consumption of paper made from bamboo and paper-mulberry bark became widespread, a demand developed for papers that were light-weight, thin, possessed of a high gloss finish, inexpensive, durable and resistant to insects, and a large variety of different qualities was manufactured to satisfy all sorts of different needs. Clearly this expansion was stimulated by the advance of printing, the progress of literary culture among the newly-arisen class of bureaucrats owing their position to the state examination system, and by the rising level of consumption among the ordinary people.

Paper made from young bamboo sprouts varied in quality according to the type of bamboo used. The poorest was often dismissed as 'only fit for the manufacture of imitation paper money for sacrifice to the gods.' Production was concentrated in southern China, especially in Kuei-chi (in Chekiang), T'an-chou (in Hunan), Jao-chou (in present-day Kiangsi), Chi-chou (in Kiangsi), Fu-chou (in Fukien) and Szechwan. The technique of manufacture appears to have improved in the course of the Sung dynasty. Ts'ai Hsiang, writing in the eleventh century, complained that when he had to use it for legal records it sometimes disintegrated 'even before a case had been decided.' Su I-chien, who flourished slightly earlier, found one merit in its fragility: 'If one uses it to write a secret letter, then no one (except the recipient) will dare to slit it open, because it disintegrates between the fingers and cannot be pasted together again.' (246) A little later, however, it won the approval of prominent officials and men of letters, and calligraphers began to appreciate for the way in which it took the tip of the brush, brought out the color of the ink, did not fade and resisted grubs. In consequence it replaced paper made from hemp and vines for the purposes of writing letters and printing.

Paper made from the bark of the paper-mulberry became the paper mainly used for government purposes in Sung times, being both cheap and light. The tree was grown almost everywhere in the empire but Kiangnan, especially Hui-chou and Ch'ih-chou, was the main center of production, followed by Chekiang, Fukien and Szechwan. Paper was also made from vines, though of what precise variety is not clear. In the T'ang dynasty it was regarded as inferior in quality only to hemp paper, but in later times it was gradually ousted by paper made from bamboo. Shao-hsing was the center of production. Hemp and ramie were also used as raw materials, usually in the form of yarn and scraps of waste or used cloth. The paper produced in Szechwan by these means was regarded by Su Tung-p'o as the finest in China, but its use seems to have been restricted to a few special purposes. Other ingredients were occasionally used, notably wheat and rice stalks mixed together, the barks and sometimes roots of trees other than the paper-mulberry, silk cocoons and even sea-weed.

The first detailed account of paper-making is probably that
given in the <u>Development of Commodities by Nature and Human Skill</u>
(T'ien-kung k'ai-wu) written by Sung Ying-hsing at the end of the
Ming dynasty,* but it is possible to obtain a fairly concrete, even
if fragmentary, knowledge of the techniques used in Sung times.
In his <u>Four Manuals On the Study</u> (Wen-fang ssu-p'u) Su I-chien
outlined the processes used in Hui-chou:

> There is much fine paper made in the counties of I and She,
> such as 'Congealed Frost' and 'Translucent Heart'. There
> is also a long variety, one sheet of which may be fifty feet
> in length. The people of She reduce paper-mulberry (bark)
> to a pulp for several days; then they macerate it in a long
> boat (in water with some chemical additive). Several tens
> of men together lift the screen on which the pulp is caught,
> while one man at the side strikes the rhythm on a drum.
> They dry it over a fire on a large (bamboo) smoking-frame.
> They do not put it on a (heated) wall (in the usual fashion)
> and so it is of an equal thinness throughout its whole
> length. (250)

This general account may usefully be supplemented by other data.
Thus Shu Yuan-yü, writing in the ninth century, mentions that along
the Yen River in Shao-hsing there were workers who specialized
in preparing vines for paper making:

> There are numerous paper workers by the banks of the
> river. They cut and hew at all seasons, making their
> living by stripping off the bark and pith. (250)

Once the materials had been gathered they had to be macerated.
The quality of the water used for this was of great importance.
The <u>Gazetteer for Hsin-an</u> (Hsin-an chih) noted that:

> For the most part, the water of Hsin-an (Hui-chou) is so
> transparent that one can see the bottom (of the streams),
> and it is useful for soaking paper-mulberry bark. Thus

---

*See the translation by E. T. Z. and S. C. Sun, entitled <u>T'ien-kung
k'ai-wu: Chinese Technology in the Seventeenth Century</u> (Pennsylvania
State University Press: University Park, 1966), pp. 223 <u>et seq.</u>

it is the quality of the water which given the finished
paper its pure white appearance. Even finer, with a
soft but tough quality, is that made with the water
obtained by breaking the ice late in the year. (251)

In similar fashion Su Tung-p'o observed:

The water of the Huan-hua River in Ch'eng-tu is uncommonly
clear and shining. It is used to steep hemp and paper-
mulberry bark for the manufacture of a fancy notepaper
endowed with an adorable close-grained whiteness.
Several tens of li away, it is no longer possible to make
it, so important is the effect of the water. ... (251)

After the bark, vines or bamboo had been steeped, they were pounded
in a mortar with a wooden pestle until they had been decomposed
into a pulp. Then they were washed with water. According to the
Szechwan Paper Manual (Shu chieh p'u):

The waters of the Huan-hua River are used in the making
of paper. The location (of the industry) is therefore also
due to the suitability of the water. By the side of the river
mortar (-like pit)s have been excavated for pounding,
forming a continuous line upstream and downstream.
All the materials used in paper-making have to be pounded
so that they are converted to a pulp, and then washed to
make them clean. Once this has been done, (the paper)
is made in the dimensions required. (252)

The pulp had then to be boiled to reduce it to a properly pasty consistency.
For this reason paper makers were sometimes referred to as
'furnace households'. Advances in printing also probably brought
about advances in the technique of bleaching paper. It is worth
noting in this connection that in Mi Fei's Critique of Papers (Mi
Yuan-chang p'ing chih-t'ieh), written towards the end of the Northern
Sung, he says:

Twenty years ago use was not yet being made of ashes
(in solution = lye) to confer translucence, but there were
some old papers with a 'boney' quality which were made
of pulp pounded so fine that they were not inferior to the
'Translucent Heart' of T'ang times. (253)

A variety of substances were added to give the pulp increased coherence when it was lifted up on and then removed from the screen. According to Chou Mi:

> Whenever one prepares paper it is essential to use
> Hibiscus Manihot and the leaves of the keng tree
> (Hemiptelea Davidi), which should be freshly pounded.
> If this is not done the paper will stick to the screen
> and be impossible to lift off. If one has no Hibiscus
> Manihot then it is possible to use the leaves of the
> willow, the peach, the wistaria (?), or the Hibiscus
> syriacus, or else wild grapes. The only criterion
> is that they should have non-stick properties. (253)

For the manufacture of some hemp paper in Szechwan, glue was apparently added to confer coherence.

The screens on which a layer of pulp was lifted from the tank varied in their construction. According to Chao Hsi-ku, a member of the Sung imperial family and a noted connoisseur of the thirteen century:

> For the manufacture of northern paper a transversely-laid
> screen is used, and the markings are always transverse.
> Its quality, moreover, is loose-textured and heavy. It
> is called 'laterally-grained paper'. ... For southern
> paper a vertically-laid screen is used, and the markings
> are always vertical. (254)

Screens also came in many sizes, according to the size of paper needed. Drying was done by means of sunlight, heated walls of a **fire.**

Colors and patterns were added to some papers. The following is a highly tentative translation of a passage from Su I-chien's Four Manuals on the Study:

> The men of Szechwan make a ten-colored paper. Usually
> ten sheets are rubbed at a time. The ends of each sheet
> are gripped by bamboo pincers, ten-colored water is
> mixed and systematically rubbed in so as to dye it. During
> the dyeing a pattern is impressed into the paper, which

stands out in marked contrast to its surroundings. It is
indescribably fine when dry. Each sheet its, moreover,
calendered on a square board, a process which subtly
enhances the innumerable forms of flowers, trees and fabulous
beasts. Sometimes the pattern is produced by means
of a stencil made of thin cloth previously stiffened with
flour-paste. This is known as 'fish-roe paper' or 'net-
pattern paper'. At the present time it may also be found
in Yen-ch'i (in Chekiang). Sometimes a paste is made
from spoiled flour and mixed with (one of) the five colors.
The paper is drawn across it, becoming dyed in an incomplet
fashion, with a charmingly irregular effect. This is
called 'flowing sands paper'. Furthermore, sometimes
acacia gum and croton oil are boiled and then spread on
the surface of some water. It is possible to drip ink
or artist's colors onto this mixture, thinning them by
immersing a piece of ginger and thickening them with
dandruff shaken loose with a fox's whisker. After this
they may be drawn into the form of human figures and
rolled into the shape of clouds or birds' feathers,
delightfully gay and variegated. The paper is then laid
on top and the pattern is transferred. (255)

In paper of the T'ang dynasty and before a yellow dye made from the
bark of Pterocarpus indicus was added at the pulp stage. This had
the additional effect of protecting the paper from insects.

A large quantity of low quality paper was made into
symbolic paper money for sacrifice to the gods. Liao Kang,
writing in the twelfth century, observed in a memorial:

I have been amazed at the popular practice of cutting
paper to serve as money to be burnt in order to seek
for happiness from the demons and spirits. I have
no idea upon what this if founded - without doubt frivolous
theories with no (Confucian) scriptural warrant. It is
passed on by the vulgar customs of the ignorant people.
As a result forty to fifty per cent of the peasantry have
become paper workers [an exaggeration] , and this
is particularly common in the Southeast. Indolent
farmers need no urging to go wherever good profits
are to be had. (256)

Persons such as those were probably the originators of the traditional Chinese art of paper-cuts. Paper must also have undergone other groms of finishing to suit it for the manifold uses to which it was put, notably paper money, paper clothes, paper armor, wrapping papers and lanters.

The main paper-making regions were northern Chekiang, Fukien, southern Anhwei, northern Kiangsi, Hunan and Szechwan. * Production of speicifc types was highly concentrated in specific localities, and those products often possessed a nation-wide reputation. There are several references to settlements of some hundreds of paper workers gathered in one spot. Lines written by P'eng Ju-k'uang in the eleventh century on Hsu-ching, which lies on the border between Hupeh and Shensi, remind us of the prevalence of paper manufacture in the mountain villages:

> In their fields they do mt work at rice or millet,
> But in their gardens.study raising hemp.
> The Tapping Households cut the lacquer trees,
> The strippers of paper-mulberry bark make paper. (263)

Large quantities of paper were presented each year to the government by various regions as tax or tribute. Thus at the beginning of the Northern Sung dynasty T'an-chou (in Hunan) contributed 1.78 million sheets annually. At the beginning of the Southern Sung Hung-chou (in Kiangsi) owed 850,000 sheets. A total of 1,448,632 sheets were produced for the state under contract at this time, in addition to 500,000 pieces of paper money made in Hui-chou.

Papers of every sort, including toilet paper, were available on the market. The public preference was for a light-weight quality, as may be seen from the following passage in the Szechwan Paper Manual:

> Our Szechwan is in the Southwest. Its nature, heavy and substantial rather than frivolous, is that of the trigram K'un ('earth') to which it corresponds. Therefore things that are produced here are heavier and solider than those from other places. ... Szechwan paper is so thick that one man can barely carry 500 sheets. It has been customary for it to be highly prized everywhere, on account of its

*See pp. 258-261 of the original text for a list of the prefectures concerned.

exotic reputation and the difficulty of transporting it. In
Szechwan, however, paper from Hui-chou and Ch'ih-chou,
and bamboo paper, are esteemed for their lightness and
thinness. Merchants who come to sell them in Ch'eng-tu
charge about three times as much per sheet as for
Szechwanese paper. (264)

The shift in the types of papers used by the government, namely hemp,
vine and silk papers under the T'ang dynasty, and paper-mulberry bark
papers under the Sung dynasty, caused the location of the chief
areas of supply to move from Ch'eng-tu and Chekiang to Kiangnan.
The Sung also witnessed the general decline of the once-renowned
Szechwan papers in the commercial market in the face of competition
from Hui-chou and Ch'ih-chou bark paper and bamboo paper.

The raw materials for paper-making were sometimes
cultivated and so, presumably, sold in quite backward areas.
Thus, according to Wang Hsiang-chih's Geography of the Empire,
in Pin-chou in Kwangsi:

The Yao people live to the West of Ch'ien-chiang county.
They have no (paddy-) fields to cultivate but depend
solely upon newly-cleared upland plots which they plow
with a knife-blade and sow after burning. Their occupation
is the production of paper-mulberry (bark). (266)

Other indications that this bark was commercially produced in the
mountain villages may be found in the passages quoted from Hsing
Yuan-lung and the poet-monk Tao-ch'ien of pages 149 and 154 below.

Tax regulations indicate the extent of the commerce in cheap
paper and paper articles. Thus in 995 'paper fans, straw shoes and
other trifling objects' were exempted from customs duties in the Liang-Che.
In 1151 a memorialist complaining that customs duties were being levied
at heavier rates than those sanctioned also mentioned that 'small
articles of daily use among the people such as oil, hemp-cloth, mats
and paper' were being taxed, a practice which was in principle
improper. It also seems that Taoists sometimes supported themselves
in part by selling such things as paper and ink at local markets.

On the structure of the business only the most scattered fragments of information are available. According to Cheng Hsia, at K'ai-feng prior to the passing of Wang An-shih's law concerning granaries and government treasuries* the so-called 'long connected paper' brought by merchants had been taxed at the Metropolitan Mercantile Tax Office (tsai-ching shang-shui-yuan) and the paper shops in the capital had then bought their paper at wholesale prices from the merchants with the assistance of this Office. Guilds of these paper shops existed in K'ai-feng and Lin-an (Hang-chou) and possibly also in other cities. A certain amount of Chinese paper was also sold abroad, especially to Annam, Cambodia, Korea and Japan.

ii. Silk

Before the Sung dynasty the production of silk was predominantly in the cities and/or under official control. Output was mainly used to meet the tax in this commodity or to satisfy the producer's own needs. Commercialization was not much developed. Shantung, Hopeh and the eastern part of Honan were the oldest centers of production, but from the end of the Han period a silk industry rapidly grew up around Hsiang-yang in Hupeh and then moved into Szechwan, where it pursued an independent course of development. The fourth to sixth centuries also saw the rise of silk manufacturing in what are now southern Kiangsu and Chekiang. During the ensuing T'ang and Sung dynasties progress in the silk industry was the result of the impressive advances made in agricultural productivity. There grew up both a long-distance trade serving the expanding urban market and the manufacture of specialized goods in the cities. Certain areas began to specialize in the rearing of silkworms, speculative transaction in mulberry leaves made their appearance, merchants served the rural textile areas as middlemen and collecters of output, and merchant capital gradually extended its control over the villages. Although under the Two Tax System introduced in 780 it remained policy that taxes should be paid in kind, the elaboration of a system of state purchase, often with payment to producers in advance, led to the disappearance of this practice. The officially controlled industry continued in existence, producing goods for consumption at the Court and for offering in exchange in the course of (official) trade with foreign countries.

---

*On which see J. T. C. Liu, Reform in Sung China (Cambridge, Mass.: Harvard University Press, 1959), p. 82.

The main areas of production in Sung times were the
Northeast, Szechwan, and the Southeast. Northern silk was
generally regarded as the best, followed by that from Szechwan.
In his Miscellany Chuang Ch'o noted that:

> Southerners rear silkworms in their houses, forcing
> (their growth) by means of (artificial) heat. They want
> to make them mature early and to economize on foodstuffs.
> The thread is therefore thin and weak, and not as good
> as that from the North.   (272)

According to Chao Hsi-ku, Hopeh silk was woven of a warp and weft
of homogeneous quality and so did not have a face side and a reverse,
whereas Kiangnan silk, which was made with a heavy warp and a
light weft, did have a distinctive face side. The passage quoted
from The Continuation of the Comprehensive Mirror on page 48
above illustrates how southern merchants came to purchase the
high-quality northern silk. In quantity of production, however,
the South far surpassed the North. In the words of the twelfth-century
official Yü Chou:

> Mulberry leaves are cheap as dirt this year;
> Wu's teeming silkworms outnumber those of Lu.   (273)

The regional distribution of the production of silk goods taken
as taxes or made in the offical workshops in the middle of the Northern
Sung dynasty is largely, though not quite completely, revealed by
the Sung Digest (Sung hui-yao). * Fancy types of silk which needed
a refined technique (such as brocades), mostly came from K'ai-feng,
Hopeh and Ch'eng-tu. Open-weave silks (lo) came principally from
the Liang-Che and Chiang-nan-tung. Figured damask (ling) was
chiefly made in Hopeh but Szechwan was also a major area of production.
Plain silks (chüan) were for the most part provided by the Liang-Che,
Chiang-nan-tung and Hopeh. Coarse silk or sarcenet** (shih-ling),
crepe silk (hu-tzu) and figured satin (ko-chih) were produced in
Ching-nan, Ho-tung, Liang-Che and Huai-nan. Pongee*** (ch'ou)

---

*All the available figures are given on pages 274-276 of the original
text. Transl.
**Cloth with a silk warp and a hemp weft. Transl.
***Coarse, heavy silk. Transl.

was manufactured in Chiang-nan-tung, Liang-Che, Ching-tung and Hopeh. Raw silk thread (ssu), silk wadding (mien) and flossy silk for embroidery (jung-mien) came from the Liang-Che, Hopeh and Szechwan.

Most of the high-quality silks used by the Court, or exchanged in the foreign trade conducted by the state or on the occasion of diplomatic courtesies, were directly produced by the state silk industry, bought through the government purchasing system (ho-shih), or else obtained by converting the regular twice-yearly tax-levy to payment in cloth (che-k'o). Records survive indicating the existence at some time or other of official silk-weaving establishments in 24 prefectures, and suggest that in a few of these prefectures there was more than one such institution.

There was an extraordinary range of special types of silk produced in different places, some with a nation-wide sale, others with merely a local one. * Chu Yü's Talks from P'ing-chou offers a good illustration of the former category:

> The inhabitants of the capital (K'ai-feng) use Lotus-flower silk from Fu-chou (in Kiangsi) for their summer clothes. It is greatly esteemed. The nuns of all the four halls of the Lotus-flower Convent make this silk and it is not permitted to impart to outsiders (how to achieve) the subtlety of the hand-twisting and the weaving. Every year each of these halls weaves close on a hundred lengths but the amount is insufficient for meeting internal needs and those of the Imperial Household. The people outside the convent weave a great deal, and this is frequently used to make up the amount required. Purchasers in the capital can naturally also tell the difference between the two kinds, and silk make outside the convent sells for twenty to thirty per cent less than that made inside it. (281)

Nuns also manufactured embroidered fabrics in K'ai-feng, Lin-an and Yueh-chou. The products of the Hsiang-kuo Convent in the first-named of these places were sold at the convent's own market, which was held once every five days, and they circulated throughout the country.

---

*Listed on pages 278-281 of the original text.

Sometimes there was competition between similar products from
different areas, which suggests that they enjoyed relatively extented
sale. According to Lu Yu's Notes from the Hall of Learned Old Age
(Lao-hsueh-an pi-chi):

> Sui-ning (in Szechwan) produces open-weave silk and calls
> it 'Yueh-chou (i. e. Shao-hsing) open-weave silk'. It also
> resembles the open-weave silk made by the nuns of Kuei-chi
> (Shao-hsing) but it is superior to it. (282)

Merchants travelled considerable distances to obtain silk. Thus
Hung Mai mentions a silk-merchant from the Ynagtze delta travelling
to Hunan for silk from Shao-yang. Another writer alludes to a
holder of the metropolitan doctorate from Nan-chien in Fukien who
bought 200 lengths of Chieh-yang silk and sold them in K'ai-feng to
defray the costs of his stay there. The brocade of the Chien River
region in Fukien was said to 'provide caps for the Empire' and it was
also exported to Indo-China.

In the main silk-producing areas the industry spread into
the villages around the towns. This is well illustrated by the
following two passages. The first, by the eleventh-century statesman
Liu Ch'ang, concerns the writer's father:

> In the Ch'ing-li reign (1041-1048) he was promoted to the rank
> of Councillor of the Grand Court and magistrate of Chin-hua
> county in Wu-chou. The people in the city that was the county
> capital made their living by weaving, and there was a saying
> that the clothes which they made clothed the Empire. They were
> for this reason particularly wealthy. (283)

The second is a decree issued in 1168 and quoted in the Sung Digest:

> In I-wu county in Wu-chou (Chin-hua) there are scattered
> storehouse proprietors and brokers who undertake the buying
> and selling (of silk). ... Previously the people in the hilly
> valleys of I-wu county made their living by weaving thin
> silk. The magistrate of this county detained all the storehouse
> proprietors of eight communities, made a note of their names,
> and confiscated the silks which they had woven. As a result
> the people suffered greatly. (283)

We also know that the old ladies in this region sometimes contracted to perform spinning for other people.

In the Southeast a distinction arose between the rice-growing and the sericultural areas. According to a memorial written by Ch'eng Chü:

> Su-chou and Hsiu-chou produce great amounts of rice.
> The purchases which the state makes there every year
> have come to exceed those made in other prefecture.
> The counties of the prefectures of Hang-chou and Hu-chou on
> the other hand mostly make their living by growing mulberry
> trees and rearing silkworms. For this reason the
> purchases of silk made there by the state are larger
> than in other prefectures. (283)

But the government continued to exact a proportion of taxes in silk from the rice-growing areas:

> The country villages of Su-chou and Hsiu-chou have from
> times past been accustomed to practise wet-field paddy
> cultivation. They do not grow mulberry or cudrania triloba. *
> Every year the population pays the summer tax in silk,
> a commodity which they do not produce. Many of them suffer
> from the fact that peddlers, some time before the day
> appointed for paying in taxes comes around, go to the
> villages of Hang-chou and Hu-chou, which do produce
> silk, and buy up cheaply goods of the sort which the common
> folk will have to pay in as tax. They then sell these at
> an inflated price, which means heavy expenditures for people
> who wish to pay before the time-limit expires. The state,
> moreover, does not get silks that are of adequate quality. (283)

The Hsien-shun reign-period (1265-1274) Gazetteer for P'i-ling (P'i-ling chih) describes how in Wu-chin county in present-day Kiangsu:

> There used to be weaving households who were skilled in
> weaving what was called 'Chin-ling silk'. They have now
> completely disappeared. Commoner households pay a tax
> in silk each year, which they meet by buying the fabric in
> the various places in Li-yang before it falls due. (284)

---

*A tree whose leaves can also be used for feeding silkworms. Transl.

Events such as these reflect an increasing regional division of labor.

A passage from Ch'en Fu's Treatise on Agriculture (Nung-shu), printed in 1154, shows how far rural specialization had gone:

> All the men of An-chi county in Hu-chou can (graft mulberry
> trees). Some of them make their living solely from
> silkworms. (For subsistence, it is necessary that) a
> family of 10 persons rear 10 frames of silkworms,
> obtaining 12 catties of cocoons from each frame.
> Each catty yields 1.3 of an ounce of thread, and from
> every 5 ounces of thread one length of small silk may
> be woven, and this exchanges for 1.4 piculs of rice.
> The price of silk usually follows that of rice. Thus
> supplying one's food and clothing by these means ensures a
> high degree of stability. One month's toil is better than
> exertions all around the year (at farming), and one is
> afflicted neither by parching drought nor by overflowing
> floods. (284)

In Wu-hsing (in Hu-chou, northern Chekiang) during the early thirteenth century some well-to-do households had 10 mou of mulberry trees, and the richest of the specialized weaving households in the mountain villages reared several hundreds of frames of silkworms. A proclamation issued by Ch'eng Pi in Fu-yang county (also in northern Chekiang) suggests the level of concentration both here and in T'ai-p'ing prefecture in southern Anhwei, with which it is contrasted:

> Mulberries are certainly grown in profusion on the level
> land in this region, but in Chiang-nan-tung and Chiang-
> nan-hsi everyone grows them on the flat places in the low
> hills as well. I have heard an old farmer from T'ai-p'ing
> prefecture say: 'When mulberries are cultivated in such
> places, one man in a day only attends to ten trees. It
> is necessary to hoe and to dig both deeply and over a wide
> area so that the roots of the mulberry tree can make their
> way without difficulty. After three years the leaves will
> be ready for plucking. - For the roots of the mulberry
> are soft and weak, and incapable of penetrating hard (soil).
> Without extensive hoeing and digging they will become twisted
> and fail to stretch out. Even if they are tended carefully they
> will still be unsteady after ten years. (284)

According to the thirteenth-century official Hsieh Fang-te, so much silk was produced in Jao-chou and Hsin-chou in Kiangsi that even the boys wore it, and women regarded the open-weave variety as of little value. There were also little market towns in which silks were woven for a limited local commercial circulation.

The tools for sericulture were often purchased. According to a poem by Su Tung-p'o and the notes accompanying it:

> Last year, when frosts were falling, they cut the autumn reeds;
> This year the silkworm frames are stacked like lines of hills.
> The wheels are made of split gourds, and the vats of clay.
> People are eager to buy these things no less than silks or gold.
> (...The reed frame is a device on which the silkworms rest. The gourd wheel and the clay vat are things used for reeling the silk. People compete to buy these objects because they urgently need them for use. It is for this reason that they attach more importance to them than to silks or gold.) (286)

And according to another poem by Su:

> The withered mulberries stretch their buds, their leaves
>   slowly grow green;
> The new silkworms may be washed at the season of Ch'ing-ming. *
> The tools used in years past are breaking in the hand,
> And by the spring this winter's clothes are tattered.
> They empty the granaries, count mouths and sell the surplus grain.
> They purchase silkworm frames, come home and wait for
>   the eggs to hatch.
> This provides not only the boxes the womenfolk require
> But also the hoes that the men use in their farming. (286)

Silkworm eggs, of which there were several varieties, were probably also sometimes bought.

Regarding transactions in mulberry saplings, The Spring and Autumn Annals of the Ten Kingdoms (Shih-kuo ch'un-ch'iu), compiled in the seventeenth century by Wu Jen-ch'en, tells the following story:

---

*A solar period roughly corresponding to Easter.

According to The History of the Five States (Wu-kuo ku-shih), *
there used to be a silkworm fair in the third moon every
year in the state of Shu (in Szechwan and parts of adjacent
provinces). When the time came round for it to be held,
all manner of goods would be gathered together for exchange
and the walled market enclosure would be filled to capacity.
(The ruler) Wang Chien (reg. 891-918) frequently gazed out
at the scene from an upper story, and once perceived that
there were not a few persons selling mulberry trees. He
turned to his entourage and said: 'There are lots of mulberry
trees; they would yield a substantial revenue if taxed.'
Word of this leaked out and the common people were so
terrified that they chopped down all their mulberry and
cudrania triloba trees in consequence. (286)

Chu Hsi also once told the people of Nan-chien in Fukien that they
should 'regularly go in large numbers during the winter months to
other provinces to buy mulberry trees.'

Traditionally there had been two kinds of mulberry tree,
the Lu mulberry and the Ching mulberry. In the writings of Sung
times, however, well over a dozen other varieties are mentioned,
suited to local soil conditions. By late T'ang times leaves were
available on the market. The Miscellaneous Records Collected in
the T'ai-p'ing Reign-period (T'ai-p'ing kuang chi), compiled at
imperial command by Li Fang and others between 977 and 981, tells
how an insect blight in 870 put up the cost of mulberry leaves in
Lo-yang and a man from Hsin-an made a modest fortune by
abandoning his own silkworms and selling his crop of leaves there
instead. In his Treatise on Agriculture Ch'en Fu says:

Many people these days do not make plans for their
supplies in advance. When they run short of leaves
they will pawn their possessions in order to buy them.
There are no lengths to which they will not go. They
are so anxious lest the silkworms go hungry that even
if they have to squander their property they do not
dare to be stingy about it. Sometimes they do not
recover their outlay from the profits which they
subsequently make. (288)

---

*A work written at the beginning of the Sung dynasty. Transl.

When prices rose high, it sometimes profited peasants to sell their leaves rather than to rear their silkworms, and those who made their living by rearing worms solely on purchased leaves would suffer severely from the shortage.

Silk thread was commonly sold rather than being woven by the spinners. This is evident from the references in the preceding pages to the commerce in thread (for example, page 48), from such proverbs as 'In the second moon sell new silk thread, in the fifth moon sell new grain,' and from a number of literary sources. Thus, according to 'The Weaver' by the eleventh-century scholar Hsu Chi:

> She does not wear the open-weave silk she's woven, but sells it
> And brings home plain silk thread bought with the cash.   (288)

Lines by the thirteenth-century official Hung Tzu-k'uei are also of interest in this connection:

> They wish they had another hundred frames of spring silkworms,
> Being delighted with the high price received for silk thread
> just sold.   (288)

Fan Ch'eng-ta wrote a poem on silk-reeling, which is included in his Poems of the Recluse from Stone Lake (Shih-hu chü-shih shih-chi) and goes in part as follows:

> The odor of cocoons boiling behind the shed
> Comes through to the front,
> The creaking of the reeling-frame
> Sounds like rain spattering in the wind.
> The cocoons are fat and their long filaments
> Unwind unbroken threads.
> How shall we find the time this year
> To weave silk clothes?
> Let's go tomorrow to the Western Gate
> And sell the thread.   (288)

Fang Yueh, writing in the thirteenth century, observed:

> My eastern neighbors boil their barley,
>> Its savor comes in pungent gusts,
> My western neighbors sell silk thread
>> And buy rice from the new harvest.   (289)

Works on elementary mathematics, such as Ting Chü's Arithmetical Methods (Ting Chü suan-fa) and The Mathematical Curtain Pulled Aside (T'ou-lien hsi-ts'ao), both of 1355, contain problems on the cost of buying specified amounts of silk thread and on the loss of weight incurred in the process of dressing it.

Chu Hsi distinguished between the silk fabrics carried by professional merchants and those that simply constituted the surplus production of peasants:

> The country people near the cities all depend on taking a
> small quantity of taxable articles into the cities to sell,
> as this enables them to make purchases of food. If we
> continue to levy the tax year in year out as before, I am
> anxious that they will have no means of paying it. It
> would be appropriate if, besides levying the tax as before
> on merchants and peddlers dealing in silk cloth, medicines,
> silk thread, silk wadding and miscellaneous items, the
> other country people who bring small quantities of local
> products into the cities for sale were all exempted one third
> of the levy. (290)

As indicated by the passage from the Sung Digest quoted on page 114 above, much of the production of silk cloth for sale was co-ordinated by storehouse proprietors, brokers, shops and other intermediaries. Some of these persons contracted to handle purchases on behalf of the government and made trips around the country villages for this purpose. Others were entrusted by the peasants with handling the paying in of the silk owed as tax. Conceivably there may also have been, as there was in parts of the hemp industry, a system of advance payments made by merchants to producers through the mediation of local brokers who also collected the finished cloth. Presumably the contractors who handled tax payments and government purchases established themselves on the basis of an already existing commercial structure.

The silk industry had thus assumed the shape shown below in Figure II:

Figure II   <u>Structure of the Silk Industry</u>
(The heavy arrows indicate the movement of tax-payments)

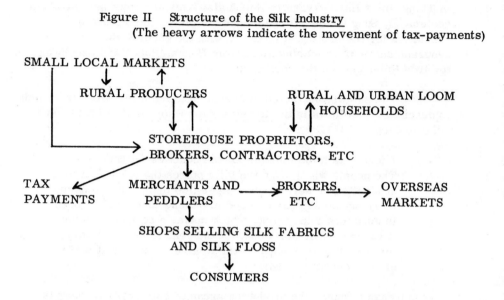

With only a few exceptions, such as Jao-chou and Hsin-chou, people in the villages wore hemp clothes. The demand for silk was therefore mainly an urban one. Fashion had a particularly strong hold in the cities and those of moderate means did their best to copy the styles in favor at the Court and among the upper classes. Even farmers and peddlers, however, as well as their wives, are known to have sometimes affected the dress of the officials when they put on their best at festival time. Chinese silk was also sold in some considerable quantity abroad.

iii. <u>Lacquer</u>

Lacquer had been used in China since antiquity for a wide variety of purposes: as a finishing coat for wooden utensils and furniture, in building, in weapons of war, in textile manufacture, in painting, in the manufacture of ink, in medicines, and as an adhesive for the repair of old objects. In the Sung dynasty, with the development of commerce and cities, the demand for it increased, the collection of sap in mountain villages became a flourishing industry. and a lacquerware industry developed in the South.

In the sixth century AD the lacquer tree was chiefly grown in Liang-chou in Honan, I-chou in Szechwan and Kuang-chou in Kwangtung. In T'ang times Hsiang-yang in Hupeh also became known as a producing center. By Sung times a large number of places had acquired a reputation for the making of lacquer, with the general shift of geographical emphasis being away from Honan, Hupeh and Szechwan and towards Hui-chou and the southeast coast.

The sap was extracted by means of a primitive process, which is described as follows in the Gazetteer for Hsin-an of the Shui-hsi reign-period (1174-1189):

> Lacquer is to be found in all the counties (of Hui-chou).
> The people who live in the hills pierce the lacquer trees
> at night and insert bamboo pipes into them. In the early
> morning the sap has dripped into these tubes and a spoon
> is used to scrape it out, which makes a squeaking sound.
> It is most laborious work. If the year is unusually dry,
> there will be less sap. If the weather is rainy, it will be
> of poor quality. (296)

That merchants toured the producing areas to collect the lacquer is suggested by a poem written by Ou-yang Hsiu on Hsia-chou in Hupeh:

> They vie in cutting the valley trees for lacquer,
> And struggle to scale the woods in search of pepper.
> Merchants from Pa congregate in their ships,
> At barbarian marts the winehouse banners beckon. (297)

Other references to the trade in lacquer may be found in the poem by Fang Hui on page 23 above and in the quotation from the Gazetteer for Hsin-an given on page 54. Because it could be used in the manufacture of weapons the export of lacquer to potential enemies was forbidden. Thus in 1018 the people of Shensi were ordered not to sell lacquer to the Hsi-hsia and Khitan.

The commercial production of lacquer in the mountain villages provided the foundation for a lacquerware industry in other areas. A good illustration of this is afforded by a passage on Wen-chou cited in Chu Mu's Triumphant Vision of the World:

> Wen-chou is situated on salty mudflats. The soil is poor
> and cultivation difficult. The people are diligent in their
> efforts and survive by their exertions. Thus the land is not
> suited to the mulberry tree and yet they work at weaving;
> nor is it suited to the lacquer tree and yet they make
> lacquer-ware. (297)

Supplies of the raw material presumably came from Ch'u-chou
upstream. Special 'Wen-chou lacquerware shops' were to be found
at both the Northern Sung and the Southern Sung capitals, and
Wen-chou lacquer bowls are known to have been exported to
Cambodia. Other places with important lacquer-ware industries in
and after Southern Sung times were Hang-chou, Hu-chou, Su-chou,
Hsiu-chou (Chia-hsing), Chi-chou, Fu-chou (in Fukien) and Tzu-chou
(in Szechwan).

iv. Iron and Copper Goods

Extensive and important work has already been done on iron
in Sung times by such scholars as Hino Kaisaburō, Robert Hartwell,
Yoshida Mitsukuni, Miyazaki Ichisada and Sudō Yoshiyuki. * Here no
more will be attempted than to present some materials not utilized
in their studies.

There is the following description of the coastal trade in iron
goods in the San-shan Gazetteer (San-shan chih) for the Shun-hsi
reign-period (1174-1189):

> In 1043 the Transport Commissioner Yang Chi requested that
> a strict ban should be placed on Fukien by which no private
> trade should be permitted on the seas with the exception of
> that in farm tools and cooking pots manufactured by commoners.
> The governor of the Liang-Che memorialized that in the
> prefectures of his province iron had never been produced, and
> that the iron brought by sea from Ch'üan-chou and Fu-chou
> to be sold every year yielded not a little revenue from the
> taxes on trade. The tax taken in commutation or a percentage
> of the goods also enabled the authorities to pay for the

---

*Bibliographical details on page 300 of the original text. Transl.

manufacture of weapons. He requested that the governor
of Fukien be told to proclaim that rich merchants would be
permitted to trade, being obliged as before to furnish
guarantors and be issued with a long certificate, but only
to sell their goods in the province of Liang-Che, the
prefectural officials of this province being responsible for
supplying them with certificates of proof (that they had in
fact complied with the foregoing regulation). (300)

This privilege seems to have been withdrawn not long afterwards.
In the middle of the fourteenth century, however, according to the
Continued Gazetteer for Ssu-ming (Hsu Ssu-ming chih) of the
Chih-cheng reign-period (1341-1367):

Pig iron comes (to Ning-po) from Fukien and Kwangtung.
Ships regularly come here to sell it. It is cast into
implements and utensils. (301)

The remark in the same source that '(Copper utensils) make somewhat
better cooking-vessels and cauldrons than those cast in iron' suggests
that the latter were in everyday use. According to an entry in the
Record of Essential Events Across the Years After the Chien-yen
Reign-period (Chien-yen i-lai hsi-nien yao-lu) for 1132:

Copper and iron are sources of profit. Great merchants
draw upon them without the authorization to do so. They
sell implements and utensils to every household, and make
a tenfold profit. In their sea-going ships they transport
these goods for sale in places as far away as Shantung. (301)

This probably refers to iron and copper produced in Fukien and Kwangtung,
and indicates the existence of an illegal trade with territories under
the Chin Tartars. Iron from these two provinces also went to Southeast
Asia.

Copper was used for coins, for weapons, for ritual vessels
and statues in Buddhist monasteries and Taoist temples, for personal
ornaments among all classes of society, for utensils and mirrors,
and for objects-d'art. There was thus an extensive demand for it.
The ore available was mined nearly to the point of exhaustion, and
the export of the metal was forbidden. Output reached a maximum

just after the middle of the eleventh century, after which time the country's resources were almost mined out, with the exception of the deposits opened up in Yunnan during the Yuan and Ming dynasties. Because of the progress made in the wet-extraction technique (the boiling of copper sulphate solution in contact with thin iron plates on whose surface the copper was deposited), the quality of copper cash, especially under the Northern Sung, was excellent. They were sought by the people of surrounding countries both as currency and treasure, with the result that a massive illicit outflow of coins became almost openly accepted. Under the Southern Sung, with the growing use of paper money, the value of copper for hoarding increased and re-casting coins, or casting them into articles of copper, became a profitable and flourishing business.

The addiction to antique bronzes, so widespread among the upper classes in Northern Sung times, led first to the writing of works of connoisseurship and then, under the Southern Sung, to manufacturing old-style articles such as gongs, bells, boilers, vases, candlesticks, horse harness, goblets, statues and cymbals. The most famous were the 'old vessels' made in Chü-jung county in the prefecture of Chien-k'ang (modern Nanking). In the eighth century these had been produced in official workshops but by Sung times they were being turned out by ordinary artisans, and a number of craftsmen personally famous for their skill in making such bronzes appeared in various parts of China. The Sung History (Sung-shih) contains the following passage relating to 1248:

> Paper money is more convenient for the purposes of transport. Copper cash are thus consigned to being stored up uselessly. ... The gold foil of the capital, the brass vessels of Ch'ü-chou and Hsin-chou and the musical instruments of Li-ch'üan (Ch'ang-sha) are all made of copper cash (in part). The copper-working artisans of Lin-ch'uan (in Kiangsi), Lung-hsing (Nan-ch'ang in Kiangsi), and Kuei-lin (in Kwangsi) are more numerous than in other prefectures. As to Ch'ang-sha prefecture, there are 64 copper furnaces in the Wu hills and several hundred copper-working households in Ma-t'an and the O-yang hills. Few coins have not been ruined by conversion into such articles. These days brass and bronze utensils made in the capital are openly sold in the markets near the Imperial Palace. (304)

These and other wares such as mirrors enjoyed a wide sale both at home and abroad.

IV. THE DEVELOPMENT OF CITIES AND MARKETS DURING THE SUNG DYNASTY

1. THE ECONOMIC MORPHOLOGY OF SUNG CITIES

While the cultural and legal aspects of the rise of cities
in Sung times are well understood, the economic, demographic and
social aspects have been inadequately studied. Nor have the villages
and the cities been considered together as part of a single whole.
There is also some confusion over concepts and terminology,
particularly as to what is meant by a 'city'.

The starting-point of the present chapter is a reconsideration
of some of the views of previous writers. Thus Katō Shigeshi saw
the breakdown of the system of controlled markets during the
T'ang/Sung transition as constituting a turning-point in the evolution
of the Chinese city; but confined himself to pointing out the facts.
He did not, for example, discuss the question of whether or not the
Chinese city, up to this time preponderantly political in nature,
and a center of consumption in an economy where exchange relationships
were but little developed, had subsequently become an entirely free
and unrestricted place, and one that in economic terms could be
simply characterized as commercial and industrial. A little later,
Fujii Hiroshi conjectured that the development of a monetary economy
among the peasantry in Sung times had brought the division of labor
between town and countryside to a new level. Miyazaki Ichisada, in
the context of a discussion of the separation of investment and
management, rightly pointed out the concentration of the population
in cities in Sung times, and the process of class differentiation towards
extremes of rich and poor. Maeda Masanori and Hori Toshikazu
suggested that the growth of cities in the late T'ang and the Sung,
and the intensification of market relationships that accompanied it,
provided certain conditions that were necessary for the establishment
of a centralized political power and changes in the status of the
peasantry. Sōgabe Shizuo, Hino Kaisaburō and Kusano Yasushi found
it possible to define the development of the Sung city in terms of the
history of taxation. Most recently, G. W. Skinner has offered an
analysis from the standpoint of cultural anthropology, though based on
materials of the late Ch'ing and Republican periods. A positive,

concrete enquiry into the Sung city is, however, still lacking.
It is the purpose of the pages that follow to put forward an outline
of what an overall view might be.

i. The City Area

        From the Ch'in dynasty until the early T'ang the 'city and
its suburbs' (ch'eng-kuo) was differentiated, as an administrative
area, from the 'country villages' (hsing-ts'un). Economically, there
may not always have been that much difference between them as the
former often contained plowland and vegetable gardens. The 'city',
however, was a center of administration and, at least in principle,
the system of controlled markets drew to it both commerce and
industry. The earliest symptoms of the decline of this system may
perhaps be traced to the period of the Northern and Southern
dynasties, but it only became of real significance as long-distance
trade and rural productive power increased after the middle of the
T'ang. Under the Sung a new social division of labor emerged.

        As the old system of market regulation collapsed, trade
came to be carried on freely both inside and outside the city walls.
Merchants settled in the cities that served as nodal points for
long-range commerce, whether these were entrepots like Ming-chou,
Ch'üan-chou, Shou-chou, and O-chou, or cities manufacturing
specialty products like Hsing-hua-chün, Chien-chou, Shao-hsing,
Hang-chou, Su-chou, Hui-chou and Ch'eng-tu. 'Most city people,'
observed Wang Chieh in the fourteenth century, 'fall into either
the category of artisans or of merchants.' (310) Urban population
expanded, and the cities overflowed their walls.

        A good example is T'ing-chou in Fukien. Its walls, built
in the middle of the eleventh century, were slightly over 5 li in
circumference; in other words, it was about half a mile in diameter.
By Southern Sung times, however, only three of its quarters (fang)
were inside these walls and no less than twenty-three outside them. *
A satellite town lying 5 li from the walls was engulfed in the conurbation.
Similar phenomena took place in many of the other important commercial
cities in the Southeast, Kiangsi and elsewhere. These new extensions

_____

*Or seventeen, according to another account.

often made it necessary to establish extra officials for the maintenance of public order. O-chou had both a satellite town to its south, handling an influx of goods from all parts of the country, and a built up area along the bank of the Yangtze containing several tens of thousands of houses, shops and taverns, and constituting in itself an important city. K'ai-feng, the Northern Sung capital, had eight urban districts (hsiang)* outside its walls in 1008, though in 1089 the entire city was regrouped into only four such districts. Lin-an, the Southern Sung capital, had nine urban districts within the walls and four outside.

Suburbs also made their appearance and were recognized as being distinctive from an administrative point of view. Thus in 1074 it was decreed that:

> The informal markets** outside city walls and the ward
> and tithing units (pao-chia) in the market towns shall not
> be assimilated into the borough and ward system (tu-pao)
> of the country villages. (311)

There is some evidence to suggest that urban residents sometimes owned agricultural land near to their cities and administered it in the expectation of a rise in the value of real estate. According to the Draft Sung Digest, 'People are greedily attached to fields in the vicinity of cities.' The same source also has a passage, relating to Lung-hsing (Nan-ch'ang in Kiangsi) in 1169, which is of interest in this regard:

> The city of Feng-hsin in Lung-hsing prefecture embraces
> the two rural areas (hsiang) of Chien-k'ang and T'ung-an.
> Customarily most of the households in the upper categories
> live in the suburbs (chin-chiao). The taxes which they owe
> for properties in other rural areas are therefore levied
> together with those due for the area in which they reside. (312)

During the Sung period countless villages developed markets and then grew into 'half-towns' (Halbstädte) and even small or medium-sized towns and cities. The meshes of the urban economic

---

*This term only acquired its later customary sense of 'suburb' in early Ming times.
**More properly perhaps, 'the commercial districts in which marketplaces were located.' Transl.

network became more closely-drawn than they had been previously. Illustrative of the new situation is a passage from the Chen-chiang Gazetteer (Chen-chiang chih) for the Chih-shun reign-period (1330-1332) on the town of Ting-ch'iao:

> These days, wherever there is a settlement of ten households, there is always a market for rice and salt. The use of the term 'market' indicates that there is business going on there. At the appropriate season people exchange what they have for what they have not, raising or lowering their prices in accordance with their estimation of the eagerness or lack of enthusiasm shown by others, so as to obtain the last small measure of profit. This is of course the usual way of the world. Although Ting-ch'iao is no great city yet its river will take boats and its land-routes will take carts. Thus it too serves as a town for peasants who trade and artisans who engage in commerce. (313)

This town clearly served a Standard Marketing Area*, that is one in which the typical transactions were the mutual exchange of the surplus products of local farms and workshops, and the purchase in return for these products of commodities brought by long-distance trade. The relationship between these basic-level markets and the constraints imposed on many of the peasants by the manorial system remains a problem. In advanced areas (that is, those with a high degree of peasant operational autonomy) peasants certainly marketed grain and other products; great merchants and landlords who held peasants in subjection also engaged in speculative sales of grain. Rural industry, however, was not so widely distributed as it was to be in Ming times and thereafter. The most appropriate provisional conclusion therefore is probably that in the Sung dynasty the peasant money economy both coexisted with and conflicted with the money economy of the landowners and great merchants.

The market-towns and 'half-towns' were established either on the borders of two counties, or on important lines of communication well away from the county capitals. Something of their density of distribution in Ch'ang-shu county in Su-chou prefecture is known from

---

*In the sense given to this term by Professor G. W. Skinner in his 'Marketing and Social Structure in Rural China,' part 1, Journal of Asian Studies, XXIV. i (1964). Transl.

the Ch'in-ch'uan Gazetteer (Ch'in-ch'uan chih) for the Shun-yu
reign-period (1241-1252). The county contained 9 rural areas
(hsiang), 50 boroughs (tu), and 386 'villages'. Of the latter, about
40 appear from their names to have supported markets of some sort,
and of these 6 to 9 market-towns were at the next higher level in
the system, while of course partially overlapping in function with
those of the first category. * The Ch'ang-shu county gazetteer for
the Hung-chih reign-period (1488-1505) also quotes an old gazetteer
as saying that:

> The fields are serried close as fishes' scales. Over a
> level plain of a 100 li villages and markets will be linked
> together continuously in all directions. (314)

A summary gazetteer for T'ung-chou in Kiangsu during the middle
of the sixteenth century noted, after having listed the market-towns,
that, 'Each of the above market-towns has its (market) area.' The
new system thus consisted of a seried of superposed levels of
markets, towns and cities normally culminating, within a given
county, in the county capital.

According to Li Yuan-pi's Guide to County Magistrates
(Tso-i tzu-chen), it was the duty of a county magistrate to lead the
elders of each village in making an itemized list of the rest-houses
(t'ing-kuan), establishments for stockpiling and storage (t'ing-t'a),
shops making and selling wine under official licence (chiu-fang), and
lodges for merchants (k'o-tien). The necessity of officials supervising
the collection of taxes and the maintenance of order was recognized.
In fact, however, an attitude of non-intervention was generally
adopted towards the appearance of small-scale markets, and no
special administrative measures were taken other than those usual
in rural villages. For larger markets, with permanently established
monopoly salt sale depots (yen-ch'ang)**, shops making and selling
wine under official license, and offices for the levy of taxes on
commerce, for all of which commoners contracted to collect the
official dues, government permission was necessary. The object of
this was to prevent mutually destructive competition between markets

---

*I.e. a ratio of one market town to about 8.65 villages. Transl.
**Not to be confused with the same term as used in Ch'ing times in
the sense of an 'official salt-producing area'. Transl.

and to safeguard the receipt of official revenues by giving officials
regulatory powers so that they could take the population in the
marketing areas and the distance between market-places as the
criteria justifying or militating against the establishment of this
latter type of market.

When a settlement reached a hundred households or, more
usually, several thousands of households, it was called a 'town' (chen)
Besides salt depots, wine-shops and tax-offices, such a town would
have its own boundaries and occasionally even a wall. There would
be a Town Supervising Official (chien-chen kuan), or a Police Inspecto
(hsun-chien), or sometimes a County Captain (hsien-wei), and there
would be the administrative subdivisions called 'quarters' (fang) and
officially sanctioned guilds. It would be reasonable to regard such
towns as constituting the lowest level in the bureaucratic system,
yet they were inflexibly classified,so far as administration was
concerned, as part of the countryside. Nor did the number of county
cities increase in Sung times; rather it slightly decreased. Thus
official categories failed to reflect the changing realities.

ii. Urban Land-Ownership

So long as the system of controlled markets was enforced,
and the conduct of business confined to the marketplaces, the
ownership of urban land and houses cannot have been an important
source of income. But, once merchants and artisans enjoyed freedom
of location, an event which probably occurred around the end of the
T'ang dynasty, renting out premises for the purpose of trade and
industry became a distinctive urban source of income, different from
renting out land in the countryside, and subject to its own particular
principles of taxation.

Some idea of the activities of an urban landlord may be had
from the following two passages, both written by natives of An-lu
in Hupeh. The first is from Cheng Hsieh's Yun River Collection
(Yun-ch'i chi):

> The Cheng family lived for generations in Ch'in (i. e. Shensi).
> Their wealth enabled them to hold a leading position in the
> area within the passes. At the end of the Five Dynasties
> my great-great-grandfather Cheng Pao-yung engaged in trade

in Hupeh and Hu-nan. He came to An-lu, was captivated
by its atmosphere, and so left Ch'in to live here. The people
of An-lu were delighted that such an important person should
come to their locality. On one occasion someone deposited
several million cash with him and more than ten years
elapsed before a merchant came by who turned out to be the
depositor's son. Cheng gave him the entire sum. ... (319)

The second is from the Historical Miscellany (Chu-shih) of Wang
Te-ch'en, who was a pupil of Cheng Hsieh:

At the end of the Five Dynasties period (Mr. Cheng) moved
to An-lu. He had enormous financial resources, and
many of the people in the city were his tenants. Whenever
there had been a heavy rainstorm he would load up a cart
with roofing tiles and go around to enquire if any of his
houses were leaking; if so, he would have them mended.
He would even repair rooms which his tenants had themselves
had built. In the depths of winter when it was bitterly cold
he would excuse them rent for several months. (319)

We also know that many small merchants in Ming-chou at this time
rented their shop-space.

With the growing demand for accomodation in the cities,
rack-renting became a problem. The Sung Digest contains the
following decree from 1107:

There are families in the capital whose business consists
of renting out houses. Recently many of them, on the
pretext of having done repairs, have raised rents - frequently
to more than twice their former level. The situation is
becoming steadily worse and making it difficult for registered
commoners and people of semi-dependent status (hsi-min)
to manage. The long-term consequences will be harmful
if these practices are not prohibited. Henceforth, landlords
at the capital, whether within or without the city walls, may
not suddenly increase rents unless they have increased the
area of the property concerned. (320)

In 1133 another decree stated that:

> The migrant people in Chiang-pei rent their accomodation.
> Many of them have been vexed by the increased rents charged
> by their landlords, and reduced to difficult financial straits.
> Furthermore, powerful property-accumulating families have
> taken possession of official land, erected houses, and let
> them to others at a heavy rental. Their wealth increases
> while humble folk are afflicted. (320)

House-owners in Shang-yuan county, in which the capital of the prefecture
of Chiang-ning (modern Nanking) was situated, are said by one
gazetteer to have enjoyed a minimum daily income of 20 to 30 strings
of cash around the middle of the thirteenth century, and those of
Chü-jung county about 150 cash daily. A further example of
urban renting may be found in the quotation from the Collection of Lucid
Decisions by Celebrated Judges which begins on page 76 above.

There was also much public land in the cities. Some of this
was used for government offices, temples, military encampments,
roads, waterways, walls, piers and markets. The rest was rented
to the common people for shops and dwellings, and often brought
in a substantial revenue. State land rented out in this fashion was
accorded favorable tax treatment, but even so it was common for
rich and powerful persons to rent strategically located sites,
sublet them to others and collect rents while defaulting on the payments
which they owed to the government. Urban land generally was a
more secure investment than commerce, and thus the well-to-do
steadily displaced the poorer classes as the owners of urban real estate.

The 'living-space tax' (chien-chia ch'ien) levied on dwellings
in T'ang times may have been the precursor of taxes which reflected
the changed relationship between city and countryside after the
breakdown of the controlled market system. In any event, the unified
taxation aimed at by the Two Tax System introduced in 780 was not
necessarily realized in practice and by the beginning of the Five
Dynasties there was emerging a tendency to distingusih between taxes
aimed at the 'cities and suburbs' and at the 'country villages'. Thus
a decree issued by the Emperor Chuang-tsung (reg. 923-925) of the
Later T'ang dynasty observed that:

> In recent times the shops, dwellings and gardens in the
> cities have not been subject to taxation, but just lately,
> because of the orders of the (preceding) illegitimate
> government, they have been being levied.   (322)

In the course of time taxes on city houses and on city land made their
appearance and when the Sung dynasty was founded a distinction was
drawn between 'taxes on the cities and suburbs' on the one hand and
the twice-yearly taxes and labor-services levied from the peasants
on the other.

   Rural taxes, which were varied somewhat according to
local conditions, were assessed on the basis of acreage, the value
of land, the extent of sowing, income from rents and income from
non-agricultural pursuits. The last category comprised pawnshops,
houses, shops, storehouses, rented draft animals and rented boats,
later also wine shops. Urban tax categories were not so rigorosly
defined, the population simply being divided into ten groups. Urban
taxes were also much less burdensome. ⌐The chief impositions
suffered by the upper classes in the cities were rather the irregular
official levies in kind (k'o-p'ei) and the provision of funds to meet
crises such as famines, brigands, flood prevention and the construction
of city walls. There were also a number of tax-exempt persons and
institutions in the cities: official families, households headed by
women, Buddhist monks, Taoist priests, and monasteries and temples.

   By the eleventh century the inequities of the tax system,
and the resulting fiscal difficulties, were already evident. Wang
An-shih therefore attempted to remedy the situation through the
provisions of the Service Exemption System (mien-i fa) and the Land
Survey and Equitable Tax System (fang-t'ien chün-shui fa). * Under
the former, previously tax-exempt households, that is urban residents,
official households, temples and monasteries, and households with
no male, no male adult or only one male adult, paid Service Assistance
Money (chu-i ch'ien). With this the fiscal privileges of the cities
almost disappeared. Thus the Service Exemption System tax categories
of 1076 listed in the Great Encyclopedia of the Yung-lo Reign (Yung-lo
ta-tien) show a general tendency, in spite of some regional variations,
to treat cities and countryside alike. Urban real estate was most

---

*See Liu, 1959, pp. 103 et seq., and 5, 39, 83. Transl.

commonly subjected to the 'charge on subsidiary-type income from
non-agricultural sources' (chia-yeh ch'ien), probably because most
of those directly engaged in trade and industry did not have fixed
property of the sort that could be made to bear taxation. Urban land
which produced income from trade or industry (chia-yeh) was
distinguished for fiscal purposes from agricultural land.

The Land Survey and Equitable Tax System of 1072 was a
synthesis and extension of earlier laws on equitable taxation dating
from late T'ang times onwards. Farmland was divided into ten
categories according to its general type and its fertility, and urban
land was also divided into ten categories according to location. An
upper limit on the density of building of 8 living-space units (chien)
per mou was laid down. Under the Southern Sung the Boundary Survey
System (ching-chieh fa), which may be regarded as the successor of
the Land Survey and Equitable Tax System, made use of still more
precise categories for rural land, and urban land was carefully
calculated. An illustration of this is provided by the Lan-ch'i County
Gazetteer (Lan-ch'i hsien-chih) for the Cheng-te reign (1506-1521),
which gives the following figures from a survey made around 1228 in
Lan-ch'i county in Wu-chou (present-day Chin-hua) in Chekiang:

Table I   Land Use in Lan-ch'i County circa 1228.

	mou
Low Irrigated Paddy Fields (shui-t'ien)	39,545
Intermediate Paddy Fields (p'ing-t'ien)	178,145
Hillside Mulberry Land (shan-sang)	17,933
Level Dry Fields (p'ing-lu)	35,705
Hillside Dry Fields (shan-lu-ti)	29,064
Bamboo Groves (chu-chiao)	8,288
Dwarf Bamboos (chu-hsiao)	8,322
(Peasants') Dwellings (wu-chi)	15,222
Ponds (t'ang)	28,393
Miscellaneous Trees (tsa-mu)	58,385
T'ung-nut and Fruit Trees (t'ung kuo mu)	15,699
Firewood Forests (ch'ai-shan)	508,935
Unplanted Farmland (pai-ti)	24,685

Table I continued

	mou

Graves (fen-ti)   8,013
Tea Lands (ch'a-ti)   146
Lime Quarries (shih-hui shan)   280

                          Chang (Frontage)

Urban Sites (fang-kuo chi-ti)   20,826

Each of the ten categories of urban land seems to have been further
sub-divided into three sub-categories according to quality.

iii. The Urban Population

       In the absence of specific statistics for the urban population
as a whole, it is necessary to make deductions from the few available
local materials. Thus the Great Encyclopaedia of the Yung-lo Reign
quotes the following figures for T'ing-chou in southwestern Fukien:

(see Table 2 on next page)

It is apparent that the rural population was almost static whereas the
urban population was growing rapidly, multiplying in a little over
half a century by more than eight times, and advancing from 6% to
28% of the total population. The percentage of Landowner/Native
Households (chu-hu) in the cities was 55% in the first period and
46% in the second. It was substantially higher in the countryside:
69% and 62% for the two periods respectively. The low population
to household ratio among the tenants/in-migrants (k'o-hu) in the rural
areas suggests that many of this class may have migrated to the
cities.

       In Yin county, in which the city of Ming-chou (Ning-po) was
situated, some 14 per cent of the population was urban in the early
thirteenth century. In She county, where the city of Hsin-an (Hui-chou)
was located, the population figures from two gazetteers reveal the
following picture:

(See Table III, p. 138)

Table 2   The Population of T'ing-chou in the Southern Sung
(Probably excluding females)

	Late 12th Century		Mid-13th Century	
	Landowner/ Native	Tenant/ In-migrant	Landowner/ Native	Tenant/ In-migrant
URBAN				
Households	2,889	2,396	33,759	39,381
Adults	5,005	2,505	82,347	39,926
Old, Young, Unmarried Adults and Cripples	2,233	8,213	1,504	26,707
Total Population	7,238	10,718	83,851	66,633
RURAL				
Households	99,825	45,221	93,857	56,436
Adults	120,447	47,405	156,257	56,507
Old, Young, Unmarried Adults and Cripples	130,691	4,581	133,738	38,465
Total Population	251,138	51,986	289,995	95,041

Table 3   The Population of She County

	1172		1208-1224	
	Households	Population	Households	Population
URBAN				
Within Prefectural City Walls	1,281	6,858	...	...
Outside Prefectural City Walls	650	3,281	...	...
Urban Total	1,931	10,139	...	...
RURAL				
She County: Landowners/Native	25,534	...	...	...
Tenants/In-migrants	409	...	...	...
County Total	25,943	...	22,613	39,783

If the difference in dates between the two sources is disregarded, it
may be deduced that the urban population of She county was about
26 per cent of the total. It is likewise known that the urban population
in Tan-t'u county, which contained the prefectural capital of Chen-chiang,
rose from 24 per cent of the total population in 1208-1224 to 33 per
cent in 1265-1274. Finally, the urban population of the two counties
in Han-yang-chün in the thirteenth century probably amounted to
about 13 per cent of the overall population of 20,000 households.

The statistics referred to above omit the urban population in
marketing centers below the level of the town (chen). They were
compiled primarily for tax purposes, and it is unclear whether or not
they included the mobile merchants population, day-laborers with
virtually no property to their name, and vagrants. Yeh Meng-te
wrote in the twelfth century that:

> When Chien-k'ang (Nanking) enjoyed peace, there were
> more than 170,000 registered inhabitants in the urban
> areas, not including the migrants, merchants, peddlers
> and itinerant laborers who came and went. (333)

There is some evidence to suggest that the mobile population was of
a considerable size at this time, and the percentages given above for
the urban population in counties containing a prefectural seat are
therefore probably underestimates.

The occupational structure of these urban populations consisted
of a relatively small number of wealthy urban landlords, well-to-do
merchants and financiers, Buddhists, Taoists, and officials together
with the members of the sub-bureaucracy, soldiers and a mass of
small traders and artisans. The richest sometimes entrusted their
funds to managers or invested it with active capitalists. To these
may be added the officials who engaged semi-openly in business,
a pursuit from which they were legally debarred. Many merchants and
industrialists also sought to buy official status, and it was inevitable
that, as the conflict between growing urban economic power and
intensifying official control became more pronounced, the upper classes
in the cities would attempt to safeguard their wealth by assuming a
politically parasitical character. This contributed to the further
division of the urban populace into very rich and very poor, and one

consequence of this was that it was on the purchasing power not of
the majority of the city population but of a minority of rich persons
that the control of the markets in the last analysis depended. This
in turn imposed a limit on the development of urban industry and
trade.

Past studies have tended to concentrate on a few great cities
such as K'ai-feng and Lin-an, and have thus overestimated the
degree of urban development in Sung times. Alternatively they have
sometimes regarded these cities as exceptional, overemphasized
the self-sufficient character of the rural villages, and so underestimated
the level of urbanization. Stressing the commercial and industrial
aspects of the newly-arisen cities has also led to a one-sided evaluation.
The division of labor between the ordinary towns and the country
villages has not always been adequately explained, a defect which it
has been the object of the present section to remedy in so far as the
economic aspects are concerned, both from the point of view of
materials and of methodology.

2. MARKETS AND FAIRS IN KIANGNAN DURING THE SUNG DYNASTY

In a sense the origins of Chinese marketing may be traced
back to the Commentaries of the Book of Changes:

> When the sun stood at midday, the Divine Husbandman
> held a market. He caused the people of the world to
> come together and assembled the riches of all under
> Heaven. These they exchanged with one another and then
> returned home, each thing having found its appropriate
> place. * (339)

A system of market regulation was also laid down in the Rituals of Chou
(Chou li). According to its provisions, trade was restricted to officially
established commercial areas within the cities, and to marketplaces
(shih) set up by the government as needed along the main communication
routes. Thus:

---

*Translation from R. Wilhelm, The I Ching or Book of Changes, translated
into English by C. F. Baynes (New York: Bollingen/Pantheon, edition of
1961), Bk II, p. 129, with considerable modifications. Transl.

> When the artificers lay out the capital of a 'feudal' lord it
> shall consist of nine square stades (li), with three gates
> on each side, and nine streets running from North to
> South and nine running from East to West. ... To the
> left (of the palace) is the hall of the ancestors and to the
> right is the altar of the local spirits. To the front is the
> palace and to the rear the marketplace. ... (339)

And:

> There shall be a kiosk provided with food and drink (for
> travellers) every ten stades along the roads between the
> capital and the provinces. Every thirty stades there
> shall be a lodge where they may find accomodation for
> the night, and where a small store of provisions will
> be kept. Every fifty stades there shall be a market(-town)
> with a lofty inn containing a large store of provisions.(339)

Prior to the middle of the T'ang dynasty at least, the principle
embodied in this system of market control was put into practice and
in consequence, to quote the words of a decree of 707, it was 'not
lawful to establish markets anywhere except in prefectural and
county capitals' unless permission to do so had been granted.

Nonetheless, as trade grew in volume, market-places little
by little came spontaneously into being in city suburbs and country
villages. Traces of informal periodic markets appear here and there
in the literary sources from the time of the Western and Eastern
Chin dynasties (265-316 and 317-419 respectively) and thereafter.
During the period of transtion from the T'ang to the Sung, the swift
tempo of economic advance in Kiangnan undermined the official
system of market control from the inside, while there was also a
rapid development of new places for the transaction of local exchanges.
As Tu Mu wrote in the ninth century:

> All the informal markets (ts'ao-shih)* of the Yangtze-Huai
> River region are situated at the confluence of rivers. In
> them reside many rich and powerful households. (338)

---

*Literally 'hay markets'. See below. Transl.

Increases in agricultural productivity in Sung times led to a notable
widening of the scale on which village markets were held, and some
of the villages supporting them grew into minor towns (Zwergstädte),
'half-towns' (Halbstädte) or even administrative centers such as
Towns (chen) or county seats. Furthermore, the number of fairs for
interregional trade increased, and also the frequency with which they
were held.

i. Village Markets

A. Terms Designating Village Markets

The terms most commonly used for rural markets were
'empty markets' (hsu-shih), 'periodic markets' (hai-shih), 'mountain
markets' (shan-shih), 'rural markets' (yeh-shih), 'small markets'
(hsiao-shih), 'morning markets' (chao-shih), 'early markets' (tsao-shih),
'village markets' (ts'un-shih), and 'hay markets' (ts'ao-shih). The
first two of these terms were peculiar to Kiangnan; the following three
were usually somewhat literary; the next two referred to the time when
markets were usually held; the last two were rather general expressions.
Regardless of these differences in nomenclature, the markets referred
to were all on a small scale and generally held either in villages,
on the outskirts of villages, or else at the roadside.

'Empty markets' may be traced back to the Chin dynasty.
According to Shen Huai-yuan's Gazetteer of Southern Yueh (Nan Yueh chih):

> The markets of Yueh (Southeastern China) are 'empty places'
> and mostly located in the village commons. The merchants
> are called together ahead of time, singing and dancing
> sometimes being used to attract them. It is the same in
> Ching-nan (Hunan) and Ling-piao (Kwangtung). (341)

There are references in T'ang times to 'empty markets' in Kwangsi
and Hunan, and in the eleventh century Wu Ch'u-hou gave the following
explanation of the term in his Miscellaneous Records from the Blue
Casket (Ch'ing-hsiang tsa-chi):

> In Ling-an the village markets are called 'empty places'.
> ... For the places where markets are held are full when
> people are present but empty when people are absent. The
> village markets in Ling-an are rarely full and frequently
> empty. It is thus appropriate, is it not, to call them
> 'empty places'? (341)

This brings out clearly their intermittent nature. Wu's interpretation
was based on a gazetteer of Fen-ning county in Kiangsi compiled
by Hsu Yün, as is clear from the section on markets in Ch'en Yuan-ching's
Extensive Record of the Forest of Affairs:

> Hai (... . Markets are commonly called hai.)
> Hsu. (Markets are commonly called hsu.) Hsu Yun's
> Gazetteer of Hsin-shui says of Fen-ning that, 'Originally
> it was an ordinary periodic market (hai-shih) of the prefecture.
> When there are markets in the villages of Ling-nan, they
> call them 'empty markets.' They do not meet frequently and
> are empty on many days. In Western Shu (Szechwan) they
> are called chieh ... in allusion to the intermittent fever
> which seizes the sufferer on every alternate day. People
> in Kiangnan find this reference to a disease distasteful and
> so simply say hai (i.e. the twelfth of the 'twelve branches'
> used for cyclical counting). In Hupeh, Hunan and Wu it is
> the custom for markets to meet every third day, hence the
> name 'periodic market' (hai-shih). (342)

Other sources confirm this three day periodicity as typical of
'empty markets', and indicate that the term was principally used in
China south of the Yangtze, especially Kuang-nan. *

The T'ang poet Po Chü-i mentions 'periodic markets where
fish and salt collect,' and elsewhere says:

> The river market is in close contact with the city gate,
> Boats in confusion throng beside the smoky village
> Where officials levy the tax on fishermen
> And others pay their dues for farming the dry hill fields.
> On the hai days of the cycle, shrimps and crabs in profusion;
> In the yin years, lynx and fox in plenty. (349)

---

*Pages 344-348 of the original work contain a geographical analysis of all
the known references to 'empty markets' in Sung and Yuan times. Transl.

Another reference to a periodic market comes in a poem written in the Yuan dynasty by Ch'en Lü:

> At the periodic market goods of all sorts are gathered;
> Though the Yao tribesmen buy nothing but salt,
> In the hills the sun has not yet risen high
> And blue-green rain is wetting the wineshop flags. (349)

The section on merchants and goods in Yeh Yen-kuei's twelfth-century Trifles from a Sea of Notes (Hai-lu sui-shih) records a name used for markets with a six-day periodicity:

> It is the custom in Ch'ih-chou (in Anhwei) to be fond of
> visiting and giving presents, but there are no exchanges
> made in the market-places.* The villages have (empty)
> places for market gatherings on specified days, which
> they call 'assemblies on the first and seventh days of the
> duodecimal cycle' (tzu-wu hui). (350)

This passage is also interesting in that it seems to imply that elsewhere the interchange of gifts had sometimes developed to the point of serving the function of economic exchange.

The term 'mountain market' appears frequently in the inscriptions and poems composed for the landscape known as Mists Clearing Over A Mountain Market**, one of the Eight Scenes from Hsiao-Hsiang***, a series of which there were many versions in Sung and Yuan times. Thus Chou Mi wrote these verses:

> The speckled bamboos
> Growing in the spring before the Huang-ling Temple.
> The k'an-k'an of the drumbeats
> That welcome the god.

---

*Possibly the text should be rearranged to read 'but there are no fixed market installations (shih-ching) for exchanges. Transl.
**See Plates VIII and XI in the original volume. Transl.
***I. e. that part of Hunan province where the rivers bearing these two names join. Transl.

The small market –
People with their bundles of tea or salt,
Chickens cackling, dogs barking,
Firewood being exchanged for rice
And fishes bartered for wine.

Here and there –
Green tavern flags,
Where elderly gentlemen sit propped,
Drowsy with drink.

They have scattered.
The market is closed,
The ferry-boat stopped.
Between us and the willows high above
Flows the sunlit mist.   (351)

And Yang Kung-yuan, a poet of early Yuan times:

The horizontal mists appear
    To hold the lofty ridges up,
While from the village market comes
    The scent of the fermenting grain.

The morning light grows brighter, people race
    To ford the river,
Carrying salt in bags, fermented wine,
    A busy throng upon its way to market.   (351)

Mountain markets such as these were not confined to Hunan but were to
be found in hilly areas or on the boundaries between the hilly areas
and the plains throughout Kiangnan.

In spite of the differences in terminology, and no doubt also
in origins and geographical distribution, the types of rural market
described in the foregoing pages were all basically similar in economic
and social function.

B. The Frequency and Duration of Village Markets

The dominant characteristics of rural markets were that they
met at periodic intervals, and that these meetings generally lasted
for only a brief time. Periodicity was based either on decades of
ten days each, of which there were three in each month, or on the
recurrent cycle of the 'twelve branches', in a manner analogous to
the reliance of Western marketing schedules on the week. Examples
of 3-day and 6-day cycles have been given above. In his <u>Miscellany
from the Ch'ing-po Gate</u> (Ch'ing-po tsa-chih) the twelfth-century scholar
and bibliophile Chou Hui mentions a 10-day cycle in Hai-nan Island:

> They do not have fixed market installations (<u>shih-ching</u>)
> but in the early morning on every fifth or seventh day
> in each decade come together to trade for a brief while,
> after which they scatter. (355)

Hsiao Chieh also refers to a 'market meeting on the fifth day of each
decade' whose din was 'like water roaring over shallow rapids. '
A 5-day cycle was also sometimes found, and so too was a 2-day cycle.
A passage in the <u>Sung Digest</u> from 997 observes that, 'In the markets
and settlements of Ling-nan (Kwangtung) there are gatherings of small
traders every other day. These are called 'empty markets'.' (356)
According to a commemorative inscription written in the eleventh
century by Lü T'ao, in Sui-ning county in Szechwan it had been
observed by the subject of his inscription that, 'The humble folk in
the villages hold markets on alternate days. ' (356) A few places of
course had daily markets. According to a gazetteer for Ning-po
in the middle of the twelfth century, 'The informal markets meet
every morning. ' (356) This seems to refer to the suburbs of the
prefectural city. Examples of this last sort of market are in general
not common. The frequency with which a market was held did not
of course indicate in and of itself the volume of commercial transactions
enacted there. This depended on the size of the market's sphere of
influence, the type of goods traded, and the distance of neighboring
markets.

Markets were held early and did not last long. This appears
clearly from various poems on the subject. Thus Chao Fan in the
twelfth century could write:

> The dawn bell tolling, I leave the country monastery -
> The early market's out on the village market ground. (357)

And Tung Ssu-kao observed in his 'Passing a Market at the Entrance
to a Forest,' written in the later part of the thirteenth century:

> This market too delights the eye.
> Those crowds that hurry to the market ground
> While it was still dark heard the bell ringing and rose. (357)

And the Northern Sung poet-monk Tao-ch'ien has these verses entitled
'On the Way to Kuei-tsung Monastery'* in his Collected Poems by the
Ts'an-liao Master (Ts'an-liao-tzu shih-chi):

> The morning sun not yet emerged from P'o-yang Lake,
> The bramble thickets for a moment seem like gates of pine.
> The aged trees steep in gloom the precipitous cliffs
> From which there comes the apes' desolate crying.
>
> With a turn of the path a valley opens
> And far ahead a village comes in sight.
> Along the road, farmhands overtaking and overtaken,
> Shouting and laughing at each other,
> Off to match wits for a few hours at the market. (357)

Finally, two verses by Fan Ch'eng-ta:

> The declining moon has sunk into the distance,
> The last few stars are dim and watery points of light,
> ... .
> Something of a crowd is gathering in the market,
> Bamboo-splint baskets come busily twisting and turning through
> > the hills. (357)

And:

> The fisherman going to the market
> > Jostles in the morning for a place on the ferry.
> The merchant who has joined in the temple procession
> > Goes home in the evening drunk. (357)

---

*A famous foundation in Kiangsi. Transl.

148

C. The Siting of Rural Markets

Local trade based on exchanges between peasants played the
main role in the establishment of local markets. The latter often
developed in connection with the local manors, as has been pointed
out by Sudō Yoshiyuki. In 1205, according to the Sung Digest, there
were in the three prefectures of Kuang-chou, Ch'ao-ch'ing and Hui-chou
some 83 local customs offices, 'all of them in the market (place) s
of country villages.' An entry for two years earlier illuminates the
nature of these markets:

> In (Ch'ing-yuan) county (in Kuang-chou) there are two high
> flat places (i. e. markets) called Shih-t'i and Shih-chin.
> They lie between two mountains. The farmland is limited
> in extent but after the inhabitants had plowed and excavated
> they were able to form settlements. The provincial governor
> gave permission for two internal customs stations to be set
> up, and invited the most powerful people in the community
> to contract for the tax-quota (mai-p'u) and themselves install
> 'customs officers in the employ of local notables' (t'u-tien
> lan-t'ou). At first there were no merchants but they levied
> a tax on all such items as the grains, hemp and beans
> harvested by the local population. (359)

Some of these market sites grew into centers of interlocal
trade. Fang Feng-chen, in his Dragon Peak Collection, described
one such in Yen-chou in Chekiang in the following terms:

> In the southern part of Ch'ing-ch'i county (present-day
> Shun-an), thirty li from the county city, there is a place
> called Yun-ch'eng, with streams and hills on every side.
> ... On the southern side of the river there is a periodic
> market (hsu-shih). Rich persons and merchants gather there.
> The water-routes reach as far as Hang-chou and Yueh-chou
> (present Shao-hsing), and to Ch'ü-chou and Chien-chou.
> Boats and carts hasten through it day and night, so spoiling
> the charm of the mountains and streams. (359)

Hung Mai tells us of a small port called Ku-pu ('Old Pier') in Yü-kan
county in Jao-chou:

There is a periodic market (hsu-shih) (in a town) of several
hundred families of inhabitants. It is a place through which
merchants are constantly passing, and there are a great
many butchers. (359)

Small towns often grew up at the sites of such markets.

Many markets arose on the ground in front of monasteries
and temples, taking advantage of the opportunities provided by the
large numbers of people gathering for religious ceremonies. Tung
Ssu-kao has a poem entitled 'Passing through the Market in front of
the Hsing-kuo Hall':

> An air of ancient times hangs over the hamlet
> Spread in a circle below the god's shrine.
> The rank smell of fish and salt is almost absent;
> Mild and pungent vegetables spread an abundant perfume.
> They barter surplus goods for those they lack;
> In the morning half-light, gather fuel and drive their herds
>   to pasture;
> And close the market well before the dusk. (360)

Tsou Hao wrote of 'The hubbub of the morning market in front of the
gates, and within the gates the silence of a mountain valley.' (360)
Another reference to the association of a temple and a market may
be found in the poem by Chou Mi translated on page 144 above. In
Sung times village markets were sometimes even called 'Taoist
gatherings' (tao-hui), 'Buddhist gatherings' (fo-hui), 'seasonal
gatherings' (shih-hui), and 'gatherings at the locality altar' (she-hui).
Finally, it sometimes happened that a periodic market would be set
up as the result of an official initiative.

It is difficult to estimate the size of the marketing areas served
by these local markets, but it is clear that if they were too close together
there might be rivalry between them. Here, from Hsing Yuan-lung's
Literary Works from the Pine Enclosure (Sung-yuan wen-chi), is 'The
Record of Yun-shih Market', written in 1208:

> In the district of Ching-i in the county of Kao-an (in Yun-chou
> in Kiangsi) there was a periodic market called Yun-shih.
> The land there was level ana it produced paper, silk thread,
> hemp, millet, wheat and wine. It was listed on the official

provincial register. Only a little more than five li away was
the periodic market of Hsin-i in Yü-chang prefecture
(present-day Nan-ch'ang), and the two markets declined
or prospered in alternating fashion. Yun-shih was destroyed
by fire in the course of the fighting in 1126, and this gave
Hsin-i a monopoly for some seven to ten years. In
consequence its people became carried away by the pursuit
of profits, and the strong and the weak merchants mutually
destroyed one another. In 1135 Yun-shih was revived, and
Hsin-i fell into an even more severe decline. (The Hsin-i
men) who were losing by this became consumed with envy and
lodged a protest with their prefect that Yun-shih was eating
up the customs levies (which they had contracted to collect),
and as a result Yun-shih was suppressed. Trade, having
no suitable place at which to be conducted, was scattered
and destroyed. In 1206 Mr. Su Sen took up the post of prefect
of Yun-chou and learned from scholarly circles of the harm
that had been done. He therefore restored the market at
Yun-shih. The people of Hsin-i collected money for bribes
in the hope of having this decision reversed. Mr. Chao Ju-tang,
the governor of Kiangsi, taking into consideration the fact that
the market at Yun-shih had had a much longer past history
of growth, issued instructions to the prefect that the people
should be allowed to do as they found convenient. ... Yun-shih
was not abolished, and the common people were therefore
content. (362)

Amano Motonosuke has made the interesting observation that in modern
times in parts of Shantung there was an unwritten law that no market
should be less than five li away from its nearest neighbor, lest it should
draw away customers from the latter and imperil its collection of an
adequate tax revenue. If such a new market were established, a
lawsuit would result. Manifestly, this sort of situation already existed
in Sung times.

It is not clear whether or not all markets invariably had a
market-square and/or market buildings. The latter were certainly
relatively common. Lou Yao, writing in the twelfth century, mentions
the proposal of a magistrate of Lin-ch'uan county in Fu-chou, Kiangsi,
that likened periodic markets to 'illegally established customs stations',
and requested that 'the buildings be razed and the markets suppressed.' (363)
Nai Hsien in the Yuan period observed:

> A ring of villages share a periodic market,
> And chiselling the green thicket put up its buildings. (363)

At the sites of the larger markets there would be permanent shops for grain and wine, if not for other commodities, and also inns for merchants. Hung Mai refers to someone 'staying overnight at the inn for merchants in a village periodic market,' and Tao-ch'ien, in the poem on a local market quoted on page 147 above, goes on to speak of the 'inns-cum-stores (ti-tien) massed like clouds.' In Chen-la (Cambodia), however, mats were simply spread on the ground.

The size of the settlement in which a market was located was not directly related to the size of its marketing area, but it is worth noting that there was a wide range in the size of the villages and towns concerned. Thus Chu Chi-fang alludes to

> People off to the morning market with their fowls and piglets,
> In a tumbledown village with pens, cottages and a few shops. (365)

And Liu K'o-chuang to

> A lonely settlement of a few homes,
> Two or three persons going to market. (365)

Ch'en Fou, the fourteenth-century poet and official, has these lines in his Ch'en Kang-chung's Drafts from Chiao-chou (Kang-chung Chiao-chou kao):

> Nine or ten huts that are thatched with reeds,
> A small bridge that spans a brook –
> Is there anything else on sale to be found in the market? (365)

These are extreme examples. Against them may be put Hung Mai's reference to Ku-pu (on page 149 above) as 'a periodic market (in a town) of several hundred families of inhabitants,' and an observation in a memorial inscription in Yang Wan-li's Collection from the Studio of Sincerity:

> There was a mountain market nearby called 'Two Fields Market'. Beside it two mountains rose up like walls, and through it there meandered a stream. Several hundreds of families lived there. (365)

Places like these had outgrown their status as villages and had become either 'half-towns' or minor towns.

As the preceding pages have made clear, markets were frequented by persons from a wide variety of classes. It was however a distinctive feature of South China that women were often in charge of bringing goods in to the markets. In K'uei-chou province, according to a poem by Fan Ch'eng-ta:

> Necks swollen with goiter, the married women
>> Come to the markets in the county capital;
> In groups of five and ten they sell their wares
>> In the southern streets.
> No passerby makes fun
>> Of their coarse and ugly looks;
> They wear the silver hairpins that
>> Their husbands bought in person (for them). (366)

Chou Ch'ü-fei wrote that:

> When I saw the women of the back-country of Kuang-nan I wondered how they came to be so numerous and enjoy such well-being. The men have scrawny little bodies, and dark complexions and sad expressions. The married women are swarthy-skinned and plump, mostly in good health and very robust. Those who carry goods on their backs to peddle in search of profit in the cities and suburbs and in the periodic markets are all married women. Polygamy is general among the ordinary people in Ch'in-chou (in southern Kuang-nan-hsi, modern Kwangtung), and all the wives take goods on their backs to sell in the markets in order to support their single husband. (366)

Other sources refer to the involvement of peasant women in mercantile activities in Hsun-chou (Kwangtung), Yung-chou (Kwangsi), Ku-t'ien (Fukien) and Chen-la (Cambodia).

D. Transactions in Rural Markets

The goods most commonly traded in rural markets were rice, wheat, millet, firewood, vegetables, fish, poultry, pigs, fruit, salt, wine and tea, * that is to say mostly articles produced in the marketing area itself and not subjected to any manufacturing process. Money was not necessarily always used. An entry on Kuang-nan market taxes in the Sung Digest for 1215 says:

> The people who live along the streams and rivers put their fresh fish on their shoulders and simply barter them in the villages. They never sell them through the markets in the county capitals. (369)

In similar vein the Record of the Country and Customs of Cambodia (Chen-la feng-t'u chi), composed around the end of the thirteenth century by Chou Ta-kuan, observes that:

> For small transactions they use rice, grain, and Chinese coins; and for somewhat larger ones they use hemp cloth. For large transactions they use gold and silver. (369)

The marketing of salt and tea, which came from areas specializing in their production, had long necessitated the services of merchants. Shu Yueh-hsiang, who wrote a series of ten poems on the various economic activities of village women, pointed out that the sale of vegetables was a source of cash income for the area surrounding T'ai-chou in Che-kiang in the verses given on page 86 above. Fang Ta-tsung, writing about his travels in thirteenth-century Fukien, observed that:

> Trade in the markets is customarily carried on by means of strings of a thousand copper cash. The people from the country villages take what they have produced to the markets and exchange it there for these strings. (370)

Lastly it may be noted that there seem to have been specialized dealings even in poultry. Teng Shen in the twelfth century mentions the 'hubbub of the duck market,' and Yang Wan-li speaks of 'people coming to the village market where the chickens cackle in their baskets hanging from the eaves.' (370) The Yuan official Chang Chih-han wrote:

---

*See the table on page 368 of the original text for a fuller listing. Transl.

> Gathering at the market early,
>> The traders' ships.
> Like squads of soldiers on the march,
>> The ducks and geese.   (370)

E. The Legal Aspects of Markets

As a small market which had sprung up more or less by accident became bigger, it seems natural to suppose that some independent code or system of unwritten law appeared to regulate such matters as the weights and measures used in transactions, the quality of goods, prices and the settlement of disputes. Materials to demonstrate this are lacking, but the continuation of the poem by Tao-ch'ien, 'On the Way to Kuei-tsung Monastery', quoted on page 147 above is suggestive in this regard:

> . . . ,
> Off to match wits for a few hours at the market.
> Numerous as clouds are the lodges and the stores. *
> They bring hemp cloth and paper-mulberry paper
> Or drive before them chickens and sucking pigs.
> This way and that lie piles of brooms and dustpans,
> So many domestic trifles they cannot all be listed.
> An elderly gentleman controls the trade,
> And all respect his slightest indications.
> The measures of length are scrupulously compared,
> And one by one turned over in his hands
> Without attention flagging or fatigue.   (371)

This old gentleman corresponded to the Market Heads (chi-t'ou) who were to be found in Chinese markets in recent times. It would be wrong, however, to regard this system of market control as pursuing an independent course of development. The setting up of markets of the periodic type was determined by a discreet alliance between, on the one hand, the powerful clans and merchants who created and maintained them, and wielded the real power there, and, on the other hand, the local government offices which provided political and legal protection, and received by way of a consideration for these services the levies sanctioned by public law. The importance which such official protection might assume is revealed by the case of the markets at Yun-shih and Hsin-i quoted on page 149 above.

---

*Or 'inns-cum-stores'. See page 151 above. Transl.

Local officials were interested in tapping the markets as a
source of revenue, and local notables or merchants would usually
contract to collect the taxes on commerce. By so doing they were
enabled to strengthen their personal control over the marketing
area and to give this control the veneer of public authority. The
Sung Digest contains a report of 1175 which illuminates the relationships
between the two groups:

> There is an institution in the villages which is known as the
> 'periodic market'. It simply consists of a market which
> meets once every three days. Initially there was no system
> for taxing it, but as the prefectures were in urgent need of
> revenue they instituted tax stations. People were induced to
> contract for the collection of the customs levies (mai-p'u)
> and to pay in cash (in advance), so that they might themselves
> collect the taxes. The tax-contractors were generally the
> powerful rascals of the local communities, and once they
> could take advantage of their right to handle the payment of
> the official levies, they acquired an immense influence over
> official affairs. The authorities benefitted from the receipt
> of the tax monies and so, even if they wanted to govern
> justly in the interests of the ordinary folk, they were powerless
> to do so. (372)

Occasionally an exemption from the tax on trade would be permitted in
the markets set up by the government in remote and undeveloped areas.
In the Collected Works from Bamboo Island (Chu-chou wen-chi), written
in the twelfth century by Wu Ching, there is an account of an official
who in fact did this:

> He went to be the magistrate of An-jen county, which had
> previously had the reputation of being a backwater. When he
> arrived he adopted a policy of severity towards the under-
> officials and generosity towards the people. He lightened
> taxes and did not press hard for their payment. Until this
> time few peddlers had come to An-jen, so he established a
> market. No official levies were exacted on market days,
> prices were uniform, and an unambiguous discipline was
> strictly imposed. Merchants gathered from all sides, and all
> obtained the goods with which they wanted to return home.
> Thus the county became so prosperous that some of the best-off
> counties in Chiang-nan-tung may well have been ashamed in
> comparison. (372)

Official need for money, however, meant that there was always the likelihood of a local government lapsing into compulsory levy of taxes. The tax on commerce (shang-shui) was the principal source of revenue, but there were others, notably the salt tax (yen-k'o) and the wine tax (chiu-shui). Of lesser importance were such taxes as market cash (hsu-shih ch'ien), market-place tax (ti-p'u) and others all of whose incidence seems to have been local rather than general.

Larger market-towns contained a Market Controller (shih-ling-ssu), whose functions were derived from the former system of controlled official markets. Prices were fixed, and there were officials responsible for supervising the collection of various taxes and police inspectors (hsun-chien) in charge of preserving law and order. There is a passage on the latter in the Sung Digest for 1175:

> The authorities of Kuang-nan-hsi stated that there was a
> market called Ku-la which was situated between the prefectures
> of Yung-chou, Pin-chou, Hang-chou and Kuei-chou, being
> in close contact with the borders of all of them. Bandits
> came and went throughout the marketing area and there
> had previously been a police inspector there. They asked
> that this official should be restored, with the title of Joint
> Police Inspector for Pin-chou and Hang-chou, and that he
> should recruit a force with an established strength of fifty
> men and officers. This was approved. (373)

ii. Fairs in Kiangnan in Sung Times

Besides the markets described in the preceding section there were numerous fairs, usually known as 'temple markets' (miao-shih) because they were typically held in conjunction with some periodic religious celebration. Gatherings at the altars of the local spirits (she-hui), which had both a religious and a social character, besides serving as an occasion for plays and street-corner entertainments, as also Buddhist and Taoist gatherings (fo-hui, tao-hui), all served to assemble large numbers of people. Markets would be set up for the sale of incense, candles and ceremonial equipment, besides all kinds of ordinary goods. A notion of the scale of the expenditures sometimes involved is afforded by Li Yuan-pi's Guide to County Magistrates:

Many of the common people promote gatherings at the altars
of the local spirits. These are popularly said to be simply
for the purpose of ensuring protection for the farmlands,
the silkworms and the inhabitants, and also for praying for
good fortune and sacrificing to avert calamities. Sometimes
they further collect fixed contributions in cash and kind from
each member in order to have vessels and other such things
made, and presented to the monasteries and temples. The
activities may last for ten days in the month and interfere
with people's working lives. The poorest among them are
able to raise these donations only if they submit to being
fleeced by the pawnshops and fall into debt.

A report of 1214 given in the Sung Digest suggests the size of the
gatherings:

From the capital to the Chiang-Che region there are many
despicable aspects of present-day popular behavior which
demand watchful attention. Regular sacrifices are owing
to the altars of land and grain, but these days stupid people
bestow obsequious flattery upon the spirits and under the
title of a gathering at the local altar often collect large
crowds of idle rascals. (377)

Hung Mai noted that:

Tens of thousands of people attend the Taoist gatherings
and the seasonal gatherings at Ch'ing-ch'eng (in Szechwan).
The inhabitants of the county often therefore set up houses
at the foot of the hills in order to sell them tea and fruit. (377)

Finally, a passage in the Sung Digest from 1133 describes the theatricals:

The temple built in Ch'ü-chou to the God of Mount T'ai is
of a vast and imposing appearance. Whenever the people of the
prefecture celebrate the god's birthday, crowds collect for
days on end. They greet the deity with hundreds of plays. (378)

It seems probable, although there is no clear statement to this effect,
that commercial activities went on in the course of the meetings
described above. This is further confirmed by the existence of a joint
prohibition in the Yuan dynasty law code of religious gatherings of this
sort and trading.

In what follows, some of the fairs of Sung times, most of them connected with religious festivals, will be detailed one by one.

The Celebration of the Buddha's Birthday at the Pao-kuo, and later at the Wan-sui Monastery, in Fu-chou

This festival was inaugurated in 1082 and took place on the eighth day of the fourth month. Over 10,000 monks and nuns took part in it. A lottery was held with clothes, fans and medicines as prizes. In 1130 it came to an end temporarily, being revived in 1133 at the Wan-sui Monastery. More than 16,000 Buddhist priests attended the first meeting. Subscriptions were solicited from all and sundry, amounting to over 3,000 strings of cash a year. The festival ceased to function after 1168 when the entire annual collection was confiscated by the authorities for use in famine relief. After recording this event, the San-shan Gazetteer goes on to comment:

> However, the landless folk of the rural communities everywhere still have their own celebrations similar to this one, and these too are thronged with people. Advantage is taken of these occasions to make profits (i.e. to trade). They do not take place at any particular time of year, but usually last for two to three days. Sometimes they are held in people's homes, and sometimes in the temples to the local gods. The old men and women from the villages who turn up to take their ease, to eat and to gossip also number several hundreds. This custom is of recent date. (378)

In Fukien, and above all in Fu-chou, the majority of the surplus rural population became monks, and this was one of the reasons why monasteries engaged in commerce to supplement their incomes. Lotteries were also used to raise funds. According to the Yuan dynasty law code (T'ung-chih t'iao-ko):

> It is everywhere the custom in the newly-surrendered territory of Kiangnan for the monks of the monasteries to assemble crowds and to seek for profits by means of a lottery, the pretext given being the need to put up new buildings. They first prepare several tens of prizes and manufacture an enormous number of lottery slips. They

allocate these to powerful families, and entrust them with
the distribution and sale to others. A vast concourse of
participants allured by these means assembles on the
appointed day. Like clouds, people from far and near
gather in their thousands. Once the monks have been paid
for the lottery slips, they make them draw lots for the
prizes. The clamor and the coming and going fill the
streets. Very big profits are made. (378)

Presumably on occasions like this and the Buddha's birthday there
were markets set up for ceremonial and other goods.

The Festival for the Deliverance of Hungry Ghosts* at the Shen-kuan Monastery in Hou-kuan County, Fu-chou

The San-shan Gazetteer records that:

The monastery contains a statue of the Buddha entering the
state of Nirvana. The figures of ten disciples are ranged
at his sides, including Self-examination, Standstill, Weeping,
Laying Hand on Breast and Passing Hand over Feet in
Grief, Lamentation, and Crying Until Voiceless. On this
day (i. e. the 15th of the 7th lunar month) the Festival for the
Deliverance of the Hungry Ghosts is held. These strange
statues are an attraction to tourists and as a result a periodic
fair (hsu-shih) has come into being. It is traditionally called
'Waiting for the Buddha of the Dead'**.

By Ming times such annual fairs were moderately common in Fukien.

The Lantern Fair at the K'ai-yuan Monastery in Shao-hsing

According to the Gazetteer for Kuei-chi of the Chia-t'ai reign-
period (1201-1204):

---

*I. e. Ullambhana. Transl.
**The birthday of Kshitigarbha, Buddha of the Nether Regions, was
held on the thirtieth day of the seventh month and brought the Festival
to its end. Transl.

The K'ai-yuan monastery is located 2 li and 170 paces to the southeast of the prefectural offices. Every year, just before the fifteenth day of the first month, the Lantern Fair is held here. Merchants come from more than ten nearby prefectures and from beyond the seas. Jades, white silks, pearls, rhinoceros horns, renowned perfumes and precious medicines, silk damasks, and goods made of lacquer and of cane pile up like mountains or clouds, dazzling the eyes of the onlookers. Buddhist books, famous paintings, bells and tripods, ritual vessels, and amusing rarities also make their appearance here. The gentry consider that it is the equal of the Medicine Fair at Ch'eng-tu. (379)

This trade in luxury items probably grew up at Shao-hsing because the latter was midway between the consuming center of Lin-an (Hang-chou) and the seaport of Ming-chou (Ning-po).

The Birthday of the Hill-god at K'un-shan in Su-chou

According to The Yü-feng Gazetteer (Yü-feng chih) for the Shun-yu reign-period (1241-1252):

The Hill-god's birthday is on the fifteenth day (of the fourth month). The people of the county city welcome the god with Buddhist and Taoist celebrations at which prayers are offered for a fortunate year. All the locality cult groups hold a joint meeting to bid the god farewell. From the Shan-t'ang River to in front of the county city there are continuous rows of tents and lodges, all reds and kingfisher blues like a picture. The peddlers with goods on their backs from other prefectures form an unbroken line. (380)

The Buddhist Festival of the Five Intelligent Beings in Wu-yuan County, Hui-chou

According to Fang Hui, writing in the Yuan Dynasty:

Every year on the eight day of the fourth month the people from every quarter bestow their flattery on the Five Shining Spirits in a Buddhist Festival. Merchants from all over the Empire converge upon this place but, apart from the annual quota of official taxes, the State obtains nothing whatever from it. (380)

The Peak Fair in Heng-chou, Hunan

The Southern Peak was one of the Five Sacred Mountains of China*, and the Peak Fair at Heng-chou was associated with it. In Fan Ch'eng-ta's Travel Journal there is the following entry for the eighth of the third month, 1173:

> We entered the Southern Peak region. Stopped half-way for a rest and something to eat. For some thirty li the road was lined with ancient pine-trees. We came to the Peak Fair and lodged overnight at Heng-yüeh Monastery. The surrounding area is entirely given over to the fairground. Goods come here from Kiangnan, Liang-Che, Szechwan and Kuang-nan. There is nothing a mortal man needs that he cannot find here. The flux of people engenders filth, clamor and confusion. Many robbers and ruffians lurk here, or make the fair their meetingplace. The government has established a Police Inspector here. (381)

Hsing An-shih also has a description of people at this fair selling combs and medicines.

The Market at the Hsiang-kuo Monastery in K'ai-feng

This was held five times a month. An astonishing variety of goods were on sale in its various sections: birds and animals; boxes, mats, screens, basins, saddles, harness, bows, swords, fruits in season, salted and dried meats; crystallized fruits, writing-brushes and inks; embroidery work and other articles made by the nuns of the city's convents; books and paintings; local specialities, perfumes and medicines sold by transferred officials; and the services of fortune-tellers and street-corner performers.

The Fair at the Ch'ung-te Temple in Yung-k'ang-chün, Szechwan

Hung Mai describes the sacrifices made here as follows:

The Ch'ung-te Temple in Yung-k'ang-chün is the shrine of the God of Drains, ** canonized as the Pa-tzu wang. An official has been appointed to supervise this temple, as in

---

*See Werner 1932 (1961), pp. 578-580. Transl.
**On whom see Werner 1932 (1961), pp. 223-224. Transl.

the case of those of the Five Sacred Mountains. The people
of Szechwan serve him with great reverence. When the
seasonal offerings are presented, or prayers said for some
particular reason, the rich and the poor alike always slaughter
a sheep. Up to 40,000 of these beasts may be burnt in a
year. A tax of 500 cash is levied on each sheep passing through
the city, and an annual revenue of from 20,000 to 30,000 strings
of cash may be obtained. It is a source of limitless profit
for the state. (382)

Shih Chieh's eleventh-century Writings of Mr. Shih from the Ch'u-lai
Mountain (Shih Ch'u-lai wen-chi) contain a record of some remarks
made to the writer by an old man from this area:

Yung-k'ang adjoins the territory of the western barbarians.
All within the four seas are united, barbarians and Chinese
have dealings with each other, and thus more than a thousand
of these tribesmen may come to the Yung-k'ang fair in a
single day. (382)

The Medicine Fairs at Ch'eng-tu and Elsewhere

The peasants of the Szechwan/Hupeh border regions gathered
and processed materia medica during the winter as a subsidiary
occupation, selling their stocks to merchants in the spring and autumn.
The earliest medicine fair was that at Tzu-chou in T'ang times. During
the Sung dynasty, the most famous were the four held in Ch'eng-tu,
in all cases but one at monasteries, at various times of the year.
Medicine fairs also took place in many prefectural and county cities
in this region. There was also one at Hang-chou. Tu Cheng, who
flourished around the beginning of the thirteenth century, has left
these verses on the autumnal medicine fair in Ch'eng-tu:

Coming in a palanquin to visit the Medicine Fair,
Our bearers' knees are caught in the press of the crowd.
Little by little we inch our way up to the gate
Already surrounded by a diversity of goods.
Passing the arcades under a careful scrutiny,
There is such profusion it cannot all be detailed:
Orpiment, seeds of aconite piled on mats on the ground,
Ginseng and glutinous millet* waiting on tray after tray,

---

*Or, just conceivably, shu here means ts'ang-shu (Atractylis lancea,
ovata), another medicinal plant. Transl.

Mica and frankincense the color of sparkling crystal,
Aloes and sandalwood wafting their fragrant scents;
The river herbs (?) are thick and dense;
From the aquatic genera come leeches;
Some things are costly, such as cinnabar,
Others are cheap, dried lacquer for example,
Others yet are bitter, like sulphate of copper,
Or like rock-honey, sweet; and some are stale
Like pemmican and mince-meat pickled in brine;
Some fresh, like dates and chestnuts.
Many are products of barbarian tribes,
Yet all have come to answer China's needs.
Merchants have buffeted the sea-winds and the waves,
And foreign merchants crossed over towering crags,
Drawn onwards by the profits to be made,
Even in crises with no spare moment for a fearful thought.
Six thousand ounces of silver is the least they carry,
And sometimes as much as two thousand ounces of gold;
The fair begins in the earliest hours of morning,
And closes in the last hours of dusk.
Here are the rich and powerful with numerous bond-servants,
And gaunt old men leading their sons and grandsons,
Carriages and horses in grand array
Scattering in clouds of dust.
When evening comes they get completely drunk
And then go home, their bags and boxes bulging. (383)

Silkworm Fairs

Silkworm fairs were held in most silk-producing areas during
the first three months of the year to provide the peasants with the
resources and equipment needed for the coming year's sericultural
activities. These included trees, buildings, silkworm frames, caldrons,
medicines, silk-reeling machines and a variety of tools. Ch'en Yuan-
ching's A Record of the Year's Activities (Sui-shih kuang-chi) suggests
that the total cost of these might be from 1,000 to 10,000 strings
of cash. A passage describing silkworm fairs may be found on page
118 above.

Others

Ou-yang Hsiu mentions a 'barbarian market' (man-shih),
or perhaps 'fair', in I-ling in Hupeh, and also a 'year-end fair'
(la-shih) in the same area. A description of the former may be
found on page 122 above. Both of them seem to have been associated
with the somewhat primitive forms of worship which were still
prevalent at this time here.

Finally, it seems reasonable to suppose that, in addition
to the well-known or unusual fairs listed above, there were numerous
fairs held in conjuction with periodic religious celebrations in
local towns and villages, being distinguished from the ordinary
markets by their concentration on the specialized products that formed
the staple of long-distance rather than merely local trade.

V. THE DEVELOPMENT OF COMMERCIAL ORGANIZATION

1. BROKERS

i. The Types and Functions of Brokers

Niida Noboru has pointed out that, 'At the very least from the time of the Chin Dynasty (AD 265-419), goods being bought and sold were divided into two categories, those for which a particular legal form had to be followed (namely, reporting the transaction to the authorities and obtaining an officially sealed contract for which payment had been made (shui-ch'i)), and those for which this was not required. In the latter was included ordinary movable property; in the former, land and houses and important movable property such as slaves, oxen, horses and camels.' From a legal point of view, the most important service rendered by brokers (ya-jen, ya-pao-jen, ya-hang), was to mediate between the sellers and purchasers of land, houses, livestock and men, and to draw up a deed of sale. They also reported such transactions to the authorities, levied the tax on them known as 'brokerage and contract tax' (ya-ch'i shui) or 'brokerage tax' (ya-shui), and collected 'broker's cash' (ya-ch'ien) as a commission. Brokers who handled important movable property on which a sales tax was levied were known as 'official brokers' (kuan-ya), a category which included those dealing in land and houses, the 'brokers for manors and mansions' (chuang-chai ya-jen); and those concerned with ordinary movable property as 'private brokers' (ssu-ya). The significance of the distinctions made between these groups appears from the passages given in the following paragraph.

A decree of 926 cited in the Digests of the Five Dynasties (Wu-tai hui-yao) lays down that:

> In the markets of the capital for all sales of one item or more of silk thread, silk cloth, grain, firewood or charcoal (or 'coal') there are brokers. When common folk begin to bargain for the sale of these goods, they cause the price to soar upwards. The ordinary people suffer in consequence. Henceforth the order shall be given that in Lo-yang all brokerage shall be entirely forbidden, excepting only for real estate, human

beings, domestic animals and vehicles, sales of which need
to be authenticated by a broker, a requirement which should
not be suddenly removed. (392)

The section on 'Brokers who measure capacity, weight and length' in
the 'Prohibitions' of the Yuan Statutes (Yuan tien-chang) mentions that
the sheep brokers in the capital and 'the brokers in the provinces who
have to draw up contracts for the buying and selling of humans,
horses and real estate' were entitled by previously existing regulations
to take a commission of not more than 2 per cent, but that 'private
brokers' might not frame deeds of sale or collect broker's cash.
Hung Mai has a story that relates how an 'official broker' (kuan-k'uai)
was commissioned to draw up a deed of perpetual sale (tuan-ku ch'i)
for some farmland and houses. A law promulgated at the end of the
twelfth century states that:

> All persons who, being old, infirm or owing indemnification,
> shall act as brokers for manors and mansions, or likewise
> as private brokers, are to be given one hundred lashes. (393)

According to Li Yuan-pi's Guide to County Magistrates:

> Every single one of the brokers for manors and mansions in
> the towns and (administrative) villages shall be registered
> with the government and given a portable ledger. Whenever
> agricultural land is sold or mortgaged he shall at once enter
> the day and the month when the contract was concluded, and
> the sum paid. Every ten days he shall send the county magistrate
> the amount (of taxes) owed for these sales and mortgages,
> requesting the issue of official sealed contracts. Twice a
> month the ledger shall be sent to the county magistrate to be
> impressed with his seal. (393)

Such brokers also handled the renting out of houses.

There were special brokers for horses, cattle and human
beings, though under the Southern Sung brokers dealing in slaves
(sheng-k'ou ya) were prohibited. The buying and selling of free
persons was illegal, and particularly severely forbidden to incumbent
officials. The law seems nonetheless to have been quite frequently
broken. On cattle and horses, Li Yuan-pi has the following interesting
passage:

It is everywhere the custom in the countryside that when cattle
and horses are being sold that, once the deposit has been paid,
the animals are given to the purchaser and an oral agreement
concluded that they shall be given water and pasture for two
or three days on a trial basis. If, however, there is an
outbreak of illness and the stipulated period of days has
already elapsed, and the seller is unwilling to give way
(and annul the sale), then the officials are pestered to give
a decision in the matter. Now, both paying the price without
completing a contract and completing the contract without
paying the price are acts which reveal an ignorance of the
provisions of the law. ... It is necessary to record these here
in their entirety so that brokers dealing in cattle and horses,
and all the country villages, may know how to avoid giving
rise to lawsuits.

T'ang and Sung law insisted that a contract be made within three days
of payment being made for slaves or livestock, and made it lawful to
cancel this contract any time within three days after its completion
if previously present diseases were detected. Cattle brokers sometimes
also functioned as slaughtermen.

Brokers handled the hiring of personnel. Thus Yuan Ts'ai's
twelfth-century Domestic Duties (Yuan-shih shih-fan) speaks at one
point of 'compelling a broker to induce the wife of some free person
(liang-jen) to abandon her husband and children to suckle our babes.'
Elsewhere he says:

> For hiring a serving-wench one needs a broker to distinguish
> clearly (between candidates for the job). What is more, a
> broker should not cause one of his own family to pe rform
> this service. (395)

In the Dreams of the Glory of the Eastern Capital (Tung-ching meng-hua lu),
written by Meng Yuan-lao in the twelfth century, the author recalls that:

> For all hiring of laborers, managerial personnel, winesellers,
> restaurateurs and artisans there were Guild Heads (hang-lao)
> who would provide them. For the hire of women servants there
> were brokers providing introductions. (395)

In similar vein, Wu Tzu-mu's Dreaming of Splendor in the Midst of
Deprivation explains how in Hang-chou every conceivable sort and
variety of laborer, servant attendant and clerk 'all had their various
guild heads to introduce them,' and adds that, ' If one of them absconded
with (his employer's) property, there was a 'foot-warden' from the
man's home area and well acquainted with him, who would proceed to
track him down.' (395-6) There were official and private female
brokers (ya-sao) and introducers (yin-chih) who would negotiate the
sale of concubines, singing-lads, dancing-girls, kitchen wenches,
needlewomen and maids to officials and well-to-do families. For
those who had to travel there were 'guild heads specializing in travel'
(ch'u-lu lao-hang) who would hire porters and undertake to provide
the necessary services along the route.

There were also brokers who dealt in tea and salt, goods under
the control of official monopoly systems. After 1131, according to
the Sung Digest, the law was that tea merchants were to take their
certificates entitling them to purchase tea to a checking station
(ho-t'ung ch'ang) in a county town for verification, and would there
submit their request to buy baskets of tea. After this, they would go on
to a mountain tea station (shan-ch'ang), buy tea there from the tea-growers
(yuan-hu), return to the checking station to have their baskets checked
for weight and sealed, and then sell it. In fact, however, many of them
did not go back to the checking station but illegally sold at a cheap price
directly to 'brokers owning (water-driven) tea mills'. They would then
take their certificates back to the mountain tea station and buy more tea
from the tea-growers, a process which could be repeated indefinitely.
In the later twelfth century a tea-broker is said to have led a band of
tea-smugglers in Hunan. According to the thirteenth-century official
Hsu Lu-ch'ing, when the price of salt was high and there were no
purchasers, the authorities would allocate it to subordinate officials
who in their turn would assign it to brokers, and these last-mentioned
would see to its distribution through rogues drawn from both the
cities and the countryside. Clearly even the circulation of monopoly
products required the services of brokers.

There were also shops run by brokers, which suggests that
they sometimes acted as their own retailers. That they could play an
important part in co-ordinating production is indicated by the passage
from the Sung Digest quoted on page 114 above, and the case of Ch'en
T'ai recounted by Hung Mai. Ch'en used a network of brokers to collect

hemp cloth for whose production he had earlier advanced money, and
he provided them with funds to build large warehouses. In general,
brokers seem to have existed for almost every known commodity from
curios and perfumes to charcoal and sites for burial.

ii. The Roles Performed by Brokers

The degree of specialization on the part of brokers depended on
the level, in the overall marketing structure, of the particular market
in which they operated. Higher-level markets acted as centers of
collection and distribution for lower-level markets, as may be seen
from the remarks of Wu Tzu-mu on the rice market outside the newly-
opened gate in Hang-chou, quoted above on page 75 . Comparable
structures probably existed for other goods besides rice. A proclamation
in a mid-thirteenth-century gazetteer for the Nanking region is suggestive:

> According to the statement made by Chu Yü and other urban
> residents of Chü-jung county in this jurisdiction, this county
> is a hilly one without communications by means of boats.
> Within the city and its suburbs are many poor persons
> registered in the lowest category, all of whom work at
> selling a variety of commodities. They also go to the
> prefectural capital to be issued with their supplies, coming
> back afterwards to the county (capital). (398)

The smaller the market, the more likely a broker was to be engaged in
other activities than simply brokerage. He might be a broker who also
ran a hostel (tien-chu ya-jen), a retailer, a weights and measures
expert, or a tax-payment agent (lan-hu) for wealthy families.

While the expansion of long-distance trade was the primary
reason for the development of brokers of this sort, the importance of
regional disparities in prices, currencies and measures deserves a
mention. Thus in 1124 two values for the ounce of silver co-existed in
Kuang-nan and Hunan, namely the Kuang-nan value of 10 ch'ien to the
ounce and the T'an-chou measure of 13 ch'ien to the ounce. Similarly,
the hu used to measure government purchases of grain in P'ing-chiang
(130 ko), An-chi (110 ko), Lung-hsing (115 ko), Chi-chou (120 ko) and
T'an-chou (118 ko) was different in every single case. The official hu
legally prescribed by the Hall for the Manufacture of Imperial Luxuries

(wen-ssu yuan) was a mere 83 ko. Measures in private use also
fluctuated widely, as is indicated by Hung Mai's story of Chang Wu-san
and his thirteen different peck measures, given on pages 70-71 above.
According to a 'Discussion of Weights' written by Su Hsun, the father
of Su Tung-p'o, in the Northern Sung:

> These days the common peole cut notches in a piece of wood
> so that it resembles (the sections in) bamboo, twist a silken
> cord and hang a stone from it in order to make the weight
> and beam of a steelyard. * Rich and powerful merchants use
> a large measure when buying in and a small measure when
> paying out. If someone from Shantung were to go to Hupeh he
> would have no idea what constituted a peck or a measure of
> grain. If one compares the foot-rules used by the families
> to the East with those used by the families to the West, one
> finds them to be as (uneven as) the ten fingers of the hands. (400)

There were comparable regional variations in currencies. The notes
to a poem by Shu Yueh-hsiang on Lang-feng in T'ai-chou provide one
example of this:

> They use neither copper cash nor paper money, but all
> employ silver which is as thin as paper and broken up into
> pieces like stars. (401)

Different conventions for the number of cash in a nominal 'hundred'
were also common.

    Further complicating factors were the secret language and
specialists' jargon employed by merchants, and the use of bargaining
to settle the price. In A Further Collection of Miscellaneous Items
(Tsa-tsuan hsu), written in the twelfth century, Wang Chih offers the
following humorous glosses:

Without guarantee:	The solemn assertions of brokers
Hard to understand:	The market talk of agents
Impossible to fool:	Someone who really knows how to bargain
Incomprehensible:	The jargon of the various trades
Not to be trusted:	A seller's assertion when he asks the price
Unable to tell good from evil:	A man watching a beheading who says brokers are fine fellows (401)

*See the lower part of the illustration on the front cover. Transl.

In the Collected Materials on Relations with the Northern Tribes, Hsu
Meng-hsin cites for the year 1126 the record of an embassy by Cheng
Chih-wang in which he describes the process of bargaining:

> For instance, if someone is buying a length of silk, the
> seller will demand 3 strings of cash and the purchaser will
> reply with an offer of 2 strings and 500 or 600 cash. To
> this a further 100 or 200 cash will then be added, and the
> exchange takes place. This is what is called 'trading'. (401)

In so far as such practices were habitual, direct transaction between
producers and customers and even between merchants were rendered
that much more difficult.

Brokers had to be somewhat better instructed and more
resourceful than ordinary people. Hung Mai hints at this in his
account of a certain Wang Keng:

> He was not of a fully adequate standard in his scholarship
> and so he became a broker. He was deeply versed in the
> ways of the world and gifted at contriving plans. Whenver
> the people of his community desired anything, they would
> go to him and be told what means they should use. The rural
> population roundabout placed great confidence in him. (402)

Brokers normally engaged in the kind of business for which the relative
size of their capital resources best fitted them. This is well illustrated
by the story told by Hung Mai about a certain Mr. Chang from Hsing-chou
in present-day Hopeh. It was normally essential for a broker to be
able to pay, or to guarantee to pay, a travelling wholesale merchant
for all or part of a large consignment of goods (in this case 5,000 lengths
of hemp cloth), and then to sell them on credit to the local retailers.
It could happen that the brokers in a local market had too little capital
to discharge their function properly. One such case is described by
Wang Yen in a passage given on page 68 above. Complaints about the
way in which brokers controlled the markets and drove up prices are
illustrated by the passages from Chu Hsi on page 68 and the Chien-k'ang
gazetteer on page 76 .

A further reason for the spread of brokers was that the government
took no direct action to guarantee the fairness of business transactions,
promoting the broker system for this purpose instead. At the same time

it served fiscal ends, being a device for the collection of the brokerage and contract tax. Its general operation emerges clearly from Li Yuan-pi's Guide to County Magistrates:

> Most of the brokers handling trade connive with merchants who willfully try to evade the taxes on commerce. They should be made to summon two or three trustworthy guarantors, and also mutually to guarantee each other. Their names will then be entered in the government registers and they will each be given a wooden plaque, which they are to keep on their persons and by which they may be distinguished. Persons over sixty-nine years of age may not perform (broker's) functions. As usual proclamations shall be put up for the information of merchants. (403)

The conditions binding upon a broker were entered on his plaque, together with his name, as follows:

> Item. Not to deal in goods (requiring contracts) without obtaining an officially sealed contract and paying the tax.
> Item. If vendor and purchaser conclude a deal by personal negotiation, the broker is not to obstruct them.
> Item. The broker is not (willfully) to force up prices; nor when goods have been sold to him on credit is he to delay the merchant concerned (by withholding payment); and if, according to the regulations, goods are sold on credit with a time-limit set for payment, then an explicit contract must be made out and numerous reliable guarantors called in, so that whatever happens no lawsuit is provoked. (403)

This plaque, bearing these rules and impressed with an official seal, was to be shown beforehand to any merchant who wanted to do business with the broker. Finally, the following announcement was to be made to the proprietors of hostels for merchants:

> When travelling merchants sell their goods, they rely upon you gentlemen for a detailed explanation of the regulations in force. They are only permitted to deal with a broker who is registered and possesses a plaque. If, through your failure to explain this regulation to him, a merchant deals with a broker who does not have a plaque, and suffers loss of either money or goods in consequence, a severe sentence shall be inflicted upon his hostel proprietor. (404)

Some additional information on the type of credit transaction which was apt to cause trouble is given by a passage in the <u>Digests of the Five Dynasties</u> for 952:

> The prefect of K'ai-feng memorialized that merchants and all classes of persons had entered plaints that they had suffered from brokers and proprietors of merchant hostels having induced the common people to buy goods on credit and then having defaulted on payment by the time-limit specified. There had also been cases in which, after having taken the goods away, they had conspired with the brokers quite openly to cheat them out of these goods. (404)

The brokerage and contract tax due on sales of real estate, livestock and human beings was levied at the rate of 2 per cent of total value during the Later T'ang dynasty (923-935) and at 4 per cent during the Northern Sung and the early Southern Sung dynasties. Later it seems to have risen to over 10 per cent, and clearly constituted an important source of local government revenue. The rate at which the brokers' commission was levied may be deduced from the statement made by Wang Chih-tao given on page 74 above, namely, from 5 to 10 per cent assuming the price of a tenth of a picul of rice to have been 200 cash at this time, that is the early twelfth century, or from 10 to 20 per cent if the lower estimate of 100 cash per tenth of a picul is adopted.

2. THE ROLE OF LODGES FOR MERCHANTS, INNS-CUM-STORES, AND ESTABLISHMENTS FOR STOCKPILING AND STORAGE AS COMMISSION AGENTS AND WHOLESALING FIRMS

Some merchants combined brokerage functions with the operation of storehouses and hostels. They were the owners of the so-called lodges for merchants (k'o-tien), inns-cum-stores (ti-tien) and establishments for stockpiling and storage (t'ing-t'a). They were often entrusted by travelling merchants with goods to be sold, and likewise commissioned to buy goods, with the result that they also fulfilled the function of wholesalers. Already in T'ang times there had been hostels along the roads which provided travellers and merchants with coach-horses and provisions. The Sung dynasty witnessed the growth along the roads of commercial establishments, some of which even developed in time into villages or towns.

i. The Spread of Commission Agents

In the largest cities there were storage firms known as 'go-downs' (t'a-fang), some of them very large and specialized. The Splendors of the Capital (Tu-ch'eng chi-sheng) written by Nai-te weng (the nom-de-plume of a certain Mr. Chao) in 1235, describes those of Hang-chou in the following terms:

> Within the northern water-gate of the city there is a stream which flows for several tens of li (to the) Pai-yang Lake. Along its banks rich families have constructed several tens of go-downs, each of which contains over a thousand units of space, or at least several hundreds. They are used for the storage of goods belonging to the shops in the capital and to itinerant merchants. They are surrounded on all four sides by water, and can so avoid being set alight by the wind (blowing flames from other fires), besides resisting the depredations of robbers. They are a great convenience for the rich families in the capital. There are few such well-equipped warehouses in other prefectural capitals. * (408)

Wu Tzu-mu adds a few further details to this description:

> Month by month those who have established these go-downs demand from those who have leased space from them a sum of cash or paper money to meet the costs of administering and guarding the premises. They hire and maintain men to go round on patrols at night, so that there is no laxness in the precautions taken. (408)

It seems, from materials presented by Katō Shigeshi, that the owners of these storage facilities also undertook to lodge merchants and to handle the sale of their goods. This type of business was probably already officially recognized in T'ang times, or so it would appear from a decree of 809:

> Henceforth, if anyone uses short hundreds of cash in transactions, let the head of the guild concerned or a broker who is the proprietor of a lodge-cum-storehouse (chü-t'ing chu ya-jen)

---

*Cp. A. C. Moule, Quinsai, with Other Notes on Marco Polo (Cambridge: C. U. P. , 1957) p. 24.

look into the matter and send him to the authorities. If they
tolerantly conceal this practice, then the vendor of the
goods and the recipient of the money shall also be permitted
to lay a plaint; and the head of the guild and the proprietor/
broker shall be punished with doubled severity. (410)

In the local markets there were also warehousemen and
innkeepers who served as commission agents and wholesalers. They
were to be found in the prefectural and county capitals, at the relay
stations of the state postal service (i-p'u), at fords and at official
stations for the conduct of frontier trade (chüeh-ch'ang). An interesting
example is that of Ho Ming-yuan, a wealthy inhabitant of Ting-chou
in the T'ang dynasty, who is said by Li Fang's Miscellaneous Records
Collected During the T'ai-p'ing Reign-period to have been in charge of
three postal relay stations, to have set up lodges for merchants
beside them, and to have had in his own home 500 looms for silk
damask, by means of all of which he became exceedingly wealthy.
Another instance is provided by Hung Mai's story, given on page 82
above, of a visiting merchant buying hemp seed oil through a local
innkeeper. On the main routes these inns and the county cities, taken
together, would seem to have been spaced out at intervals of between
five and ten miles. The Yuan Statutes contain provisions which
give some idea of the overall density:

> The prefectural and county capitals are located far distant
> from each other. In those villages and settlements around
> inns which lie between them every 50 to 70 li (17 to 23 miles),
> and in which there are twenty families or more, archer patrols
> shall be set up. ... Where they do not amount to twenty
> families, the difference shall be made up. Where there are no
> villages or settlements around inns every 50 to 70 li, villages
> and inn-settlements shall be founded, likewise being made to
> amount to twenty households. The patrolmen established
> there shall be separate, and not count in the number of
> households. At passes, fords and ferries, inns must be set
> up and archers installed, without any reference to the 50 to
> 70 li limit. (411)

The section on the issuing of proclamations in Li Yuan-pi's Guide to
County Magistrates throws further light on the importance of these
inns:

In each of the large and small market towns and in each of
the numerous outlying towns, riverine ports, country villages
and inns, one copy should be posted up. Furthermore, a
printing-block in small type should be made, and whenever a
village elder visits the county city for an overnight stay,
he should be given a copy and told to make it widely known. (412)

Inns for merchants were sometimes found in ordinary villages. Thus
Hung Mai tells us of a certain Mr. Mu who 'lodged overnight in a small
village in an inn which had only one room.' As mentioned on page 130
above, it was the duty of village elders to inform the magistrate about
the lodges for merchants in their area, and any changes which took
place regarding them. Significantly, in 1169, 'establishments for
stockpiling and storage', 'shops' and 'work premises and marketing
arcades' (fang-lang) were added to the list of taxable sources of
non-agricultural rural income (on which see page 28 above).

Speculative purchase of goods in bulk was the main business
of the owners of large storage facilities in the local cities. A brief
reference to investment in such stockpiling and storage may be found
in the passage from Hsu Meng-hsin's Collected Materials on Relations
with the Northern Tribes given on page 32 above. The urban
landlord Cheng Pao-yung, described by his great-great-grandson
Cheng Hsieh in a passage translated on pages 131 and 132 above, made
a business of accepting other people's money on deposit. Liao Kang,
in the work cited on page 69 above, mentions the way in which
storehouse owners bought up large amounts of rice as it come onto
the market. Chu Hsi's strictures on the powerful families who made
huge purchases of rice, given on page 71 above, probably refer to
the same phenomenon.

ii. The Functions of Commission Agents and Wholesalers

The Guide to County Magistrates contains the following
instructions to be proclaimed to the proprietors of merchant hostels:

Item. Each hostel shall regularly keep two or three of its
best rooms sprinkled, swept and spread with fresh, clean
matting to await the exclusive use of officials and holders
of a degree won in the imperial examinations.

Item. When officials or degree-holders are residing at the
hostel there shall be no hubbub or improper behavior.
Item. If a travelling merchant remains in residence for
many days, so becoming somewhat the object of suspicion,
and uses his money in unreasonable ways without a sense
of what is suitable, or if there are any persons the purpose
of whose actions is not apparent, then the innkeeper should
secretly report them to the authorities or to the officers
nearby in charge of catching robbers.
Item. If a merchant falls ill and is unable to proceed on his
way, the innkeeper shall, at his convenience, report the
matter to the heads of the administrative village and their
constables. A nearby doctor shall be summoned to examine the
sick man, and to write out a diagnosis on the same day for
submission to the county magistrate. If the heads and the
constables pick up an ill person on the road and lodge him at
an inn, he too must be examined according to this
procedure, so that nothing needful is overlooked. Once
his condition is relatively better, he shall visit the county
magistrate's office together with the heads and constables
to provide witness on the basis of which money or goods may
be given to the proprietor of the inn and the doctor.
.... . [As on page 172 above]
Item. They should explain to travelling merchants that before
they sell goods on which a tax is payable they should first
go to the tax-office, pay the tax and receive a sealed contract,
so that they avoid being blackmailed out of goods or cash by the
threats of unprincipled rogues. What is more, if they do so
this will ensure a plentiful revenue for the local tax-office.
Item. They should explain to the travelling merchants that
the brokers are not to be trusted. They will talk them into
raising their prices and selling on credit, after which there
will be delays and no payment will materialize. It is much
better to sell at a low price for ready cash. If, in accordance
with the old practice, purchases are made on credit, there
must be reliable guarantors and an explicit contract. (414)

In fact, however, many inn proprietors also doubled as brokers. Thus
Ch'en Yuan-ching observed in his Extensive Record of the Forests of
Affairs (in the passage quoted on page 31 above) that when hiring a
boat the services of 'a broker who is the master of a shop or a lodging-
house' (tien-chu ya-chia) were necessary.

On the activities of storehouse and inn owners as commission agents, the following account written around the end of the twelfth century by Liao Hsing-chih and included in his Works from the Studio of Perception (Hsing-chai chi) is illuminating:

> Just recently there was an inn on a road in Pa-ling (Yueh-chou in Hunan) which was one evening gutted by fire. Travelling merchants had entrusted their goods to its proprietor to hawk around and so, when it happened to burn down, the prefect suspected foul play. He ordered an investigation, and fish-glue was found scattered among the ashes. It was estimated that there still remained several hundred catties which the fire had spared. When enquiries were made as to the reason for this it was learned that the merchants had been coming from Ning-po and were on their way to Hsiang-chou. (416)

Inn proprietors and brokers with storehouses were also commissioned by merchants to buy up goods on their behalf, and sometimes advanced the necessary funds. A case in point is Ch'en T'ai, the hemp cloth merchant, whose activities are described on page 168 above.

iii. Tax Contractors

A special type of broker was the agent for paying in taxes (lan-hu). Sometimes he would use his own capital to ensure that payment was made on time, and then charge heavy interest for this service. This practice is alluded to by Yuan Ts'ai:

> Inevitably, if one owns property, one has to pay taxes. It is essential, therefore, to set aside a portion of one's funds in advance for paying them, allocating the remainder for everyday expenditures. If the harvest is a poor one, the only proper course is to make economies. One should not encroach on the tax-payment funds. Otherwise, when the time for payment approaches and one is hard pressed by the officials, one will either have to take out a loan at interest, or entrust a tax-payment agent with paying them, reimbursing him at a heavy price. Both of these are means whereby a family's substance may be dissipated. (417)

In the thirteenth century Yuan Fu described how in Hui-chou the tax
payment agents would push up their price when receiving their
commissions from the households owing tax but, when they were
buying the silk required from the weavers, would haggle the price
down and buy coarse sub-standard silk that was almost unsaleable.
They were able to pay in these inferior articles by taking advantage of
the government's need to send off the tax-quota quickly. An entry in
the Sung Digest for 1154 states that the tax-paying agents would sometimes
form alliances with officials, with the consequence that the latter would
accept the inferior silks proffered by the agents but judge those paid
in directly by ordinary households to be deliberately sub-standard and
therefore smear them with persimmon oil and ink, while even articles
that did come up to standard would be made to be paid in at double the
proper rate. The Record of Essential Events Across the Years After
the Chien-yen Reign-period says, with reference to 1135, that the
government compulsorily purchased 4,400-odd piculs of rice in Hu-chou
every month for army supplies, but paid only 300 cash for one-tenth of
a picul, so that the tax-paying agents had to levy the money needed over
and above this amount before they could supply the full quantity. The
Sung Digest also states, with regard to 1162, that the manner in which
the poll-tax silk (shen-ting chüan) was levied as one whole piece for
every four or five men caused such difficulties for the peasants in the
more remote villages of Hu-chou that they had to entrust the task of
making payment to agents, and suffered financially in consequence. (418)

It was illegal for lower-level local government personnel
(kung-jen) to act as tax-payment agents, and if upper-level local
government personnel (li-jen), village tax-records secretaries
(hsiang shu-shou) or grain-tax receivers (chuan-tou) did so they were
not supposed to accept any renumeration in cash or kind for their
services. The laws of the Southern Sung dynasty prescribed flogging
and even exile for tax-payment agents who failed to pay on time.

The analysis presented in the preceding pages may be
expressed in the form of the following diagram:

180

Figure II   The Place of Brokers, Owners of Storage Facilities,
Innkeepers and Tax-Contractors in the Commercial Structure

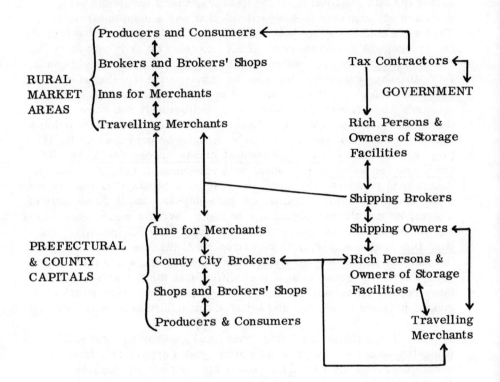

VI. THE CHARACTERISTICS OF COMMERCIAL CAPITAL

1. THE SOCIO-ECONOMIC BACKGROUND OF THE ACTIVITIES
   OF THE FUKIENESE MERCHANTS OF SUNG TIMES - A CASE STUDY

Fukienese merchants only became of importance in the world
of commerce during and after the Sung dynasty. The main reasons for
this were the growing surplus of population relative to cultivable land
in the province, and the impulse provided by contact with new commercial
opportunities.

Prior to the T'ang dynasty, Fukien had been an independent
and little civilized region cut off from the North China plain by
natural barriers. Within the next three or four hundred years, however,
this situation was rapidly reversed. Fukien came to occupy a leading
cultural and economic position in South China. The immediate reasons
for this change were the stimulus provided by long-distance trade and
the development occasioned by the southwards migration of Northern
Chinese. Fukienese coastal trading became active towards the end of
the T'ang dynasty, and during the period of the Five Dynasties the State
of Min used the formal structure of tributary relations to develop a public
and a private trade with the dynasties ruling in North China. In 1087
a Superintendency of Foreign Trade (shih-po ssu) was set up in Ch'üan-chou,
and by Southern Sung times this port had become, both in name and
reality, the linch-pin of trade with Southeast Asia. Fukienese pre-eminence
in shipbuilding at this time may be inferred from the passage by Lu
I-hao quoted on page 6 above, and Fukienese navigational skill from
the passage written by Liao Kang on the occasion of his assumption of
official duties in Chang-chou on the southeastern Fukien coast, and
given on page 9 . The province's quota for the tax on commerce increased
from about 130,000 strings of cash at the beginning of the dynasty to
about 240,000 strings in 1077.

The influx of migrants from the North which began in the
middle of the T'ang period contributed to the cultural development of
the province and by Sung times it was producing more holders of the
metropolitan doctorate than any other, and also numerous high officials
who built up Fukienese power in the central government by means of
mutually recommending one another. Fukienese scholarship held a
leading position. According to the Yuan official and teacher Wu Ch'eng:

A high regard among the Fukienese for the metropolitan
doctorate began with the people of Ch'üan-chou; and from
them culture diffused and spread until by the end of the Sung
dynasty Confucian mores were more highly developed in
Fukien than anywhere else in the Southeast.   (424)

Lin Shang-jen observed that:

Just as the 'seven provinces' of Fukien excel in their
scenery so too do the people surpass others in talent...
and therefore half of those in the Empire who put their
satchels on their shoulders and come to take the examinations
at the capital are customarily Fukienese.   Families have
schools where instruction is given; the people are imbued with
the good influence of the Book of Odes and the Book of Documents.
Half of those who hold positions at Court and wait upon the
Emperor, being officials who enjoy an intimate relationship
with him, and of those who go out to govern the provinces,
holding the imperial commission and occupying office, are
likewise regularly Fukienese.   (424)

Chu Hsi and others remarked on the flourishing state of Fukienese higher
education and Fang Ta-tsung had this to say about the general level of
literacy among the people:

In my own county (of Yung-fu) every family is adept at music
and the chanting of texts.   People know the laws; and this
is true not only of the scholars; every peasant, artisan and
merchant teaches his sons how to read books.   Even
herdsmen and wives who bring food to their husbands at work
in the fields can recite the poems of the men of ancient times. (423)

This advanced educational level was of great importance for the formation
of the Fukien merchant class.

A shortage of arable land was a basic constraint on the
province's agriculture.   Double-cropping was practised in the warm
coastal regions, but this provided at best a partial answer from which
not too much could be expected.   Rather, the land in the hilly prefectures
of the interior was utilized to the utmost.   Terracing is referred to by
several authors.   Thus according to Fang Cho, whose From the Anchored
Dwelling (Po-tse pien) was written early in the twelfth century:

> The land in the 'seven prefectures' of Fukien is limited
> in extent and not very fertile. Rivers and springs are shallow
> and remote. The people work extremely hard but the means
> by which they make their living are inferior to those
> anywhere else. Rich persons open up terraces on the hills
> for cultivation, and these rise level upon level like the
> steps in a staircase. (425)

Chu Mu's Triumphant Vision of the World quotes a poem on Chien-ning
prefecture as saying:

> There is no drop of water that they do not use,
> Farming the mountains even to their summits. (427)

Cultivation was labor-intensive, and advanced techniques were
employed, but there was a limit to what could be achieved by these
means, and even the rich in Fukien were much less well off than their
counterparts in Chekiang and the lower Yangtze region. Agriculture
offered little scope for development and demand for land pushed its
price up to the point where it was apparent that there was a limit to
the amounts that could usefully be invested in it. People were induced
to turn to commercially-orientated farming or to take up non-agricultural
pursuits. Fang Ta-tsung (page 54 above) mentions fish-ponds, and the
cultivation of rice with a high gluten content suitable for the manufacture
of wine, and of sugar-cane. Melons, oranges, plums and timber were
grown for sale, and so were lychees, as is indicated by the quotation
from Ts'ai Hsiang given on page 88 above. Wine was fermented
and Fukien tea was renowned throughout China. The Gazetteer for
Kuei-chi in the Chia-t'ai reign-period (1201-1204) mentions that,
'These days the men of Yueh (Chekiang) wear clothes of pueraria
fiber cloth that comes from Fukienese merchants.' (426) In Ch'üan-chou
cotton was grown, and further supplies were imported from Hai-nan
Island. Cloth was woven and exported to Kuang-chou. The shipping
and sale of Fukienese iron and ironware to Kiangsu and Chekiang is
described in the passages from the San-shan Gazetteer and the Continued
Gazetteer for Ssu-ming given on pages 123-124 above. Chien-chou
produced silks, porcelain, paper and books; Ch'üan-chou paper and
tortoise shell combs. Fu-chou made a widely-sold cloth and lampshades;
while Min county in Fu-chou manufactured straw matting, some of which
was sold to Kiangsu and Chekiang for use as salt sacks. Fukien also
served as the main commercial entrepot for goods coming to China from

Southeast Asia.   Markets and fairs became widespread phenomena,
and the passage from Fang Ta-tsung cited on page 153 above is
testimony to the diffusion of an exchange economy among the
peasantry.

The extension of this exchange economy led to rising prices,
increasing consumption, and a mood of extravagance which was further
fostered by the popularization of the Buddhist religion.   Ts'ai Hsiang
felt obliged to utter a warning against the exorbitant expenditures and
the excessive debts incurred in the country villages on the occasion of
coming-of-age ceremonies (when youths attained twenty Chinese years
of age), marriages, funerals and festivals.   Changes in class relationships
also took place, as the San-shan Gazetteer reveals:

> It is the custom of Fukien to treat New Year's day as the
> greatest of the festivals. ... From the degree-holding
> gentry downwards, the scholars, rich commoners, government
> clerks, merchants, and government runners all used to observe
> a sequence of gradations in their dress, which no one dared to
> transgress, be it even so slightly.   Scholars wore caps and
> sashes, or sometimes capacious gowns of a dull brown
> color; rich commoners and clerks wore black gowns; and
> peasants, traders and households in the lower grades of
> registration wore gowns of white hemp cloth.   Married women
> who were not the wives of officials did not dare to put on the
> ceremonial collar; and those who did not belong to great
> families did not venture to wear caps or sleeveless jackets.
> These were the customs thirty years ago, and no one dared to
> change them in the smallest degree.   It was the same with terms
> of address.   A person from the scholar class who did not in fact
> study would not be termed a 'cultivated talent'.   In great
> households the father (tieh) would be called 'father' (fu) and
> mother (niang) 'mother' (mu), while the male and female serfs
> and those below them would style these persons 'lord'
> (lang-chün) and 'lady' (niang).   Peasants, traders and households
> in the lower categories would call males senior to them (pa)
> 'father' (fu) and women senior to them (nai) 'mother' (mu).
> Their equals and below they would address as 'uncle' (shu-po)
> or 'aunt' (sao).   These fine distinctions were extremely strict.
> Even if people became suddenly rich or suddenly poor, no
> changes were permissible.   Status divisions were thus

established from of old, and the salutations and obeisances
at the various seasons of the year might be observed to follow
a regular order. Over the last thirty years these distinctions
of rank have gradually disappeared, and this has been most
particularly the case during the last five years. Peasants,
traders and humble folk even wear Taoist dress, sleeveless
jackets and purple gowns, while their wives even wear
sleeveless jackets and ceremonial collars. Terms of address
are likewise quite different from those previously in customary
use. (428)

Ts'ai Hsiang observed that, 'It is human nature for everyone to desire
riches. Even peasants, artisans and merchants all scheme away night
and day in search of profit,' and it was increasingly agreed that a
desire for wealth was both natural and acceptable. This was reflected
in the sharing out of the inheritance before the death of the father
and the mother, a practice known as 'distribution while alive' (sheng-fen)
and subject to a taboo but nonetheless widespread, and in infanticide,
which was illegal but still prevalent in the hill regions. It was also to
be seen, in a more muted fashion, in the out-migration of Fukienese
farmers, especially to Kuang-nan. Wang Hsiang-chih, in his Geography
of the Empire, quotes another source as saying that in Mei-chou in
present-day Kwangtung:

> There is plenty of land in the prefecture, but the people are
> idle and few of them work at agriculture. They rely entirely
> on migrants from T'ing-chou and Kan-chou to do the farming. (430)

Many peasants went into other occupations. Wang Ying-chen,
who was the assistant prefect of Chien-chou for a time in the later
twelfth century, observed that:

> In Fukien the land is restricted and the population dense.
> People give birth without limit, and since the number of
> persons has multiplied in this fashion, when there are three
> adult males in a family, generally one or even two of them
> will abandon secular life and enter a Buddhist or Taoist
> monastery. (429)

Liu Yen had written in a similar vein in the later eleventh century:

Fukien is bounded on either side by southern Chekiang and
P'an-yü (the Canton region). The dense population exerts
pressure on the land. The men are well-endowèd with
ability and struggle to better themselves. Thus five or six
out of ten regularly attain the rank of scholar and a further
one in five becomes a follower of the Buddha. (429)

Tseng Feng, an official of the mid-twelfth century, noted that:

Everywhere these days there are persons leaving agriculture
to become scholars, Taoists, Buddhists or professional
entertainers; but those from Fukien are the most numerous.
The land of Fukien is cramped, and inadequate to feed and
clothe them, so they scatter to all the four quarters. For
this reason wherever studying goes on, there Fukienese
scholars will be found. Wherever there are Buddhist or
Taoist halls there will be Fukienese Taoists and Buddhists.
Wherever there are markets there will be Fukienese professional
entertainers. More and more of them every day spread all
across the country, yet those living in Fukien never grow
any fewer. The explanation for all this is the following:
when men are few then success is easy; and when men are
numerous then success is difficult. When it is easy because
(competitors) are few, even if fortune has only endowed one
with mediocre talents, one can still spread one's wings;
but in the case of difficult circumstances because of numerous
(competitors) it is only if one has skills that greatly exceed
those of others that one will obtain success. Thus of those
whom the Empire knows as scholars, Taoists, Buddhists and
professional entertainers, the Fukienese are the most skillful.
The reason is that there are many of them (in their homeland)
and it is difficult for them (to make the grade). Among many,
it is easy not to compete and hard to compete; and amid
difficult circumstances not to compete is the mark of the
maladroit and to compete the sign of the skillful. Some have
obtained success without having skill, but those who are skillful
have always obtained it. Therefore those Fukienese who are
professional entertainers have no rivals when they tour the
mansions of the great and the central markets; those who are
Taoists and Buddhist monopolize the famous mountains and
important centers; while those who are scholars are pre-eminent
in promotions in the state examinations. (429)

Taoists made a subsidiary business out of selling incense and drugs, and Buddhist monks also engaged in commerce.

Commercialization spread throughout society. For the upper levels, the following remarks by Chu Mu on Shao-wu prefecture may be instanced:

> If a family has surplus funds, they will regularly take them to distant places and trade in other prefectures. (429)

For the lower levels, Chu's observations on Ch'ang-lo county are pertinent:

> Among the criss-crossing lines of the market-place there are more stalls run by women than by men. (429)

Ch'en P'u, a scholar who lived at the end of the Southern Sung and the beginning of the Yuan, wrote in a piece on the women of Ku-t'ien county that:

> (The married women) stick flowers in their hair and act as brokers. They have the reputation of dominating the markets in the county city. They sit in the rows of shops and comb their hair, their laughing chatter all deception judged to suit the moment. They put on fine clothes in the most outre fashions and come to agreements among themselves to keep prices up. The stupid laborers and simpleminded serfs receive outrageous treatment at their hands with hanging heads. Such is our Fukien! (429)

It was Su Tung-p'o's opinion that, 'The entire province of Fukien makes its living by the practice of sea-borne commerce.' Its merchants ranged from Kuang-nan, Liang-Che, Shantung and Chien-k'ang (Nanking) to Korea, Japan and places in Southeast Asia such as Champa and Java. * The Sung History's chapter on Korea states that:

> There are several hundred Chinese in the (Korean) capital, most of them Fukienese who have come by junk for the purposes of trade. (The Koreans) secretly try out their abilities and entice them with salaries and official positions. (430)

---

*On pages 431 and 432 of the original work there are tables showing the occasions when Sung merchants who visited Japan or Korea may clearly be identified as Fukienese. Transl.

In comparable fashion the <u>Continuation of the Comprehensive Mirror</u> mentions a decree of 1076 that states:

> Men from Fukien and Kuang-nan go to Vietnam for purposes of trade. Sometimes we hear that some of them have remained there to serve as officials. (432)

It may be significant that one tradition has it that the Vietnamese royal house was of Fukienese descent.

Overseas shipping ventures might be managed by one wealthy businessman on his own, either as the owner of the ship and the cargo, as in the case of Fo-lien, the Moslem from Ch'üan-chou who owned eighty sea-going vessels, or as owner of the ship, captain, and owner of the cargo, as in the case of Yang K'o from the same city who had amassed 200,000 strings of cash in the course of ten years as a sea-faring merchant. Collective financing and management, according to some variety of either the <u>societas maris</u> or the <u>commenda</u>, were also common, as may be seen from the passages by Chu Yü on page 15, Ch'in Kuan on page 27 and Pao Hui on page 33. A measure of government control was imposed on ventures overseas. Thus a decree of 1094 laid it down that:

> The Department of State, Imperial Secretariat, Imperial Chancellery and Bureau of Military Affairs proposed that when merchants went trading across the seaways they should write out a list of the persons, ships, kinds and quantities of goods and the destination involved, which should then be submitted through the prefectural authorities. Those who were going to Korea should be required to have a capital of at least 30 million strings of cash, and the number of boats should not to be allowed to exceed two. As before, they would be required to return by the following year. They were to call upon three rich persons of the same place of origin to furnish them with guarantees. (433)

Under the Yuan, official capital was also invested in overseas trading expeditions.

Fukienese merchants, managers, fortune-tellers and professional entertainers also spread out along the land routes both North and South. According to Wang Hsiang-chih's <u>Geography of the Empire:</u>

Nine out of ten pawnbrokers in Hua-chou (in Kwangtung) are
Fukienese. The Fukienese resolutely put their empty hands to
work, and those who come south over the mountains often
become rich. (434)

The significance of the activities of the Fukienese merchants
and their socio-economic background becomes clear when these are
considered against the overall picture of change in Fukienese society
at this time.

2. THE CHARACTERISTICS OF COMMERCIAL MANAGEMENT

The terms 'manager' (kan-yun, kan-jen) and 'agent/broker/
petty trader' (ching-chi, ching-chi-ken) frequently appear in T'ang and
Sung historical records. Their original meaning was simply 'a person
who takes charge', and they were generally applied to the head of the
family or some relative or guardian who showed skill in the direction
of a family's affairs. In the course of time they also acquired the
more specific sense of someone who made the management of a business
his profession, or a broker. Even in this latter sense, however, the
terms had become obsolete by Ch'ing times, as may be inferred from
A Collection of Customs (T'ung-su pien) written by Chai Hao in the
eighteenth century:

> Note. 'Agent' has the sense of 'manager'. In times past
> they referred to the practice of commerce as 'acting as an
> agent/broker/petty trader.' (438)

A detailed account of the problems faced by an upper-class
family in its selection of managers is given in the Description of Domestic
Duties (Yuan-shih shih-fan) compiled by Yuan Ts'ai in the twelfth century:

> The manager who is in charge of the treasury should pay
> constant and careful attention to his accounts, and watch the
> balance in hand. The manager who is in charge of the grain
> and rice should keep meticulous records and maintain a
> scrupulous guard over his keys. One should also select
> conscientious persons to serve as watchmen. One should
> choose as one's manager to be entrusted with funds for the
> practice of commerce someone who is possessed of integrity
> and parsimonious in his family expenditures. The reason for
> this is that even families of moderate means still have

difficulties in meeting their everyday costs. Even more
does this apply to those who are hired by others. How can
they adequately deal with hunger and with cold? It is the
nature of a person of intermediate status that if he sees
something desirable he will be thrown emotionally and
mentally off balance. These considerations apply even more
forcefully to ignorant persons from the lower classes. How
can the attractions of wine, food, music and fornication fail
to exercise their influence over him? If someone who has
hitherto had insufficient money to satisfy his wishes, and has
repressed his desires, sharing hunger and cold at home
together with his relatives, and when away from home looking
on what he sees as though he did not see it, now has money
and goods in profusion before his eyes, then, even if he is
strict and careful every day, his (scrupulous) attitude of mind
will in the course of time be lulled to sleep. If his master
acts a little laxly, he too will have no compunction about
failing in his duty. To begin with, so long as his misappropri-
ations are extremely small, he imagines that he can make
them good again and so still feels no anxiety. If over a long
period his master shows no awareness of what is happening
then he will increase (his depredations) day by day and month
by month until after a year has elapsed they have become
substantial. Although he feels disturbed and unhappy, he has
no alternative but to seek to conceal them. After two or three
years he will have embezzled so much that tell-tale signs will
be impossible to hide. His master will want to inflict harsh
punishment upon him, and it will be all but too late for him to
repent. For these reasons, whenever one entrusts one's
affairs to managers, one has to take precautions against this
happening. (439)

Managers were thus able persons, without wealth of their own in most
cases, who were employed by others in the capacity of agents, stewards
or servants.

Managers' status vis-à-vis their masters varied. The well-to-do
sometimes had managerial serfs (kan-p'u) who handled for them such
matters as tax-payments, the collection of rents and even the management
of their personal funds generally. This was true both of manors and of
trade. Thus Han Yuan-chi wrote a piece entitled 'On Merchants' in the
twelfth century in which he observed:

It is the custom of Yueh (i. e. Chekiang) to be fond of trading.
There was a great merchant who in nearly ten years of
business had amassed a vast fortune, after which he no longer
engaged in commerce. He then deliberated as follows:
'I am beyond doubt a merchant, and it is hardly possible
now for me to abandon commerce or forget it. Although I
have become old and have to sit at home, even if I am
incapable of being a merchant myself, why shouldn't I send
my son to trade in my place?' But, since his son lacked
the capacity to do a merchant's work, he summoned one of
his serfs and taught him about commercial matters. He
watched how the serf conducted himself and, placing ever
greater confidence in him, entrusted him with everything. (441)

Other managers were professionals. Some even owned their own land
and had their own managers subordinate to them (known as t'a-ch'uang-erh).
Hung Mai describes the following case of a professional commercial
manager:

Shen Shih-meng from Tsao-yang (in Hupeh) had a reputation
as a manager of commercial affairs throughout Kiangnan,
Hunan and Hupeh. The wealthy Mr. P'ei sought and obtained
his services, making him extremely welcome and entrusting
him with a capital of 100,000 strings of cash with which he
was allowed to do as he liked. Within three years Shen had
doubled this sum, and gave the profit to his employer. He
then further increased the total to 300,000 strings. When old
Mr. P'ei died a few years later, Shen went to Lin-an to
mourn him, and as before to return the funds. P'ei's sons
gave him thirty per cent of it, which amounted to 20,000
ounces of silver. (442)

Nonetheless, a certain element of serf-like status seems to have
inhered in the position of managers in most cases.

This is also evident in a form of borrowing closely akin to the
management of a master's funds, the characteristic feature of which
was that the profits were shared equally. According to the Sung author
Lien Hsuan:

The Chang family of Ta-t'ung (in K'ai-feng) held a leading
position in the capital on account of their wealth. It is
general practice for the rich to entrust their money to others,
to calculate the profit gained therefrom and to take half of
this sum, a practice known as 'putting one's money to use'
(hsing-ch'ien). The rich regard those who borrow on these
terms (hsing-ch'ien) as equivalent to semi-servile retainers
(pu-ch'ü). If it so happens that they have to go past a borrower's
house they are installed in a position of honor and wine is
set before them. The married women emerge and urge them
to drink, while the host will stand and wait upon them. The
rich will politely decline, and only after having been forcefully
urged two or three times will (the host and his wife) dare to
take their seats. The son of the Chang family was a young man
whose father and mother had died, leaving him in charge of
his family's affairs before he had yet married. Having gone
to sacrifice at the Drain-god's shrine west of the prefectural
capital, he returned past the house of Sun Chu-chiao, who had
borrowed money from him on a profit-sharing basis. Sun set
several rounds of wine before Chang and his as yet unmarried
daughter came out to urge Chang to drink. She was of an
extraordinary beauty, and Chang gazed at her and said, 'I should
like to make her my wife.' Sun became alarmed at this and
expressed the view that it was not possible, adding: 'I am
Your Honor's serf. The neighborhood would laugh at the oddity
of a serf becoming his lord's father-in-law.' 'Not so,' replied
Chang; 'I have merely troubled you with a little of my money
and goods. How can you venture to liken this relationship to
the subjection of a serf?' ... . (442)

A person borrowing money on a profit-sharing basis might sometimes
hold a powerful position with many men under his orders. Hung Mai
recounts the following story:

Wang Yuan-mao was a Ch'üan-chou man. In his youth he
worked as a mere handyman in a Buddhist monastery. His
masters taught him how to read the books of the southern
barbarian lands, with all of which he was able to become closely
acquainted; and he accompanied sea-going junks to Champa.
The king of that country admired his ability to read both
barbarian and Chinese books, invited him to become a member
of his staff, and gave him one of his daughters in marriage.

Wang lingered for ten years before returning, with a
bridal trousseau worth a million strings of cash. His lust
for gain became still fiercer, and he next went trading as
the master of a sea-going junk. His wealth became limitless
and both Prime Minister Liu Cheng and Vice-Minister Chu-ko
T'ing-jui formed marriage connections with him (through
their children). In 1178 he despatched his borrower (hsing-ch'ien)
Wu Ta to act as head merchant (kang-shou) in a ship setting
out to sea with a total crew of thirty-eight men under a chief
mate. They were away for ten years, returning in the seventh
moon of 1188, anchoring south of Lo-fu Mountain in Hui-chou.
They had obtained profits of several thousand per cent. (443)

The use of the term hsing-ch'ien in Yuan dynasty drama in the pejorative
sense of 'servant' or 'handyman' probably derived from this relationship
of financial dependency.

A merchant who used capital provided by others for his ventures
might also be known as an 'agent merchant' (ching-shang), a term
which corresponds to the Latin tractator. Li Fang's Miscellaneous
Records Collected During the T'ai-p'ing Reign-period tell the following tale:

Towards the end of the T'ai-chung reign-period (847-859) of
the T'ang dynasty, there was a certain T'ung An-yü, a rich
countryman who lived in the market-town of Ju-k'o in the county
of Kuai-ch'i in Hsin-chou (in Kiangsi). Originally he had been
quite penniless, but had struck up a friendship with Kuo Kung,
a man from the same canton as himself, and Kuo had lent him
sixty or seventy thousand cash. This he had used to trade as
an agent. When he subsequently became rich and Kuo asked
for the return of the money which he had lent, T'ung declined
to do so. ... (444)

Finally, there were the 'agents/brokers/petty traders'
(ching-chi). If the meanings of this term which refer to the managers
of family affairs and to brokers, the latter of these usages being common
enough in the Ch'ing dynasty but little met with in Sung times, are
excluded, it would seem to have referred to small merchants who
sometimes but by no means always had their own shops. A decree of
820 on taxation laid it down that, 'The petty traders (ching-chi) who live
in the shops in rural villages and towns should be liable for contributions

in the same way as ordinary folk.' In the Sung dynasty Chu Hsi wrote,
in connection with certain relief measures, that:

> In the various country communities there are prosperous families
> who operate shops. The written sanction for a relief quota
> originally allocated to them should be taken back from them.
> If there are some small shops which do not do a great deal of
> business, and are incapable of supporting themselves, and if
> they have already requested written sanction for a relief quota,
> it should not be withdrawn from them.   (445)

And:

> The first category comprises shop businesses which do
> business daily, and whose affairs are prospering, having
> taxable property and able to support themselves. They may
> not request to be given written sanction for a relief quota. ... .
> The second category comprises families that manage to get by
> at a certain standard, and also the lower level of government
> personnel. They may go to the county granaries to purchase
> rice. ... . The third category comprises indigent petty
> traders (ching-chi) and those who even if they have a small
> shop business do not have a big turnover, and also very poor
> holders of the provincial academic degree. These persons
> may request written sanction for a relief quota. ... . (445)

Thus management and the ownership of capital became separated.
This may be seen from materials already presented, notably the passage
by Hsu Meng-hsin on pages 31-32, the story told by Yang Wan-li given
on page 28, and the account of a lawsuit over a rice-shop on pages 74-76.
The Continuation of the Comprehensive Mirror also has the following
remarks by Ou-yang Hsiu as of the year 1040:

> How can the means by which a great merchant is able to amass
> his fortune consist of personally selling in trifling amounts in the
> market? He has to have peddlers and lesser merchants among
> whom he shares out this task. Peddlers and lesser merchants will
> work not for a profit but only for a livelihood. Therefore the
> great merchant does not resent their sharing in his profit,
> since he relies on them to market his goods. Even if his
> takings are small (on each item), if his merchandise circulates
> rapidly these small (profits) will mount up to a great deal. (448)

Yuan Ts'ai stressed the importance of putting money to work:

> Sometimes when brothers, sons and cousins are living together
> the head of the family will keep the funds to himself, anxious
> lest the disaster of the family estate splitting up should occur.
> He will buy gold and silver and hoard them away. This is an
> act of great folly. Assuming that one has 100,000 pieces of
> gold and silver, and that these are used to buy income-yielding
> property, the yearly takings are bound to be 10,000 pieces.
> After ten years or so one will have recovered what may be
> regarded as the 100,000 and the rest will all be profit. What
> is more, this 100,000 may be made in its turn to yield profits.
> If it is used for a pawnbroking business, a profit of a hundred
> per cent will be realized within three years. One will have
> recovered what may be regarded as the 100,000 and the surplus
> will all be profit. It can, moreover, be doubled again in the
> next three years, until one loses account of the amount. What
> reason can there be for storing it in strong-boxes rather than
> taking advantage of it as a source of profit and benefitting
> everyone? I have seen people make available their private
> funds to everyone (in the family), causing them to be managed
> by the family, and then, after a long time has elapsed, take
> back only the capital sum. The wealth in these people's
> families reaches the brothers, sons and cousins in equal
> shares, and for generation upon generation no division takes
> place. This is the reward for having thought about this matter
> to good effect. (448)

The management of a pawnshop by a non-kinsman is described in the
Southern Sung collection of verdicts, The Collection of Lucid Decisions
by Celebrated Judges:

> Lo Yu-ch'eng received in instalments from Chou Tzu-tsun the
> sum of 270 strings of cash with which to open a pawnshop. A
> written contract was drawn up in proof of this. It is now more
> than eight years since this took place. Since his master is
> suing him for defaulting on this debt, Lo has stated that the
> money which he received never amounted to this much, and
> that what was referred to as opening a pawnshop was in fact a
> gambling den (kuei-fang)*. This is greatly at variance with

---

*A term which in T'ang times had been used to designate a safe-deposit
firm or proto-bank, but whose meaning had now changed. Transl.

what is written in the contract, from which one can see that it is not true. How can the authorities, however, for all that they are concerned with right principles and with laws, discipline every single case in which some low fellow lays his hands on funds and then misuses them? It is fortunate that Chou Tzu-tsun has already recovered 216 strings. If the capital and the interest are reckoned together then he has merely obtained half of the interest, but he is merely 40 to 50 strings short if only the capital is taken into consideration. With matters having turned out as they have done, he is lucky to have his capital. How can one find the time to take the interest into account as well? If one lends one's money to a bad man, one must simply acknowledge that one has made a mistake. (449)

Such a manager of a pawnshop was usually known as a 'head clerk' (chang-shih). A story from Hung Mai shows comparable managers running lodges for merchants:

Yeh Ch'ing was a commoner from Ch'u-chou whose family had for generations managed an inn-cum-store belonging to a great family. Poverty obliged Yeh to give up this profession, and he enlisted as a constable with the Kua-ts'ang Constabulary, showing himself to be brave and fearless. ... Outside the prefectural city wall there was a large hostelry which had only been built three years previously, and was extremely new and clean. A great number of merchants lodged there. In 1189 the proprietor was the commoner Chou Erh-shih. His son was stupid and lacked understanding. ... The hostel subsequently fell into a decline but in 1192 someone mentioned to the proprietor that Yeh Ch'ing was a suitable person to whom to entrust it, and the owner invited Yeh to take it over, offering a year's exemption from rent as an inducement. (449)

In a variety of ways a new career was thus opening up to those endowed with a talent for commerce.

3. THE CHARACTERISTICS OF COMMERCIAL WEALTH

Large profits could sometimes be made from mobile commerce, especially the sea-borne variety, based upon the exploitation of opportunities as they presented themselves; but hazards of both a natural and a social kind caused it to remain a speculative and dangerous pursuit. More fixed and permanent commerce, notably of the type exemplified by brokerage, though comparatively free of the speculative element, required not only energy and dedication to the search for profit but also the possession of large capital resources and the ability to utilize them, if the rivalry offered by competitors was to be successfully overcome. The prevalence in the literary sources of tales of fortunes acquired at a single stroke by the unearthing of buried treasure also attests to the difficulty of accumulating further capital simply by extending the exploitation of that which one had already.

Some instances of the accumulation of capital have been given in the preceding pages. Ch'in Kuan's story of Lin Chao-ch'ing recounted on page 27 above hints at the speculative and opportunistic nature of the sea trade in which he made his money. Hung Mai's life of Wang Yuan-mao, who learned the languages of Southeast Asia from his masters in a monastery (which was clearly itself engaged in trade) shows how fortune and high social position could be won through knowledge, desire for gain and fearless resolve. (See pages 192-193 above.) Hung Mai also describes the success of Hsu Ta-lang, a small K'ai-feng flour merchant who set up three mills and in order to supply them bought thirty to forty donkeys with whom he went out to other counties to buy wheat, becoming wealthy after ten years of strenuous work. The case of Shen Shih-meng, given on page 191 above, illustrates how a financial manager with a good reputation might be entrusted by another with capital already accumulated.

A distinction was often drawn in Sung times between 'large' and 'small' merchants. Thus in 1142, for the purposes of the frontier trade with the Chin Tartars, the Southern Sung government defined 'small merchants' as those dealing in goods worth less than 100 strings of cash and required them to join together into ten-man groups. Chou Ch'ü-fei mentions that the rich Szechwanese merchants who made annual trips south to Ch'in-chou with the figured silks of their native province only engaged in transactions worth at least several thousand strings of cash. They would ordinarily leave it to the smaller merchants who were their dependents to deal with the Vietnamese in small quantities of paper, writing-brushes, rice and cloth. The linking together of large and small merchants into networks for combined operations is also suggested by passages from Ou-yang Hsiu (page 194), Yang Wan-li (page 29) and Yeh Shih (page 14).

For much the same reasons that these networks of subsidiaries were formed to engage in joint operations, namely enhanced competitive power, and also protection against such risks as shipwreck and robbery, merchants of approximately equal standing would often form partnerships with each other. Early evidence of this may be found in the ironical phrases of Yuan Chen's poem 'The Pleasures of the Travelling Merchant', written in the latter half of the T'ang dynasty*:

> He leaves home in search of associates,
> and
> The associates swear an oath together
> To sell the counterfeit and not the true. (456)

Such combinations were common in Sung times. Hung Mai, for example, mentions a Lin-an tea merchant and his thirty companions peddling tea in Ch'ang-shu county in 1194, a group of twelve associated merchants passing through Lien-chou in Kwangtung in 1189, a wealthy merchant from Ch'ang-lo county in Fu-chou and numerous other merchants buying up cloth and then taking a ship north to Chekiang to sell it, and other instances. Yeh Shih tells the story of Lin Hsing-hsiang from T'ai-chou, a poor man when young who had become a travelling merchant. Once, after having shared out some profits with his fellow merchants, he redid the calculations and discovered that he had been allotted more than was due to him, and hurried after the others to return the surplus. The formation of temporary associations of merchants for overseas ventures is described by Chu Yü in a passage translated on page 15 above.

Associations were also formed by merchants engaged in the Kiangsi to Kuang-nan cattle trade, with its overtones of coercion and brigandage (see pages 98-99 above), and for illegal trading in tea and salt. Wang Shih-p'eng, the twelfth-century official, observed that:

> Furthermore, those of the inhabitants of the Southeast who know how to make use of weapons, such as those from Kiangsi, Fukien and such places as Hsien-chü in T'ai-chou and Tung-yang in Wu-chou (Chin-hua), are all sturdy and good at brawling. They frequently form into groups under tea merchants or salt merchants. (457)

---

*See the note on page 45 above. Transl.

Groups of associated tea merchants constituted the background to the rebellion raised by the tea broker Lai Wen-cheng at the beginning of the Southern Sung, and the invasion of the Chin Tartars at the end of this dynasty was resisted by a Tea Merchants' Army.

The passage from the Draft Sung Digest given on page 33 above seems to distinguish between three possible forms of association, namely the association of partners (chiu-ho huo-pan), the joint-capital partnership (lien-ts'ai ho-pen), and the association of members of the same trade without joint capital (fei lien-ts'ai ho-pen erh chiu-chi t'ung-hang). An alternative but less plausible interpretation of the text would indicate only a distinction between partnerships with and without joint capital. Work has already been done on the joint-capital partnership (lien-ts'ai ho-pen, ho-pen, or tou-niu) by Miyazaki Ichisada, Hino Kaisaburo, Kusano Yasushi and Imabori Seiji. In particular, Hino analyzes a passage for 1201 in the Sung Digest in which certain officials pointed out that investment in 'long life treasuries' (ch'ang-shang k'u), i.e. tax-exempt monastery pawnshops, was a means by which rich persons sought to evade taxes, and that it generally took the form of joint capital:

> The practice known as 'collecting and tying' (tou-niu) whereby rich people combine to pool their resources and accept a common set of rules, is much the same everywhere. As regards these regulations, ten persons will join into a group, whose capital may amount to anything from 1,000 strings of cash to 5,000 strings of cash in all. The period of the operation is usually set at ten years, and at the end of each year the group will meet to work out its profits, which are never less than several fold, while leaving the capital sum invested as before. No money is initially paid in to the government for the purchase of ordination certificates; it is merely a scheme to aim for profits under false pretences. (459)

To this example may be added the problem posed by Ch'in Chiu-shao, which is given on page 32 above: Four merchant partners in an overseas venture, having paid off the owner of their ship, have to calculate the ratio in which they must share out the goods which they have bought if these are to correspond to the amounts of capital which each has invested. As Imabori has pointed out, although the capital here is temporarily treated as a single sum, this unification is achieved by means of individual loans made between the four partners, and the

corporate character of the partnership is not complete. Pao Hui
describes yet another form of share-capital in the passage given on
page 33 above. Yuan Hao-wen who flourished in the Chin dynasty,
also tells the story of two young rascals who dressed up a beggarwoman
as their mother, took up lodgings in a hostelry in Hsin-kan county in
Kiangsi, and won everyone's confidence with their traveling outfits
and display of filial piety. They then borrowed 300 strings of cash
from a wealthy family by the name of P'i to whom they entrusted their
mother and their effects while they set off to trade. They were back
six months later with a several-fold profit, which they returned along
with the capital. They were then able to obtain 2,000 strings of cash
from a number of well-to-do persons, including the P'is, after which
they absconded under the pretence of setting off on a journey. Yuan
comments that:

> Everyone observed their practised skill as agent merchants
> (ching-shang) and the manner in which they daily associated
> with people, as the result of which they lent them all they
> wanted. (460)

The share capital was thus contributed by a large number of people.
Among other evidence of joint-capital partnerships at this time may be
mentioned a law of 1034 permitting up to ten households to contract
collectively for the franchise of an officially licensed wine shop. One
instance is known in which three families pooled funds in order to buy
a calf, and another in which three peasants farmed their lands cooperatively,
sharing the harvest equally between them.

While Sung times saw the rise of more advanced forms of the
accumulation and concentration of capital, yet it is clear, if one takes
a general view, that at all levels those who possessed capital resources,
rather than pursuing a course of concentrating and rationalizing their
commercial undertakings, preferred to invest their wealth in a dispersed
fashion, entrusting it to others and concealing it, seeking profit through
activities of an opportunistic nature conducted through subsidiaries.
Wealth acquired through commerce was also constantly being diverted
into land and buildings, particularly the former. The rapid rise in the
price of land during the Southern Sung, though partly due to inflation,
was also in some measure the result of this. Li Hsin, writing around
the beginning of the twelfth century, observed that:

> If seafaring merchants do not prize pearls and jade, then they esteem rhinoceros horn and tortoise-shell. If merchants who travel overland do not greatly value salt and iron, then they have a high regard for tea. They grasp their counting-slips, their steelyards and their measures of capacity until they have amassed great gains, so that they may seek to own fields and houses, their principal wives be resplendent with hairpins and ear-rings, and their subsidiary wives pluck the strings of the zither. This is what merchants want. (464)

While land was often desired as the most permanent and secure of investments, there was sometimes an element of the irrational in its acquisition, as may be seen from this story told by Li Fu, who flourished in the latter part of the Northern Sung:

> I had a neighbor who inherited his father's property of over ten ch'ing of fine farmland just outside the (county) city. He was provided with an ample sufficiency of clothing and food, but being incapable either of energetic farming or competent management he succumbed to temptations laid before him by others. Enamored of the idea that if he had many acres he would acquire an impressive reputation, he used every penny of his family's fortune to obtain a further several tens of ch'ing of poor arable land far off in the hills. He hoped that people would admire the extent of his holdings, but the distant fields brought in no income and he regularly had to subsidize them from his fields near the city. ... (462)

When people purchased lands, their acquisitions would usually be scattered in several places, the reason for this probably being that land would normally come onto the market only to the extent that its owners found it necessary to resolve some pressing financial crisis. Absentee landlordism on the part of officials, the rich, upper level local government personnel and merchants thus became quite common in some areas. Merchants' funds were also put into urban real estate (see the passages from Cheng Hsieh and Wang Te-ch'en on pages 131-132, into private and commercial buildings (see Hung Mai's story on page 91 and the remarks of Hsu Meng-hsin on page 32, slaves and other luxury items.

VII. COMMERCE AND SOCIETY

1. THE EXPANSION OF CONSUMPTION

The diversification of consumption, a phenomenon causally related to the development of a commercial economy during the Sung dynasty, took two forms. The consumption of luxury items became more generalized and items of mass consumption became more varied. Each of these aspects will be examined here in turn.

i. The Generalization of the Consumption of Luxury Items

Extravagance was general at the Sung court. For the construction of the Yü-ch'ing chao-ying Palace, Emperor Chen-tsung mobilized 30,000 to 40,000 workmen, and assembled precious materials for it from all over the empire. The Emperor Hui-tsung's collector's passion for rare objects and plants necessitated, or so one critic alleged, a special convoy of boats to bring new acquisitions north to the capital. On the urging of a geomancer he had an artificial hill constructed to the northeast of K'ai-feng, in the hope of thereby multiplying the imperial progeny. He excelled as a calligrapher, originating the style called 'Slender Gold', and as a painter of landscapes, birds and flowers; and further wasted his time in the pleasures of connoisseurship. Extravagance was likewise common among the high officials. Thus in Ts'ai Ching's kitchens each kitchen-maid is said to have specialized in a particular task; Wang Fu is reputed to have had three larders stuffed with pickled orioles; T'ung Kuan owned several thousand catties of materia medica; and Chia Ssu-tao is reported to have had some hundreds of jars of sugar and eight hundred piculs of pepper stored away in his cellars.

The Sung official class, whose economic foundation was the intensive and highly productive agriculture of their tenants, and who could gain access to official position only by means of success in the imperial examinations, differed from the aristocrats of the Six Dynasties and the subsequent period (i.e. from about AD 400 to 900), for whom rank and fortune were a hereditary birthright, in that as officials they had to make their own way by their own efforts and most of the privileges of status which they enjoyed did not descend to their children. It cannot have been easy for them to maintain their families at a good standard

of living in the urbanized and commercialized society of the times.
Their official prerogatives, however, and laws that were in fact tolerant
of official investment in commerce, particularly in the covert form of
investment of funds with others, meant that they were well supplied with
opportunities for becoming rich; and as rank and wealth increased
they tended to move into the cities, where their extravagant expenditure
provided the basis for the flowering of a distinctive official-gentry
culture. Yang Fang, writing in Southern Sung times, drew the following
contrast with the preceding era:

> It is popularly said that, 'Only after three generations of
> holding government office can a family really know how to
> dress up and dine upon dainty fare.' I would rather say that
> after three generations of holding government office, the sons
> and grandsons are bound to be extravagant, and given to the
> utmost indulgence. They will be unwilling to wear coarse cotton,
> coarse silk, coarse padded garments, worn-out hemp quilting
> or any clothes that have been laundered or patched, insisting
> on openwork silk, thin silk, damask silk, crepe silk, figured
> silk, natural silk (i. e. silk not passed through boiling water)
> and fresh, fine and luxurious linens and silks, whether plain
> or fancy, surpassing those of other persons in their costliness
> and in the oddity and ingenuity of their patterns and styling.
> They will be unwilling to eat vegetables and will look on greens
> and broth as coarse fare, finding beans, wheat and millet
> meager and tasteless, and insisting on the best polished rice and
> the finest roasts to satisfy their greedy appetites, with the
> products of the water and the land, and the confections of
> human artifice, set out before them neatly in ornamentally
> carved dishes and trays. This is what is meant by 'being
> able to dress up and to dine!' (468)

Official-gentry extravagance was also to be found in their buildings,
gardens, drinking-vessels, objets-d'art and servants.

These customs spread downwards from officialdom into the
lower classes and outwards from the capitals into the provinces. So
much at least may be inferred from the sumptuary laws repeatedly
issued by the Sung government, especially those relating to dress,
furniture and buildings. * These were widely disobeyed, as may be
seen from one of Su Hsun's observations:

*On pages 470-473 of the original work there is a chronological list
of the relevant ordinances. Transl.

These days the families of artisans and merchants trail white
silks and brocades, and adorn themselves with jades and
pearls. In nine cases out of ten, if one looks a person over
from head to foot, one will find that he is breaking the law. (473)

Wang Mai, a thirteenth-century official, was of the opinion that:

The customs of the empire have now become extravagant.
Limitless sums are squandered on the construction of lofty
and elegant mansions, something which used to be forbidden.
These days such is the practice of spendthrift emulation that
roofbeams confront each other in unbroken succession. There
is no end to the waste of money on gliding and kingfisher
feathers, something on which restraints used to be imposed.
There are at present rows of shops which do gold-plating,
competing with each other for profit. One drinking-bout among
the gentry may squander property worth ten pieces of gold.
It is not only officials of long standing who do this; the
pernicious practice is imitated by those who have just entered
the government service. Trifles like women's ornaments and
clasps may cost up to a hundred thousand cash. Nor does this
happen only in the great households; those of moderate means
also strive to do the same. Adornments which make their
appearance in the Rear Palace* in the morning will have become
the fashion among the commoners by evening. What is
manufactured yesterday for those in high places will be spread
throughout the capital tomorrow. (474)

Yuan Shuo-yu, referring to Lin-an, noted regarding the use of gold
foil costume jewelry that, although it was illegal, 'Powerful and titled
families are firmly attached to the custom, and all those commoners
who have a little money try to have ornaments made of it.' Gold and
silver vessels were much used, being found even in the wineshops,
tea-houses, and restaurants of K'ai-feng and Lin-an. Shops that dealt
in gold and silver, and silversmiths, were to be found in many prefectural
and county capitals, and even in some market towns. In some areas
ordinary townsfolk and villagers wore gold and silver ornaments.

_____

*The quarters of the Empress and the imperial consorts. Transl.

The latter half of the Southern Sung saw an outburst of extravagant fashions and the overthrow of the old conventions of dress. This is attested to by the passage from the San-shan Gazetteer for the Shun-hsi reign-period (1174-1189) quoted on pages 184-185 above, and also by Wu Tzu-mu:

> Since the Shun-yu reign-period (1241-1252) there has been a change in dress. There is a class of latter-day young men who do not conform to the old conventions. They wrap themselves in strange turbans and bizarre garments, form groups of three to five, and vie with each other in showing off their finery, to the point where everyone else is heartily weary of having to watch it. There is no longer the pure simplicity of former times. (481)

Luxurious tastes were also prevalent among the upper classes of the various peoples that constituted China's neighbors: the Liao, the Japanese, the Vietnamese and the Cambodians. They obtained the Chinese goods they needed either through trade or in the form of gifts made by the Sung in return for tributary offerings.

ii. The Diversification of Items of Mass Consumption

It was often said that seven commodities were necessary for everyday life, although there was some slight disagreement among various authorities as to which they were. In his Dreaming of Splendors in the Midst of Deprivations Wu Tzu-mu wrote that:

> There is a dense population within and without the city walls of Hang-chou. Through the length and breadth of the prefecture wherever there are city quarters, groups of houses, bridges or gateways, and also in out-of-the-way places, one will find street stalls and buying and selling going on. - For firewood, rice, fermented soya bean sauce, * vinegar and tea are articles which people need every day, and soup is indispensible as a side dish for those who are better off. Even the poor cannot do without these things. (476)

---

*See S. H. Shih, A Preliminary Survey of the Book 'Ch'i Min Yao Shu', An Agricultural Encyclopedia of the Sixth Century (Peking: Science Press, 1958), pp. 84-87. Transl.

Wine, vegetables and charcoal were also sometimes found in such lists
of essentials. In a humorous piece about the pampered beauties of
Hu-chou, Hung Mai gives their 'seven requisites' as oil, salt, fermented
soya bean sauce, salted soya bean relish,* ginger, pepper and tea,
a more luxurious assortment altogether, mentioned in order to illustrate
the cost of these ladies' upkeep. The Ming writer T'ien I-heng has the
same list as Wu Tzu-mu:

> It is proverbially said that firewood, rice, oil, salt, fermented
> soya bean sauce, vinegar and tea are the seven necessities
> which no one can do without. There is a brief composition
> by an author of Yuan times which runs:
>> Leaning at the window thick with creepers,
>> Sighing but saying nothing,
>> With the seven essentials all used up
>> What sort of life can one lead?
>> Firewood's scarce as purple mushrooms,
>> Oil as sweet dew, and rice as cinnabar.
>> I dreamt just now of a dribble in the sauce-jar -
>> The salt-jar will soon be empty too.
>> There's not much tea and little vinegar.
>> What difficulties these seven essentials give! (476)

Of the various articles just mentioned it seems likely that rice, tea
and pepper only became widely consumed in and after the Sung dynasty.
The materials presented in Chapter III show that there was a great
increase in the varieties of rice available during this period, and that
many kinds of oils, condiments, meats, poultry, fish and fruits, as
well as tea, salt and sugar, were on sale in city and village markets.

Some further insight into the nature of items of mass consumption
may be obtained from the exemptions granted from trade tax and ship
tonnage tax (li-sheng-shui) to 'goods in daily use among the people.'
The supplementary regulations issued in the T'ien-sheng reign-period
(1023-1031) exempted grains, firewood, charcoal, hay, old housing
materials, wood and iron destined for use in farm tools, hemp and silk
cloth in lengths of less than a p'i (40 Chinese feet) and fish caught for
the fisherman's own consumption. Regulations promulgated on this
matter at other times were broadly similar.

---

*See Shih (1958), pp. 87-88. Transl.

2. THE INCREASE OF NON-AGRICULTURAL OCCUPATIONS IN THE COUNTRYSIDE

The Sung dynasty saw a growth in the number of significant social classes. Already in T'ang times Han Yü had observed that the traditional four-fold division into 'scholars', 'farmers', 'artisans' and 'merchants' needed to be supplemented with the further categories of 'Buddhists' and 'Taoists'. In the eleventh century Ch'en Shun-yü extended Han Yü's six classes to eight:

> It has been said that, 'Alas! Of all the hardships of the people, none is worse than farming! In the agriculture of times past, one man received a 100 mou of land* but these days ten men do not dispose of a 100 mou between them. Of old everyone farmed for himself, but now farming is all done for the benefit of others. ** Anciently the rulers employed the people (on corvées) when they were at leisure and made the taxes light so that they would be contented. They exerted themselves at farming in order to make it an honorable calling. Today the government afflicts the people with strenuous labor-services and heavy exactions, setting up the gradations of superiors and inferiors in order to spur them to effort. Long ago there used to be only four classes of commoners, of whom the farmers were one, but now there are eight in all, namely scholars, farmers, artisans, merchants, Taoists, Buddhists, soldiers and vagrants, and of these the farmers are but one. Scholars in the past did not practise farming nor did the great officers of state pursue the kind of profits suitable for gardeners or workmaids. Our present-day nobles and high officials build up vast landed estates. Once the artisans and the merchants on the one hand and the peasants on the other supported each other in interdependent fashion, and acted with moderation; but now artisans and merchants practise extortion upon the peasants and never grow tired of cheating them. (483)

Several other Sung writers expressed much the same sentiments.

---

*The full allotment for an adult male under the T'ang equitable field system. Transl.
**I.e., on the basis of tenancy. Transl.

The emergence of a class of professional soldiers may be traced to the collapse of the T'ang divisional militia system in the first half of the eighth century. Those recruited were poor persons who had lost their connections with the agricultural world. They sometimes exchanged the rice which they received as pay for ready money, and made use of a part of this to finance business activities. Former landless peasants also made up a certain proportion of those who became Taoist priests and Buddhist monks. Many of the Taoists toured around the country selling medicines, stocks of which they acquired at the medicine fairs in Szechwan, Hunan, and Kwangtung, or else telling fortunes, practising alchemy or medicine, and selling incense, papers, ink, writing-brushes, candles and fans. Buddhist monks also sometimes ran shops or pawnbroking businesses in conjunction with their main work, or sold lottery tickets. As may be seen from the remarks of Chu Yü quoted on page 113 above, Buddhist nuns sometimes made a speciality of the manufacture of embroidered silks; and both they and Taoist nuns acted as brokers and peddlers. Vagrants, who were often remarkably numerous, especially in poor areas such as Ching-hsi (western Honan and northeast Hupeh), engaged in tea and salt smuggling, and in counterfeiting, gambling and swindling. They might also act as agents, hired laborers, butchers or local government personnel.

Even in T'ang times, self-sufficient villages lacking economic contacts with the outside world had become sufficiently rare to make it worthwhile for the ninth-century poet Po Chü-i to record an instance of one such which he had seen in Hsu-chou, in what is now northwestern Kiangsu. There was a general tendency, already noted by Po, for peasants to give up farming either wholly or in part in favor of the more profitable occupations of the merchant and the artisan. Thus the thirteenth-century scholar-official Tai Hsu had this to say about the class of peasant-artisans which grew up around Ting-hai (present-day Chen-hai) in Ming-chou (now Ning-po):

> Since, even if they do own a few mou of land, they do not farm, how are they to obtain their food? And, since the rural communities are all poverty-stricken, even if they do work as artisans, craftsmen, knife-smiths or peddlers, who will give them employment? Since, however, they do possess a few mou of land, one has to regard them as practising agriculture; and yet, since they work as artisans, craftsmen, knife-smiths or peddlers, one must speak of them as pursuing skilled trades. (486)

Evidence already presented in this book indicates the existence of rural paper-cutters (108), peasants who doubled as carriers to local markets (68 -69 , 151 -152), and country folk who joined boats as helmsmen or sailors (22-23). Hung Mai mentions cases of villagers who became merchants, brokers and keepers of merchant hostels. Shen Kua also tells the story of a smallholder in Yang-ti county, in what is now Honan, who farmed 50 <u>mou</u> of land jointly with his elder brother. When his elder brother's son was married, the division of the property would have meant bankruptcy for them all and so he relinquished his share, took some other goods in exchange, and moved his family to rented accomodation thirty <u>li</u> away. Local peasants kindly provided him with 30 <u>mou</u> of land, on which he set his son to work, while he himself sold medicines, practised divination and labored as a hired farmhand, later being compelled by a competitor to give up the first two of these occupations.

Hired laborers such as he was did not only work at agriculture. Both in villages and in cities they were in demand in smithies, water-mills, threshing yards, rice-cake shops, oil shops, tea plantations, orchards and fish-rearing pools, as also for the cultivation of sugar-cane and vegetables, building, transport and communications, and the handling of cargoes. In the cities the heads of the appropriate guilds also provided pawnshop clerks, servants of various kinds, porters, attendants, actors, musicians and chessplayers for hire. Hung Mai tells how country folk too would sometimes come into a city in search of employment:

> Every day the villagers who live close about the prefectural city hasten in to the bridge in the lesser eastern suburb of Ch'eng-tu to sell their labor. Anyone with money may hire them. They act as carriers for local distribution. (487)

It is clear that peasants engaged in commerce. Thus Yao Ho, the ninth-century poet, left the following lines describing a journey which he had made:

> Touring away from home through country fields,
> In house after house the doors were shut.
> From asking after the inhabitants
> One learnt that they had all gone off to trade.
> No tax is placed by government on commerce, *
> While heavy burdens lie upon the farmer. (487)

---

*A systematic network of internal customs stations was not created until Sung times. Transl.

In the course of an account of the defects of the Service Exemption System* , the uniform application of which was ruining some peasants by forcing them into the money economy, Liu Chih argued that:

> It is to be feared that these people will not be content to remain farmers. The (registered) population of the empire is wasting away daily. Lesser folk are becoming merchants, tenants or idle vagrants; sometimes the members of a family will no longer serve as guarantors of each other's good behavior but illegally scatter and become enrolled in the lowest category of (free non-immigrant) household (hsia-hu)**. The more powerful folk join forces and become bandits. (488)

There is also some evidence to show that tenants engaged in trade although it was Lu Nan-kung's opinion that, 'Tenants do not have sufficient insight to permit them to carry on business; they are only capable of devoting their energies to plowing and digging for their masters.' He went on to make the following observations about those who combined farming and trade:

> At the present time the population consists of numerous tenant/in-migrant households (k'o-hu) and few landowner/native households (chu-hu). Distinctions must be drawn between the various grades of those termed 'landowner/native households'. They include persons with tax quotas of over a hundred, a thousand or even several thousands of cash, as well as those who are only liable for ten or a hundred cash. Now those whom one is sorry for are not the well-to-do families but only those who owe ten to a hundred cash. While they have the titular status of 'landowner/native households' they are in fact worse off than the tenant/in-migrant households. The reason for this is that they do not have sufficient land to supply them with food and clothing, and for their livelihood they regularly have to depend on their entrepreneurial ingenuity. (489)

It was not only the rural poor who engaged in commercial activites. Fan Chün described the rich speculators and money-lenders as follows:

---

*On which see page 134 above.
**Which included besides farmers, those who combined farming their own land and trading, traders, and those who combined farming others' land and trading. Transl.

There are some who put gold and pearls in sacks, and bundle
up white silk gauze, taking advantage of the seasons when
these things rise and fall in value, and growing fat on their
winnings. Others store grain in their granaries, taking
advantage of the peasants' difficulties to buy it cheap and sell
it dear, waiting without exerting themselves for cereals to
rise in price. Others yet again are able to lay their hands
on large sums of money, which they lend out at interest,
fleecing the poor commoners by receiving back double what
they have lent. Such persons as these drink strong wines and
eat rich foods. They sing in the mornings and pluck the lute-
strings at night. They smile when they see the afflictions of
the people, looking over their shoulders with a satisfied
appearance. For these reasons, respectable men and upper-
class families get rid of their houses and their lands, sell off
their plows and cattle, abandon their fields, relinquish
agriculture and seek to evade taxes by so doing. (489)

Hung Mai's account of Chang Wu-san Chiang-shih, which is given on
pages 70-71 above, offers a typical example of this sort of person.
It is clear from the passage by Chu Hsi quoted on page 194 that rural
businesses covered a wide range from the prosperous to the very poor;
and it is also interesting to note that Chu's definition of the lowest
category of household (in Tu-ch'ang and Chien-ch'ang counties in present
day Kiangsi) specified three types of person, namely, owner-farmers
who might also possibly be engaged in commerce, non-farmers engaged
in commerce, and tenant-farmers who might also be engaged in commerce.
The diversification of occupations in the countryside thus clearly affected
all classes.

The reasons for this development were of course multiple. They
included the favorable treatment accorded to commerce in comparison
with agriculture by the policies of the early Sung state, the ruin of
independent farmers of moderate means as the result of heavy taxation,
and also the way in which the tax system forcibly called a money economy
into existence. Especially important, however, was the phenomenon of
urbanization, which may be conceived of as part of an increasing social
division of labor, and the appearance of a nationwide hierarchy of markets
reaching down to village level. It was these circumstances which made
it possible for the money economy to prove more attractive to many
than an agriculture burdened with heavy taxes.

3. THE COMMERCIAL SPIRIT

By the Sung dynasty the traditional taboo on the overt pursuit of profit had been somewhat relaxed. One early indication of this was Po Chü-i's remark, made in the ninth century, that 'Men in their myriads none of them but love riches.' For Sung times it is possible to instance such observations as those of Ts'ai Hsiang quoted on page 185 above, Ssu-ma Kuang's 'Both townsfolk and countrymen, whether in the fields or away from them, seek only for profit from morn till night,' and Li Yuan-pi's 'Most of the foolish populace give priority to business activities and wealth.' The older viewpoint of blunt opposition to such behavior was still sometimes expressed, as by the eleventh-century official Feng Shan:

> Heaven and Earth bring things forth in constant (quantity), and the piling up of wealth is not a policy to be approved of. (494)

Others accorded a partial affirmation to the pursuit of wealth, seeing it as a necessary evil and stressing the need for moral restraint. One such was Li Chih-yen the thirteenth-century traveller:

> What is profitable is the opposite of what is hurtful, and there is thus some good in profit-making. Moreover, in this world it is not possible to avoid planning for profits if one is to make one's living. What people should be careful to avoid is riches gained in disregard of human fellow-feeling. To be able in these matters to limit one's desires and take but little is to come close to perfection. The most heartless practice of all is to be found in the grain trade when those with funds accumulated and capital mobilized take advantage of the seasonal abundance of rice to buy it up cheaply. ... (494)

There was also some notion of the wrongfulness of asking more than a fair price. Thus Hsu Hsuan in the tenth century asserted that:

> All the profits which townsmen make by selling things are taken at a constant rate. To take profit at an excessive rate would be extortion. (494)

It was customary to urge the seller or lender of money to show a certain compassion towards the buyer or borrower; but it is open to doubt how far this was observed in practice. *

We may conclude with Yuan Ts'ai's realistic account of the ways in which the younger members of an official's family might hope to make their living:

> If the sons and younger brothers of an official have no hereditary stipends by which they may be maintained, and no landed property on which they may depend, and they want some way of serving their parents and caring for their dependents, the best thing for them to do is to become Confucian scholars. Those of them who are endowed with outstanding talents and able to pursue the calling of a scholar fitting himself for appointment to office will, if of the first quality, gain riches and honors through success in the examinations, and if of the second quality, give instruction to disciples and receive the offering due to a master; while those who are not able to pursue the calling of a scholar fitting himself for appointment to office will, if of the first quality, be able to fulfill the tasks of writing letters and drawing up documents for others, and if of the second quality, be able to give primary instruction to boys in the arts of punctuating and reading. Those who are not capable of being Confucian scholars may make their living without disgracing their ancestors by working as spirit-mediums, doctors, Buddhists, Taoists, farmers, merchants or experts of some sort. It is the greatest disgrace to the ancestors if sons or younger brothers degenerate into beggars or thieves. ... (495)

---

*See the concluding remarks on the legal case on page 78 above.

AUTHORS AND SOURCES REFERRED TO IN THE TEXT

Chai Hao	翟灝	T'ung-su pien 通俗編	189
Chang Chih-han	張之翰	Hsi-yen chi 西巖集	153
Chang Hsieh	張燮	Tung/hsi-yang k'ao 東西洋考	16
Chang Ju-yü	章如愚	Shan-t'ang ch'ün-shu k'ao-so hsu-chi	46
		山堂群書考索續集	
Chang Pang-chi	張邦基	Mo-chuang man-lu 墨莊漫錄	36
Chao Fan	趙蕃	Shun-i kao 淳熙稿	146
Chao Hsi-ku	趙希鵠	Tung-t'ien ch'ing-lu 洞天清祿	107
Chao Shan-kua	趙善括	Ying-chai tsa-chu 應齋雜著	13
Ch'en Fou	陳孚	Kang-chung Chiao-chou kao 剛中交州薰	151
Ch'en Fu	陳尃	Nung-shu 農書	116
Ch'en Fu-liang	陳傅良	Chih-chai wen-chi 止齋文集	53
Ch'en Lü	陳旅	An-ya-t'ang chi 安雅堂集	144
Ch'en Mi	陳宓	Fu-chai hsien-sheng lung-t'u Ch'en-kung	
		wen-chi 復齋先生龍圖陳公文集	97
Ch'en P'u	陳普	Shih-t'ang hsien-sheng i-chi 石堂先生遺集	187
Ch'en Shun-yü	陳舜俞	Tu-kuan wen-chi 都官文集	207
Chen Te-hsiu	真德秀	Hsi-shan hsien-sheng Chen Wen-chung	
		kung wen-chi 西山先生真文忠公文集	61
Ch'en Yuan-ching	陳元靚	Shih-lin kuang-chi 事林廣記	31
--		Sui-shih kuang-chi 歲事廣記	143
Ch'eng Chü	程俱	Pei-shan hsiao chi 北山小集	115
Cheng Hsia	鄭俠	Hsi-t'ang hsien-sheng wen-chi 西塘先生文集	111
Cheng Hsieh	鄭獬	Yun-ch'i chi 隕溪集	131
Ch'eng Pi	程泌	Ming-shui chi 洺水集	59
Chia Ssu-hsieh	賈思勰	Ch'i-min yao-shu 齊民要術	103
Ch'in Chiu-shao	秦九韶	Shu-shu chiu-chang 數書九章	32
Ch'in Kuan	秦觀	Huai-hai chi 淮海集	27
Chou Ch'ü-fei	周去非	Ling-wai tai-ta 嶺外代答	7
Chou Hui	周煇	Ch'ing-po tsa-chih 清波雜志	146
Chou Mi	周密	Kuei-hsin tsa-shih pieh-chi 癸辛雜識別集	102
--		Ts'ao-ch'uang yun-yü 草窗韻語	144
Chou Pi-ta	周必大	Chou I Wen-chung kung chi 周益文忠公集	61
--		Erh-lao-t'ang tsa-chih 二老堂雜志	84
Chou Ta-kuan	周達觀	Chen-la feng-t'u chi 真臘風土記	153
Chu Chi-fang	朱繼芳	Ch'ing-chia lung-hsun kao 靜佳龍尋薫	151
Chu Hsi	朱熹	Chu Wen kung chi 朱文公集	71
Chu Mu	祝穆	Fang-yü sheng-lan 方輿勝覽	65
Chu Yü	朱彧	P'ing-chou k'o-t'an 萍洲可談	15

(Titles for which no author is given)

GLOSSARY OF CHINESE TERMS

a-pan 阿班	mast watch mate	16
ch'a 樣	(a type of tree)	93
ch'a-ti 茶地	tea lands	136
ch'ai-shan 柴山	firewood forests (land category)	135
chang-nien 長年	senior seaman (cp. next entry)	17
chang-nien san-lao 長年三老	captain and senior sailors	16
ch'ang-sheng k'u 長生庫	'long life treasury', (monastery) pawnshop	199
chang-shih 掌事	head clerk managing a business	196
chao 棹	sweep (oar)	11
chao-shih 朝市	morning market	142
chao-t'ou 招頭	engager (of crews)	18
che-k'o 折科	converting regular twice-yearly tax-levy to payment in other commodities	113
chen 鎮	town	131, 139
cheng (fu) ch'uan-chu 正(副)船主	chief (assistant) ship's master	18
ch'eng-kuo 城郭	city and suburbs	127
chi-t'ou 集頭	market head	154
chia-yeh 家業	estate producing income from trade or industry	135
chia-yeh ch'ien 家業錢	charge on income from non-agricultural sources	135
Chiang-ch'uan 江船	Yangtze River boats	10
chieh 痎	intermittent fever, periodic markets	143
chieh-chih 解質	pawnbroking	32
chien 間	unit of housing space	135
chien-chia ch'ien 間架錢	housing-space tax	133
chien-chen kuan 監鎮官	Town Supervising Official	131
ch'ien-hu 縴户	trackers	19
chih-k'u 直庫	arsenal comptroller (on a ship)	18
chih-ma 脂麻	oil-hemp, sesamum	80
chin-chiao 近郊	suburbs	128
ching-chi(-jen) 經紀(人)	one who manages affairs; agent; estate agent, broker, money broker; petty trader	31, 193
ching-chieh fa 經界法	Boundary Survey System	135
ching-shang 經商	agent merchant (trading with a commendator's capital), tractator	31

chiu-fang 酒坊 　shop making and selling wine under official license　130

chiu-ho huo-pan 糾合夥(夥)伴 association of partners　33

chiu-shui 酒稅 　wine tax　156

ch'ou 紬 　pongee　112

chou-shao 舟梢 　helmsman　24

chu-chi 朱記 　vermilion seal issued to leaders of overseas trading expeditions　15

chu-chia 主家 　owner (of a ship)　32

chu-chiao 竹脚 　bamboo groves (land category)　135

ch'u-hai 出海 　'he who goes to sea', executive in charge of business operations on a sea-going trading venture　16

chu-hsiao 竹篠 　dwarf bamboo (lands) (land category)　135

chu-hu 主戶 　landowner/native household　136

chu-i ch'ien 助役錢 　Service Assistance Money　134

ch'u-kuan 處館 　tutor, secretary　77

ch'u-lu lao-hang 出陸行老 guild head specializing in travel　168

chu-po ta-ku 主舶大賈 　chief merchant on board　28

chu-t'ing chu-jen 居停主人　broker who is the proprietor of a lodge-cum-storehouse　174

chu(-yü) 株(梗) 　(a kind of hardwood)　94

ch'uan 絹 　plain silk　112

ch'uan-chu 船主 　ship's owner(s)　15

ch'uan-hang 船行 　shipping broker　26

ch'uan-hu 船戶 　shipmaster, boat owner　13, 36

chuan-tou 專斗 　grain tax receiver clerk　179

ch'uan-ya 船牙 　shipping broker　26

chuang-chai ya jen 莊宅牙人 broker for manors and mansions　165

chuang-yuan 莊園 　manor　1

ch'üeh-ch'ang 権場 　official station for the conduct of frontier trade　175

chün-t'ien 均田 　'equitable fields' system of land tenure　1

erh-ch'ien, san-ch'ien 二仟三仟　leading seamen in charge of second and third sails　18

fan-t'ou jen 飯頭人 　(shipping) brokers　40

fang 坊 　city quarter　127

fang-kuo chi-ti 坊郭基地 urban sites　136

fang-lang 坊廊 　market arcades-cum-warehouses　176

fang-t'ien chün-shui fa 方田均稅法　Land Survey and Equitable Tax System　134 fei lien-ts'ai ho-pen erh chiu-chi t'ung-hang 非連財合本而糾集同行   association of members of the same trade without joint capital   34

fen-ti 墳地   graves   136

fo-hui 佛會   Buddhist gathering, market, fair   149

fu 父   father   184

fu kang-shou 副綱首   assistant group leader of a number of merchants (on board ship)   15

fu-ling 茯苓   China root   49

fu-tan 負担   carrying (grain) on the back (to market) vendor   67

hai 亥   12th of the '12 branches'; periodic market   143

hai-ch'uan 海船   sea ships   10

hai-po 海舶   sea junks   10

hai-shang 海商   merchant engaged in maritime trade   24

hai-shih 亥市   periodic market   142

hang 行   guild   1

hang-lao 行老   guild head   167

hao-ch'uan 耗券   wastage tickets   24

ho-ku 合股   (Ming and Ch'ing) business partnership   3

ho-ku 和顧   'harmonious hiring' (of commoners' boats by the government)   29

ho-pen 合本   joint capital (partnership)   32

ho-shih 和市   government purchasing system   113

ho-t'ung ch'ang 合同場   checking station (for tea certificates)   168

hsi-min 細民   persons on semidependent status   132

hsia-hu 下戶   lowest category of free non-in-migrant households, consisting of farmers and full and part-time merchants   210

hsiang 鄉   rural area, community   128

hsiang 廂   urban district   128

hsiang-kung 香工   incense offerer   18

hsiang-mu 香木   fragrant wood   94

hsiang-shu-shou 鄉書手   village tax-records secretary   179

hsiang-ts'un 鄉村   country villages   127

hsiao-shih 小市   small markets   142

hsiao-ssu 小廝   servants (on board ship)   18

hsien-chieh shang-ch'i yin 先借上期銀   silver paid before hiring   35

hsien-wei 縣尉   County Captain   131

hsing-ch'ien 行錢   'putting one's money to use' by entrusting it to someone else in receipt for half the profits he gained; the borrower of money on such terms; servant, handyman   31, 193

hsu 虛 (墟)	empty place, intermittent market	143
hsu-shih 虛市	'empty market', periodic market	142
hsu-shih ch'ien 墟市錢	market cash	156
hsun-chien 巡檢	police inspector	131
hu-ch'uan 湖船	'lake-boat', i.e. sea-going shallow-draft oared galley	9
hu-ma 胡麻	sesamum	80
hu-tzu 縠子	crepe silk	112
Huai-ch'uan 淮船	Huai boats	12
huo-chang 火(夥)長	chief mate of a ship	18
huo-pan 火(夥)伴	partners in a trading venture	28
i-ch'uan fa 義船法	the system of voluntarily contributing ships	13
i-p'u 驛鋪	relay station of the state postal service	175
jen-ch'ing 人情	sense of mutual obligation	77
jung-mien 茸綿	flossy silk for emroidery	113
kan-jen 幹人	manager	31, 189
k'an-k'u 看庫	storekeeper (for a superior)	78
kan-pan kung-shih 幹辦公事	public business manager (of a ship provided for the government service)	28
kan-p'u 幹僕	managerial serf	190
kan-yun 幹運	manager	189
kang 綱	convoy	20
kang-shou 綱首	head merchant (on an overseas trading venture)	15
k'ao-she 犒設	feast	25
kao-shih 篙師	chief poler	18
keng-mi 粳米	rice of moderate gluten content	51
k'o 客	outsiders	29
k'o-chang 客長	chief merchant (on board ship)	18
ko-chih 隔織	figured satin	112
k'o-hu 客戶	tenant/in-migrant household	136
k'o-p'ei 科配	irregular levy imposed on urban residents (and peasants)	134
k'o-tien 客店	lodge for merchants	130, 173
ku-ch'ien 雇錢	hiring cash	24
ku-chou ch'i 顧舟契	contract for the hire of a boat	36
k'uai 塊	bale (=2 hu)	35
kuan-ch'uan 管船	shipmaster	40
kuan-k'uai 官儈	official broker (see kuan-ya)	166
kuan-pin 館賓	resident tutor	78
kuan-ya 官牙	official broker, i.e. one handling transactions in property and goods on which a sales tax was levied	165

kuei-fang 櫃坊	(T'ang) safe-deposit firm or proto-bank; (Sung) gambling-shop	195
kung-jen 公人	lower-level local government personnel	179
kung-she 工社	sailors	18
la-shih 臘市	year-end market	164
lan-hu 攬户	tax-payment agent for wealthy families	169
lang-chün 郎君	lord	184
lao-ta 老大	chief seaman	18
li 里	stade, approx. 1/3 mile	141
li-jen 吏人	local government personnel	179
li-sheng-shui 力勝稅	ship tonnage tax	27
liang-jen 良人	free person	167
lien-ts'ai ho-pen 連財合本	joint-capital partnerhsip	34, 199
lin-hu 賃户	tenant	20
ling 綾	damask silk	112
lo 羅	open-weave silk	112
lu 櫓	fishtail oar	11
mai-p'u (=p'u-mai) 買撲(朴)	auction	155
man-shih 蠻市	barbarian market or fair	164
mi-chu 米主	rice-owner	67
mi-ch'uan 米船	rice boat	67
mi-hang 米行	rice brokers	68
mi-k'o 米客	rice merchants	67
mi-p'u 米鋪	rice shops	68
mi ya-jen 米牙人	rice brokers	68
miao-shih 廟市	'temple market', i.e. fair	156
mien 綿	silk wadding	113
mien-i fa 免役法	Service Exemption System	134
mu 母	mother	184
nai 妳	woman senior to speaker	184
nan 楠	camphor-tree	93
nan-ch'uan 南船	southern ships	9
niang 娘	mother, lady	184
niu-shui 牛稅	tax on sales of oxen	98
niu-tsu 牛租	rent charged on oxen rented out by the government	98
no-mi 糯米	rice of high gluten content	51
pa 罷 (?=爸)	male senior to speaker	184
pai-ti 白地	unplanted farmland, unbuilt site, (land category)	135
pan-chu 板主	ship's owner	18
p'an-po(-jen) 盤剝(人)	transship (per)	19

MICHIGAN PAPERS IN CHINESE STUDIES

No. 1. The Chinese Economy, 1912-1949, by Albert Feuerwerker.

No. 2. The Cultural Revolution: 1967 in Review, four essays by Michel Oksenberg, Carl Riskin, Robert Scalapino, and Ezra Vogel.

No. 3. Two Studies in Chinese Literature, by Li Chi and Dale Johnson.

No. 4. Early Communist China: Two Studies, by Ronald Suleski and Daniel Bays.

No. 5. The Chinese Economy, ca. 1870-1911, by Albert Feuerwerker.

No. 6. Chinese Paintings in Chinese Publications, 1956-1968: An Annotated Bibliography and an Index to the Paintings, by E. J. Laing.

No. 7. The Treaty Ports and China's Modernization: What Went Wrong? by Rhoads Murphey.

No. 8. Two Twelfth Century Texts on Chinese Painting, by Robert J. Maeda.

No. 9. The Economy of Communist China, 1949-1969, by Chu-yuan Cheng.

No. 10. Educated Youth and the Cultural Revolution in China, by Martin Singer.

No. 11. Premodern China: A Bibliographical Introduction, by Chun-shu Chang.

No. 12. Two Studies on Ming History, by Charles O. Hucker.

No. 13. Nineteenth Century China: Five Imperialist Perspectives, selected by Dilip Basu, edited by Rhoads Murphey.

No. 14. Modern China, 1840-1972: An Introduction to Sources and Research Aids, by Andrew J. Nathan.

No. 15. Women in China: Studies in Social Change and Feminism, edited by Marilyn B. Young.

No. 16. An Annotated Bibliography of Chinese Painting Catalogues and Related Texts, by Hin-cheung Lovell.

No. 17. China's Allocation of Fixed Capital Investment, 1952-1957, by Chu-yuan Cheng.

No. 18. Health, Conflict, and the Chinese Political System, by David M. Lampton.

No. 19. Chinese and Japanese Music-Dramas, edited by J. I. Crump and William P. Malm.

No. 20. Hsin-lun (New Treatise) and Other Writings by Huan T'an (43 B.C.-28 A.D.), translated by Timoteus Pokora.

No. 21. Rebellion in Nineteenth-Century China, by Albert Feuerwerker.

No. 22. Between Two Plenums: China's Intraleadership Conflict, 1959-1962, by Ellis Joffe.

No. 23. "Proletarian Hegemony" in the Chinese Revolution and the Canton Commune of 1927, by S. Bernard Thomas.

No. 24. Chinese Communist Materials at the Bureau of Investigation Archives, Taiwan, by Peter Donovan, Carl E. Dorris, and Lawrence R. Sullivan.

No. 25. Shanghai Old-Style Banks (Ch'ien-chuang), 1800-1935, by Andrea Lee McElderry.

Prepaid Orders Only

MICHIGAN ABSTRACTS OF CHINESE AND JAPANESE WORKS ON CHINESE HISTORY

No. 1. The Ming Tribute Grain System, by Hoshi Ayao, translated by Mark Elvin.

No. 2. Commerce and Society in Sung China, by Shiba Yoshinobu, translated by Mark Elvin.

No. 3. Transport in Transition: The Evolution of Traditional Shipping in China, translations by Andrew Watson.

No. 4. Japanese Perspectives on China's Early Modernization: A Bibliographical Survey, by K. H. Kim.

No. 5. The Silk Industry in Ch'ing China, by Shih Min-hsiung, translated by E-tu Zen Sun.

NONSERIES PUBLICATION

Index to the "Chan-kuo Ts'e", by Sharon Fidler and J. I. Crump. A companion volume to the Chan-kuo Ts'e, translated by J. I. Crump (Oxford: Clarendon Press, 1970).

Michigan Papers and Abstracts available from:
Center for Chinese Studies
The University of Michigan
Lane Hall (Publications)
Ann Arbor, MI 48109 USA

Prepaid Orders Only
write for complete price listing